THE WORLD NEEDS MORE CANADA

"Nous dédions ce livre aux citoyens du Canada ainsi qu'aux créateurs de culture du pays qui nous inspirent, qui nous interpellent et qui reflètent notre identité aux yeux du monde entier."

l'équipe**Indigo**

"We dedicate this book to the citizens of Canada and to the culture makers of our land, who inspire us, challenge us, and reflect who we are for all the world to see."

team!Indigo

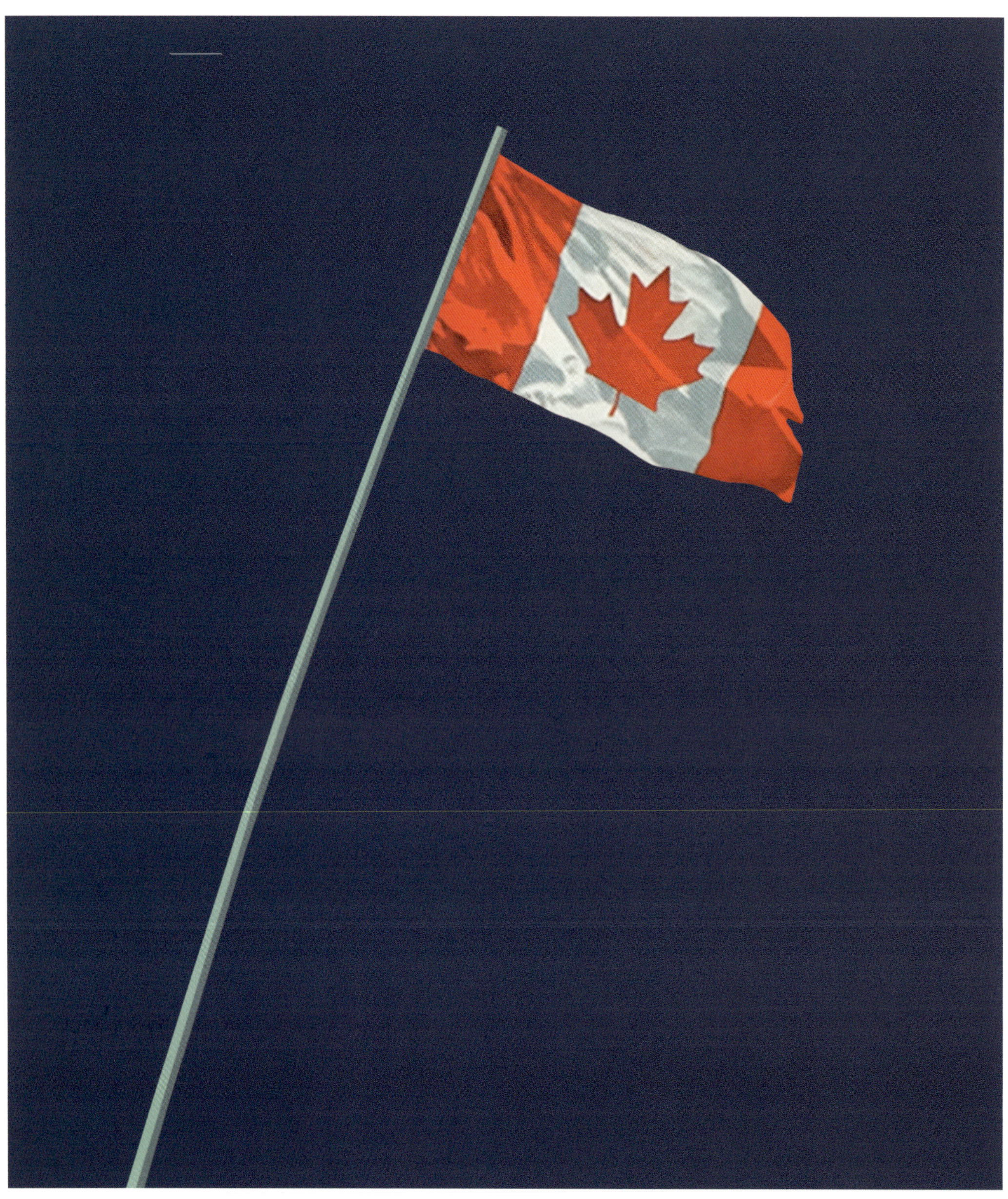

TRUE NORTH, TRUE LOVE

We all have our own Canada—a subjective take on what it should be, what it means, and why it matters. Given our vast size, diverse regions, multiple languages, and citizens who hail from all over the globe, it's little surprise we interpret and experience Canada in different ways. Still, as you will clearly see in the pages that follow, we Canadians know in our hearts and minds what it means to be Canadian.

This book is a collaboration between Indigo and many of Canada's great culture makers. It is our big, love-filled birthday card to this great land and the people who live here. From one end of the country to the other, Canadian poets, writers, artists, chefs, architects, musicians, painters, and photographers share feelings, memories, and messages to commemorate our 150th.

The World Needs More Canada will leave you thinking about this country and its elusive cultural identity in a special light. It will make you proud. It may even bring you to shed a few tears.

How fitting that Canada's 150th birthday comes at a time when the world is sitting up and taking note. Without basking in the glory—which would be so un-Canadian—it's hard not to enjoy our moment in the sun. Canada is seen as cool and progressive. Foreign media can't seem to get enough of our cultural exports, the stories of our generous embrace of those who land on our shores, and our amazing "second-generation" prime minister.

Marshall McLuhan once famously said, "Canada is the only country in the world that knows how to live without an identity." Today, as is evidenced here, it is clear we know exactly who we are.

At only 150, we are still a work in progress. But there can be no doubt that our future is bright. We must only honour our history and stay true to the overarching values and ideals that beat deep within us.

Happy Birthday, Canada!

AMOUR
BORÉAL

Nous avons chacun notre propre version du Canada, soit une opinion subjective de ce que le mot signifie, de ce que le mot devrait représenter, de son importance. Étant donné sa vaste superficie, ses diverses régions, ses multiples langues et ses citoyens venant des quatre coins du monde, ce n'est pas étonnant que nous interprétions et vivions le Canada de différentes façons. Toutefois, en regardant entre les pages de ce livre, vous verrez que nous les Canadiens savons ce que cela signifie être «Canadien», dans nos vies quotidiennes, dans nos cœurs et dans nos esprits.

Ce livre constitue une collaboration entre Indigo et plusieurs des grands créateurs de culture canadiens. C'est notre carte d'anniversaire regorgeant d'amour que nous offrons à notre pays merveilleux et à tous ceux qui y habitent. D'un bout à l'autre du pays, poètes, écrivains, artistes, chefs de cuisine, architectes, musiciens et photographes canadiens ont partagé leurs pensées, émotions et messages pour commémorer le 150e anniversaire du Canada.

The World Needs More Canada vous invite à faire une réflexion sur le Canada et sur son identité culturelle furtive. Ce livre vous remplira de fierté et il pourrait même vous faire verser quelques larmes.

Il est tout à fait opportun que le Canada célèbre son 150e anniversaire à un moment où le monde entier commence à nous remarquer. Sans pour autant baigner dans un sentiment glorieux (après tout, ce ne serait pas très canadien de le faire!), il est difficile de ne pas profiter de notre place au soleil. Le Canada est perçu comme un pays tendance et progressiste. Les médias de pays étrangers raffolent de nos exportations culturelles, des histoires témoignant de notre accueil chaleureux des nouveaux venus et de notre illustre premier ministre de seconde génération.

Marshall McLuhan dans une déclaration devenue célèbre avait dit : «Le Canada est le seul pays du monde qui sait comment vivre sans identité». Il est clair toutefois que nous savons aujourd'hui exactement qui nous sommes.

À l'âge de 150 ans à peine, notre pays est toujours un projet en cours, mais il n'y a aucun doute que notre avenir est prometteur. Il suffit d'honorer notre histoire et de respecter les valeurs et idéaux qui nous sont communs.

Joyeux anniversaire, Canada!

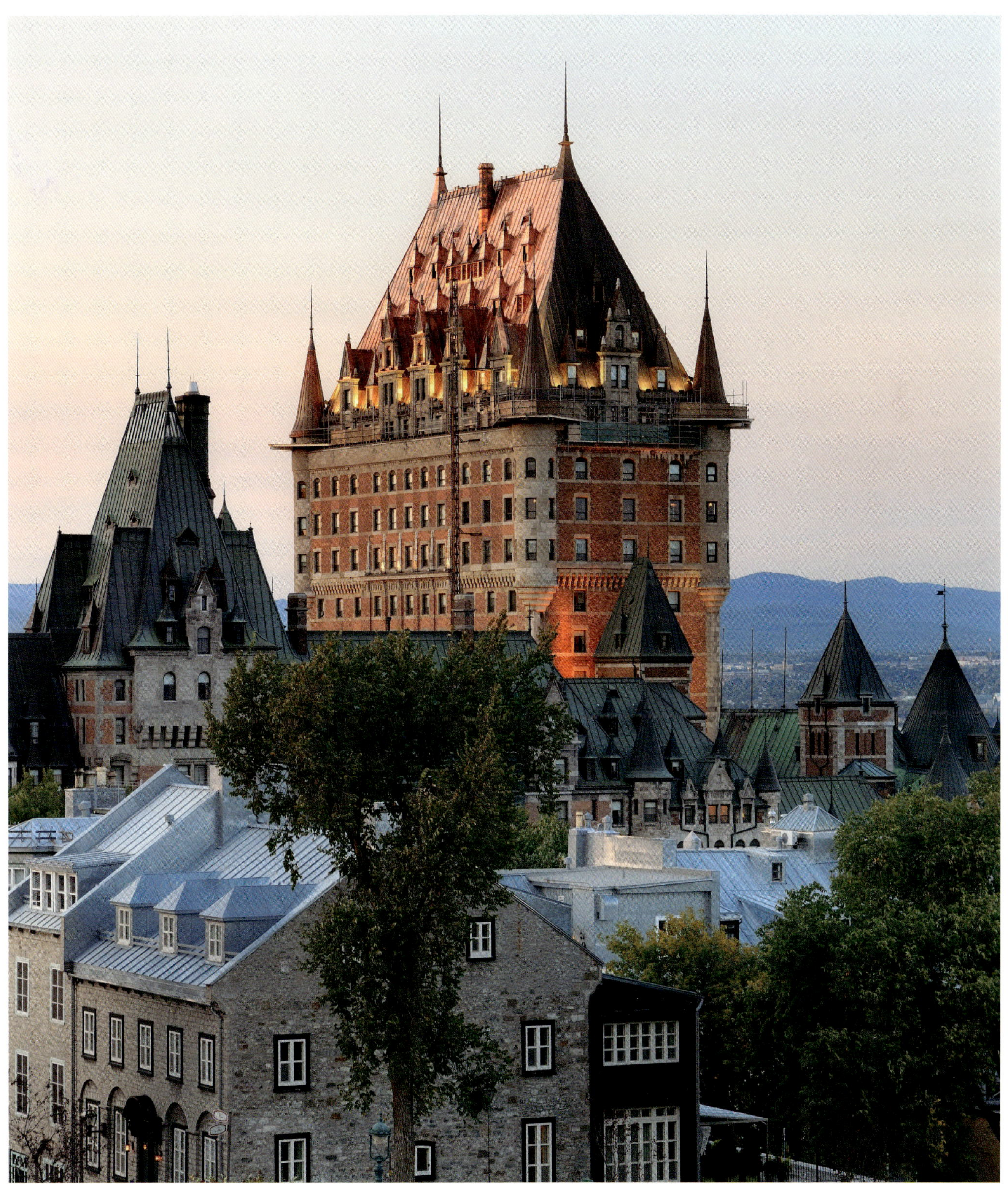

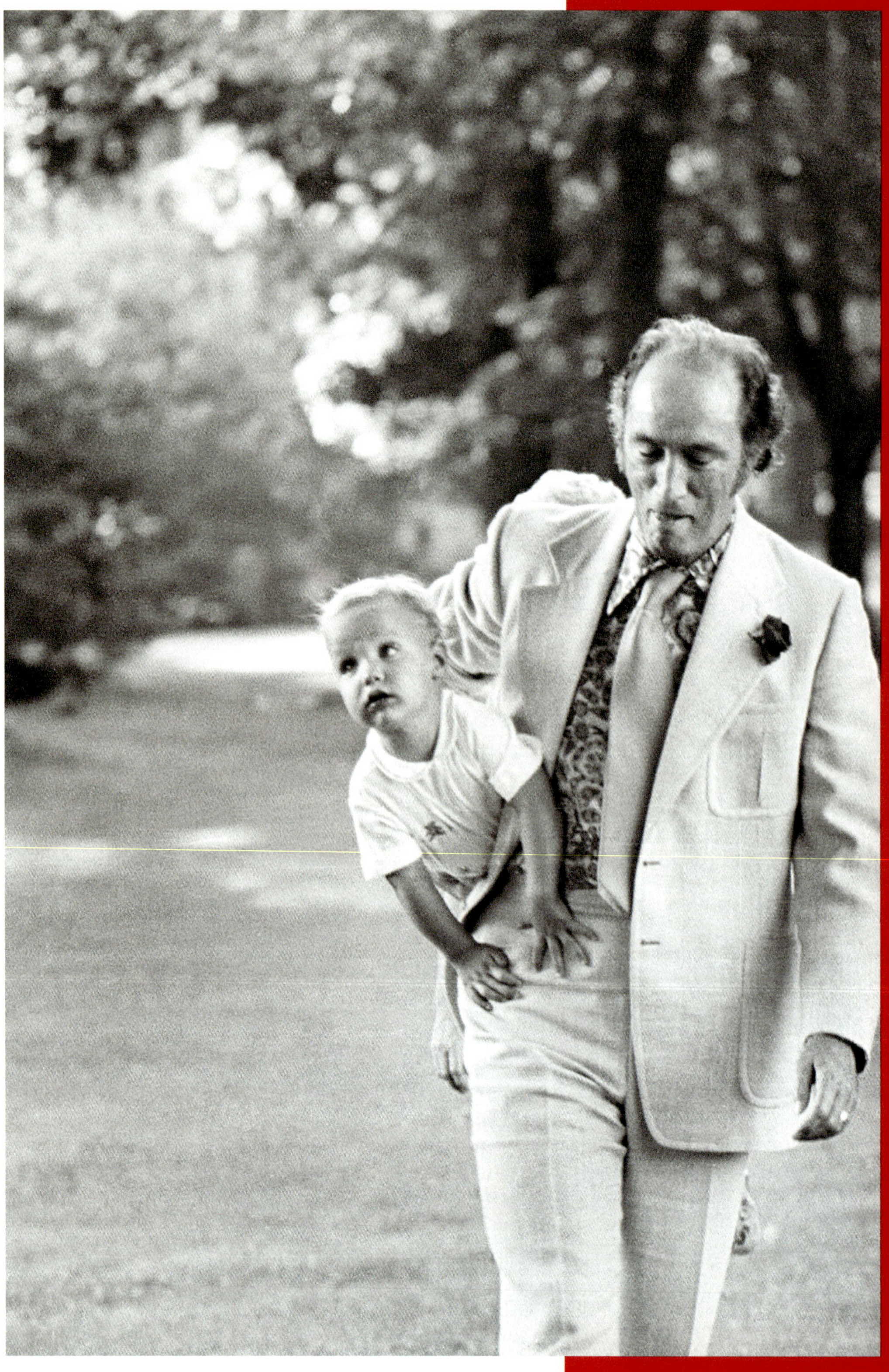

"As we celebrate our nation's birthday, let us also celebrate our diversity. It united us in the past. It binds us together today and it is at the very heart of our future success. No matter our faith, where we were born, what colour our skin, what language we speak, or whom we love, we are all equal members of this great country. We have all worked very hard to build this diverse, inclusive, and prosperous nation that we all love so much."

«Alors que nous célébrons l'anniversaire de notre nation, profitons-en pour célébrer en même temps notre diversité. Elle nous a unis dans le passé. Elle nous unit aujourd'hui, et elle est au cœur de notre réussite future. Peu importe notre foi, l'endroit où nous sommes nés, la couleur de notre peau, la langue que nous parlons ou la personne que nous aimons, nous sommes tous des membres égaux de ce magnifique pays. Nous avons tous travaillé très fort pour bâtir cette nation diversifiée, inclusive et prospère que nous aimons tant.»

JUSTIN TRUDEAU
PRIME MINISTER OF CANADA
PREMIER MINISTRE DU CANADA

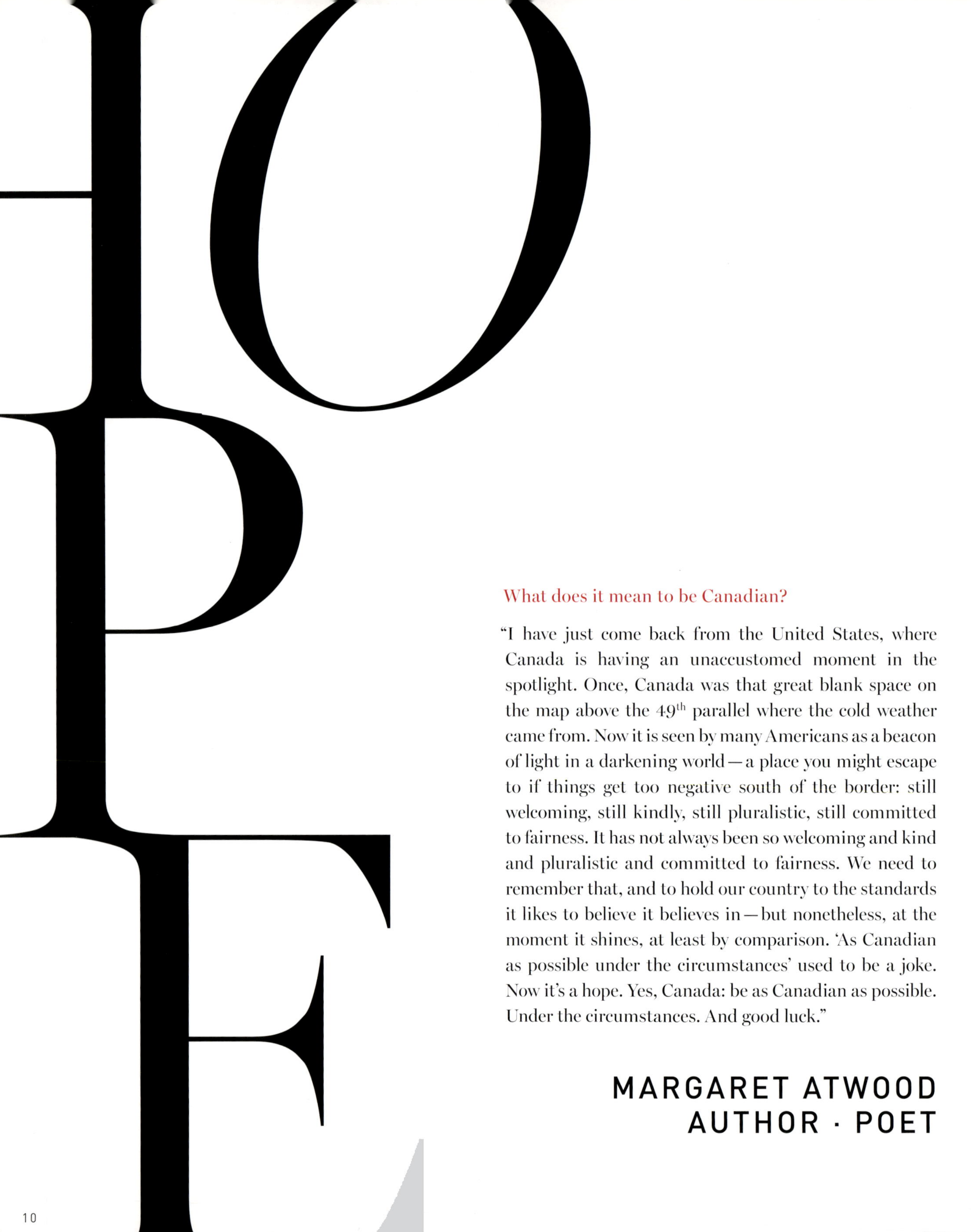

What does it mean to be Canadian?

"I have just come back from the United States, where Canada is having an unaccustomed moment in the spotlight. Once, Canada was that great blank space on the map above the 49th parallel where the cold weather came from. Now it is seen by many Americans as a beacon of light in a darkening world — a place you might escape to if things get too negative south of the border: still welcoming, still kindly, still pluralistic, still committed to fairness. It has not always been so welcoming and kind and pluralistic and committed to fairness. We need to remember that, and to hold our country to the standards it likes to believe it believes in — but nonetheless, at the moment it shines, at least by comparison. 'As Canadian as possible under the circumstances' used to be a joke. Now it's a hope. Yes, Canada: be as Canadian as possible. Under the circumstances. And good luck."

MARGARET ATWOOD
AUTHOR · POET

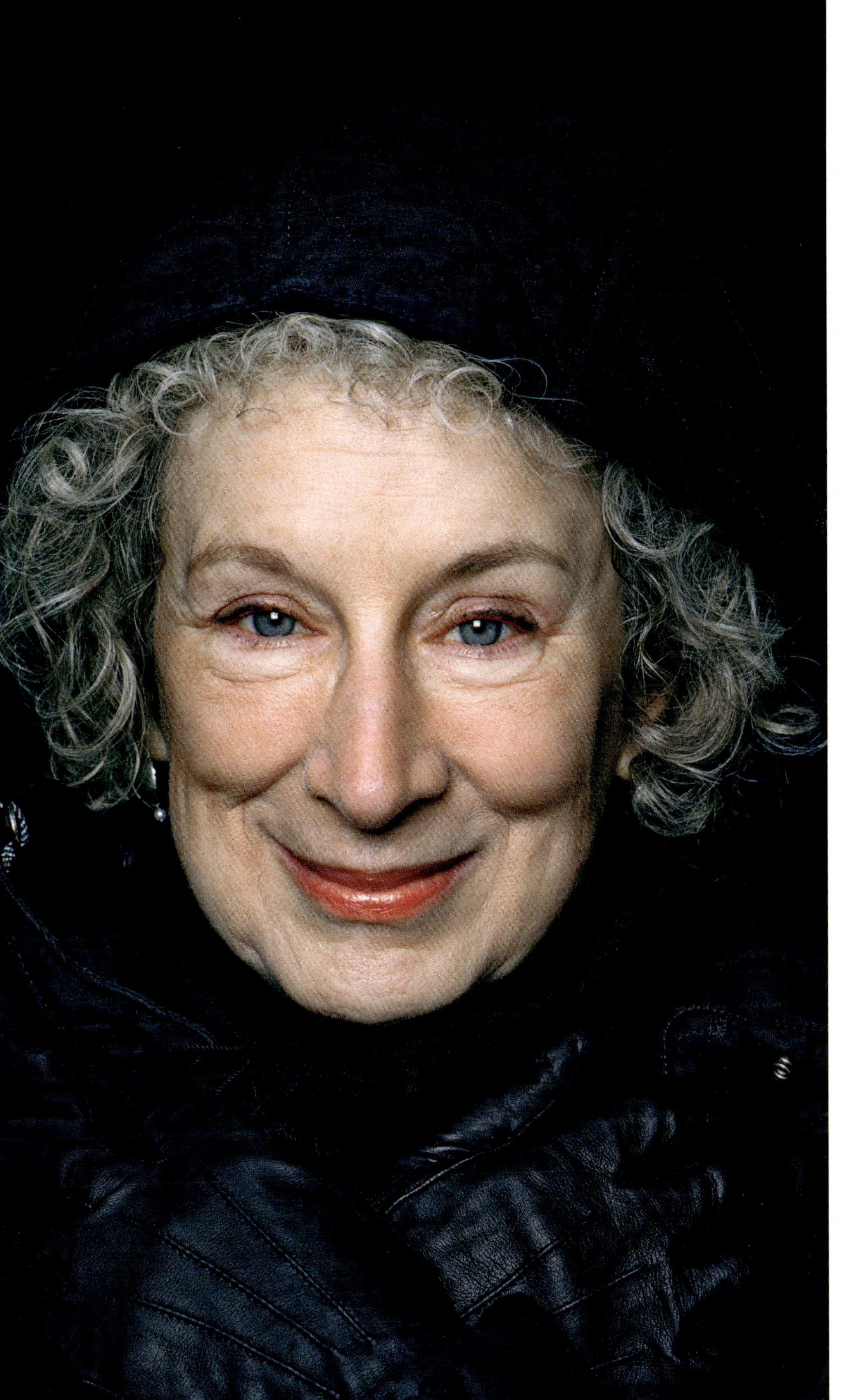

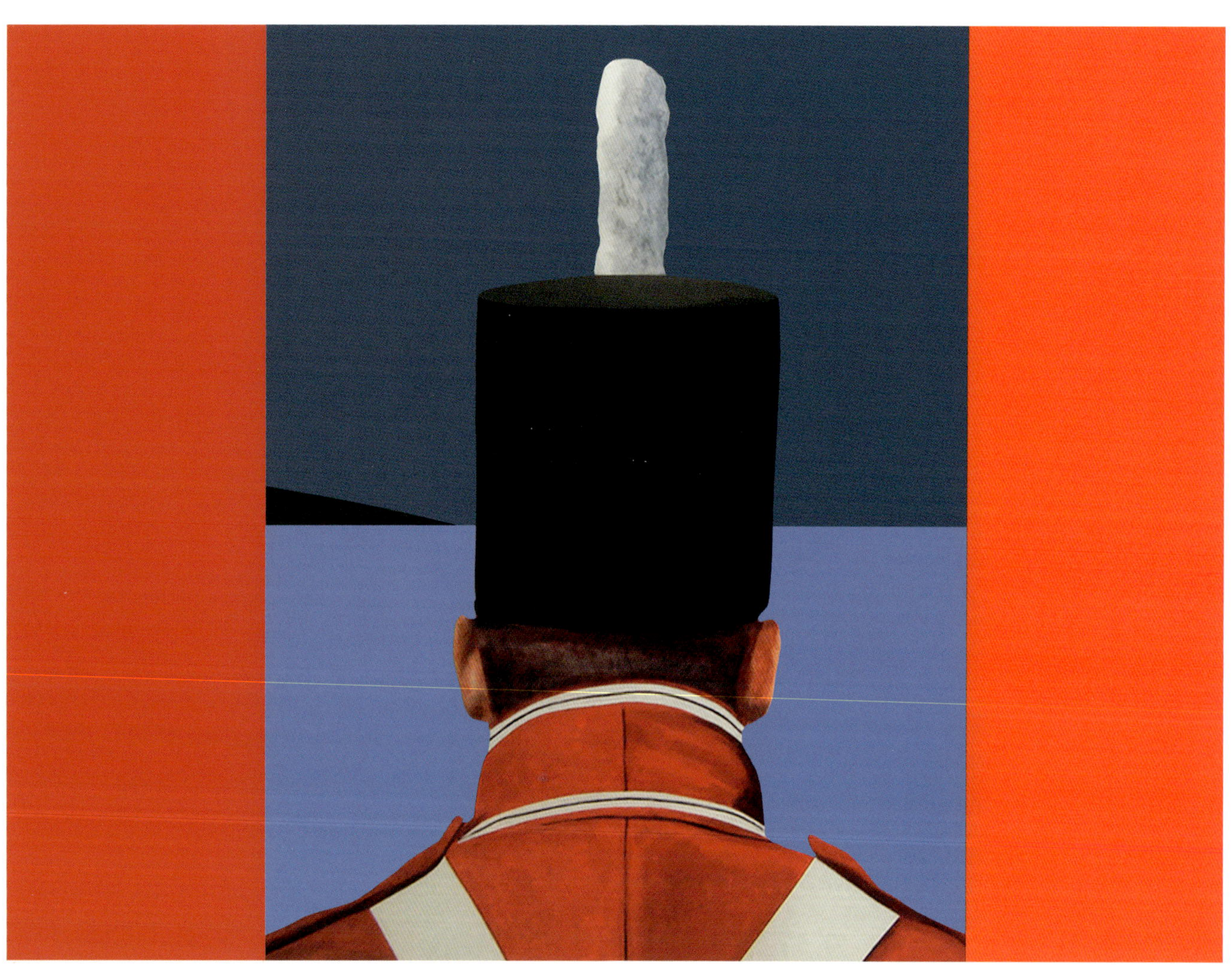

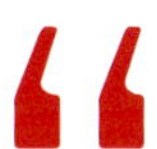

As a visual artist, I have spent five decades probing the psyche of the nation in my work. **'Qui sommes-nous, d'où venons nous, où allons-nous? Who are we? Where do we come from? Where are we going?'** These are themes I have explored, from the Queen riding a moose to illustrating Margaret Atwood's poems for *The Journals of Susanna Moodie* to painting variations of our maple leaf flag fluttering in the wind. As a historian, I have studied the contributions of First Nations, the French, the English, and All the Rest of Us to Canada's spectacular heritage.

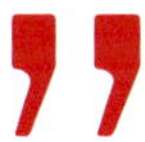

CHARLES PACHTER
ARTIST

BARBARA REID
AUTHOR · ILLUSTRATOR

"After a fabulous day at the Vancouver Island Children's Book Festival in Nanaimo, the authors, illustrators, and organizers were ready to celebrate. On the invitation of the founder and spirit of the festival, Thora Howell, we took a little ferry to the Dinghy Dock Pub on Protection Island. The setting sun was blinding. Within moments an assortment of hats arrived at the table. They had been rounded up by Protection residents and loaned for our comfort. Happy conversations around a table including Roch Carrier in an ancient borrowed floppy straw hat felt like a pretty Canadian moment."

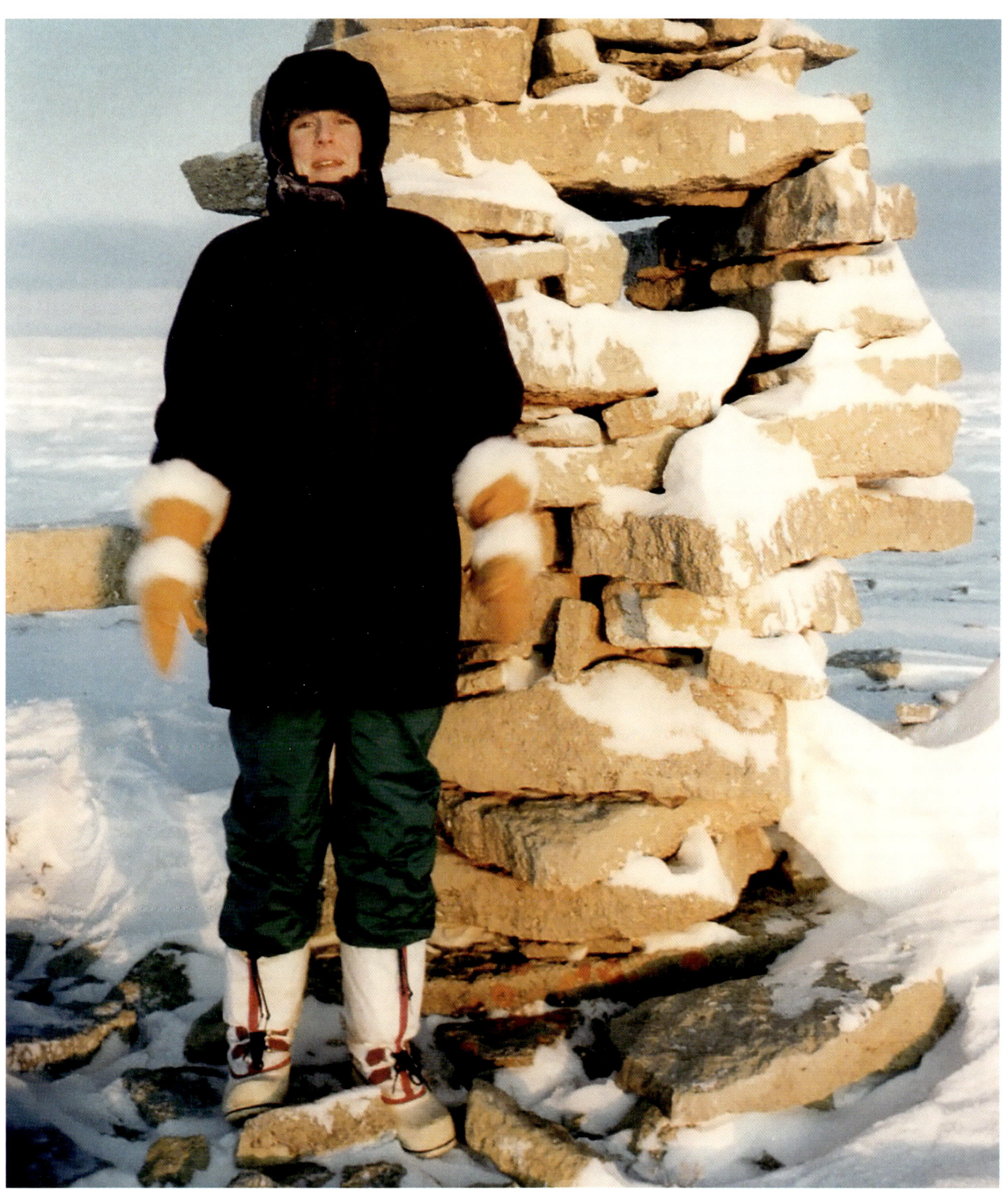

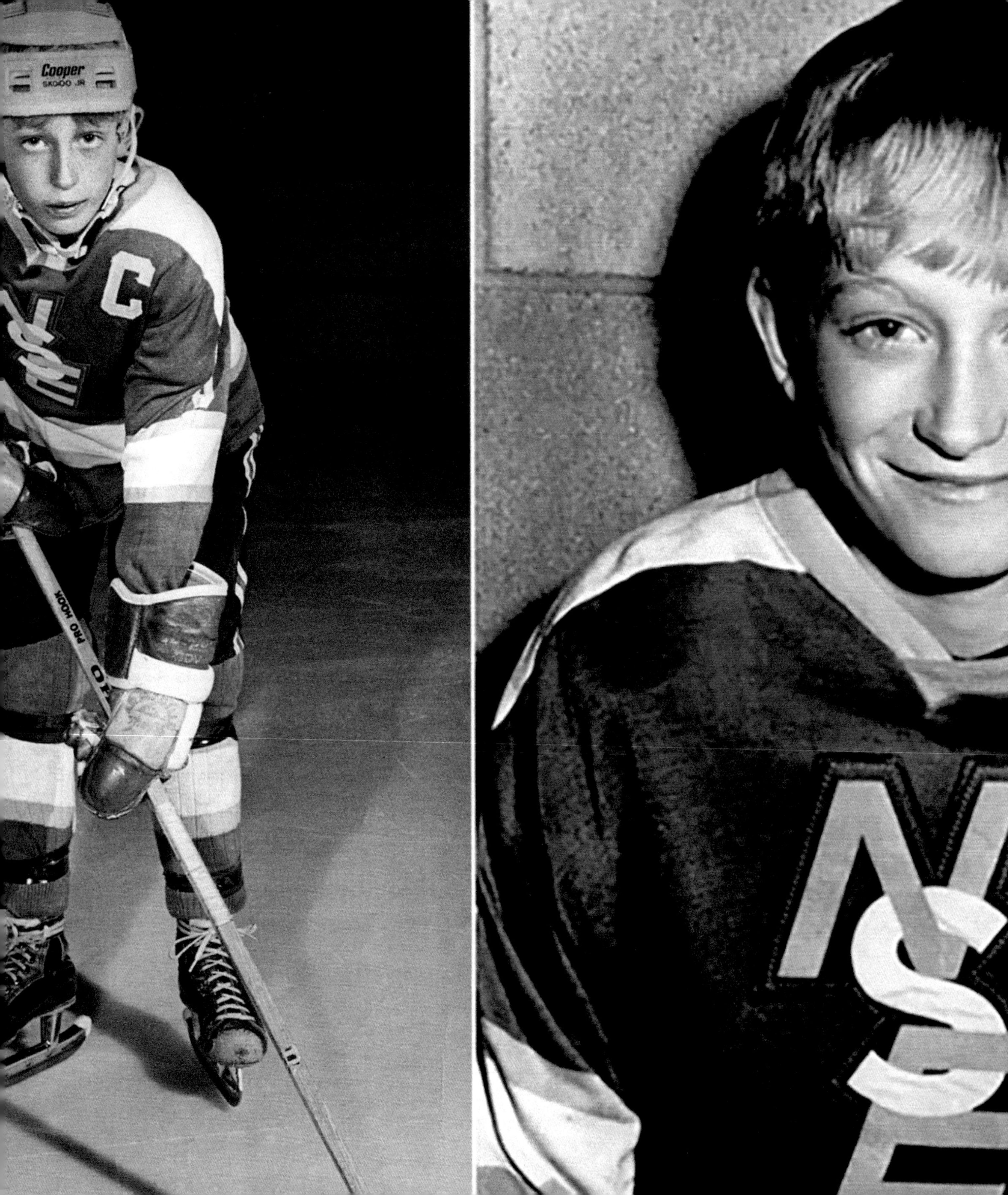
Cooper
SK100 JR
PRO HOOK

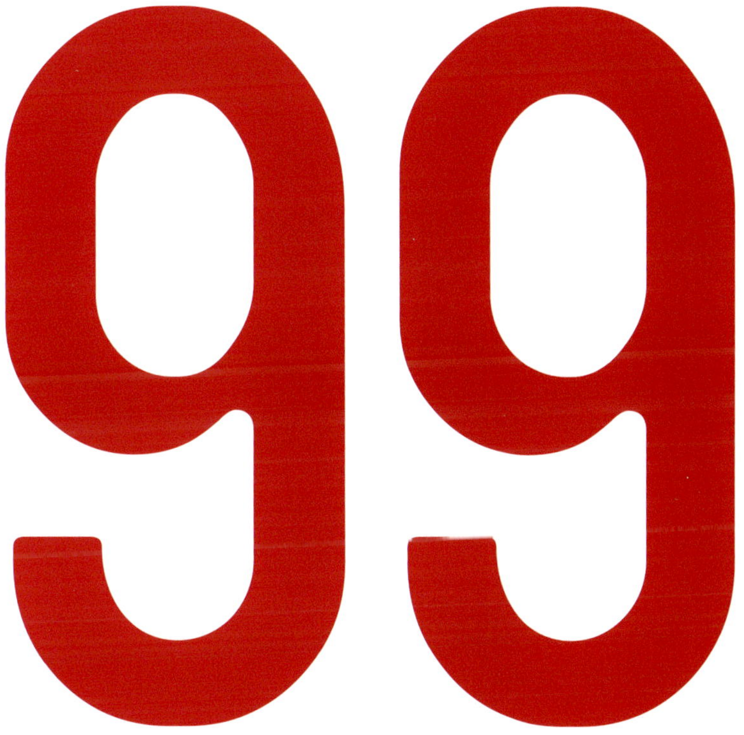

"In 2002, Canada and the U.S. played the gold medal game in Salt Lake City and I was told that somewhere between 26 million and 27 million out of the 35 million Canadians watched that game. And they said, 'What do you think of that?' And I said, 'What do I think of that? What were the other nine million doing?' That's how much we love hockey in Canada."

WAYNE GRETZKY · ATHLETE

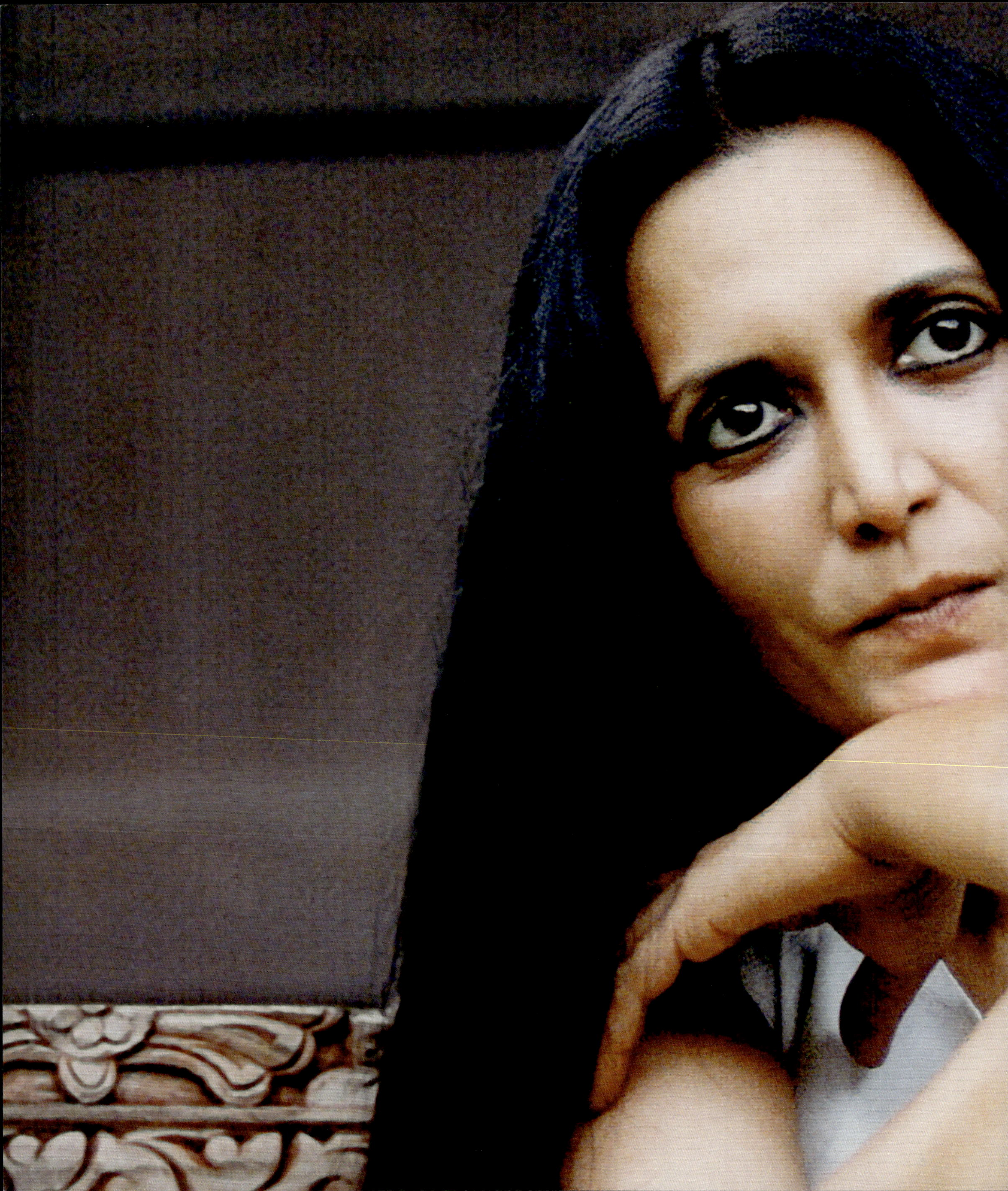

“MY MOST CANADIAN MOMENT WAS POURING **MAPLE SYRUP ON PANCAKES IN A RAMSHACKLE SHACK** ON THE BANKS OF THE GANGES IN VARANASI.”

DEEPA MEHTA
FILMMAKER

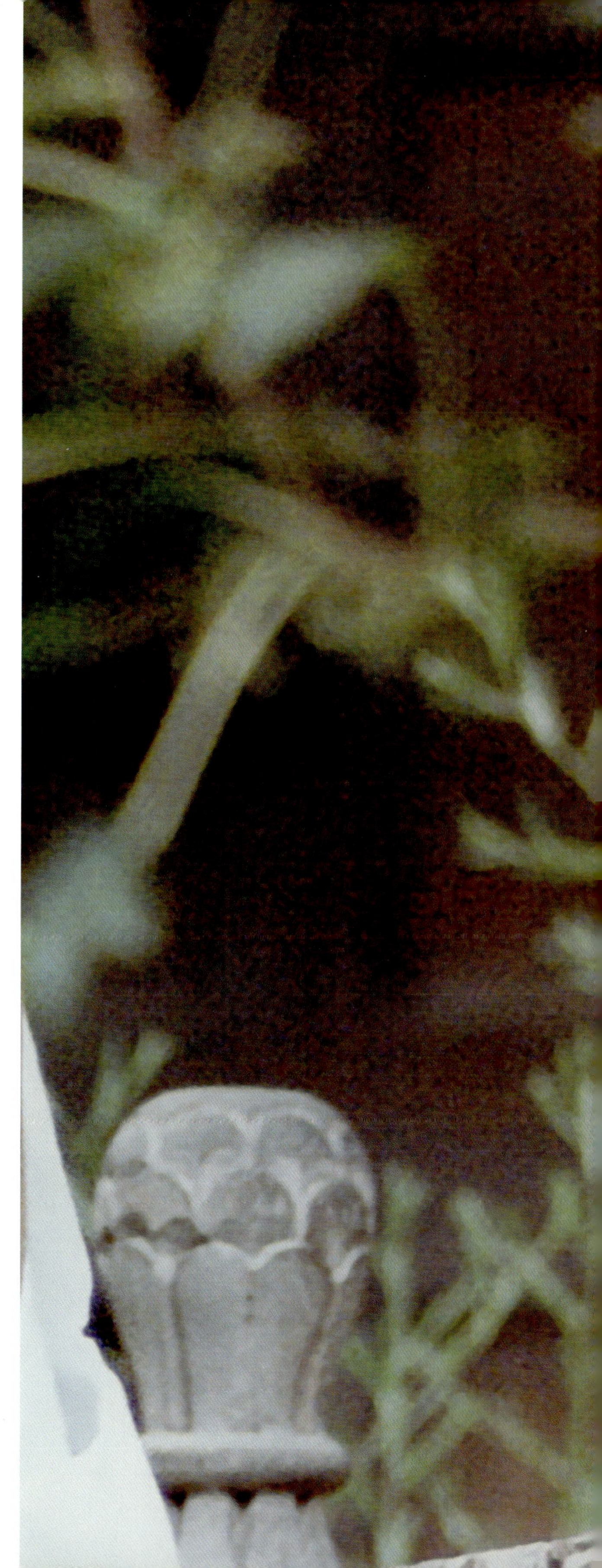

“WE ARE VERY WELCOMING PEOPLE AND KNOWN THROUGHOUT THE WORLD FOR OUR KINDNESS. IF YOU BUMP INTO SOMEONE ELSE, THE CANADIAN WILL ALWAYS BE THE FIRST ONE TO SAY ‘SORRY.’ ”

MALIN ÅKERMAN · ACTOR

GEDDY LEE
MUSICIAN · SONGWRITER

"My most 'Canadian' memory is going to a recording session with Bob and Doug McKenzie to sing the chorus to *Take Off from The Great White North* while my wife, Nancy, my eight-month-old son, Julian, and I were all wearing toques."

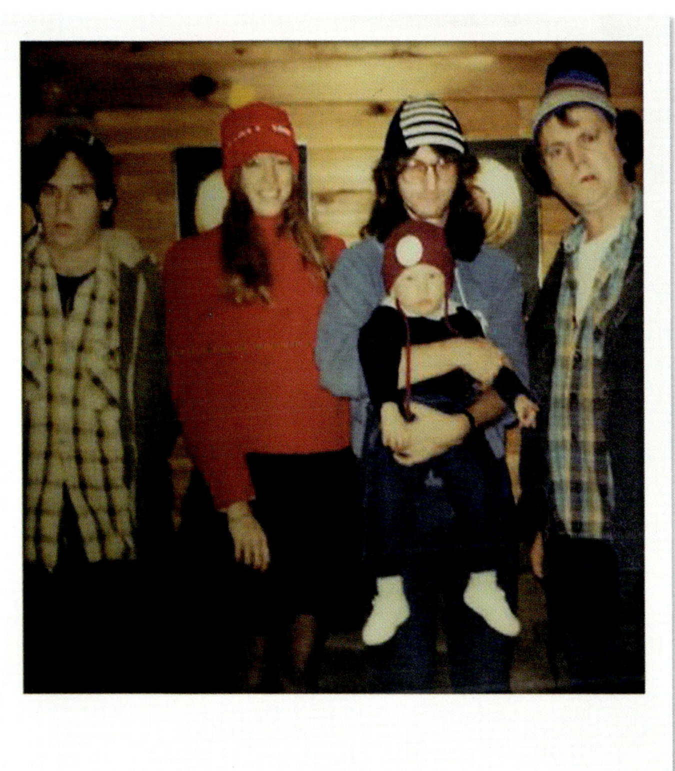

“Now I barely remember the year or month or where it took place. But I remember exactly where I was when it occurred. It took place one evening in Canada, though it was really happening in a distant country within its own later time zone. My son and I in a car had just left the 401 and were driving north on Highway 37. It was almost dark. The radio did not have strong reception, for it was reporting the event all the way from Seoul. The announcer began in a hushed voice and then became manic as the crowd in that far-off place began screaming, and my son and I, though unable to see what was happening and not quite hearing what exactly was happening, were screaming, too. For the man's name was still being mentioned and was still part of the story. After a moment as brief as a long sigh, he had won. **Ben Johnson had won the men's 100 metres in 9.79 seconds, while we were only imagining it within all that noise. That is when the moment always stops. On September 24, 1998. That is the moment I still remember, when I was so proud to be a Canadian.** In spite of what happened so soon after, when things went wrong for him, the public turning away from him. What kind of life did he have after those few seconds? I still think of him. I still want to go up to him and shake his hand.”

MICHAEL ONDAATJE
AUTHOR

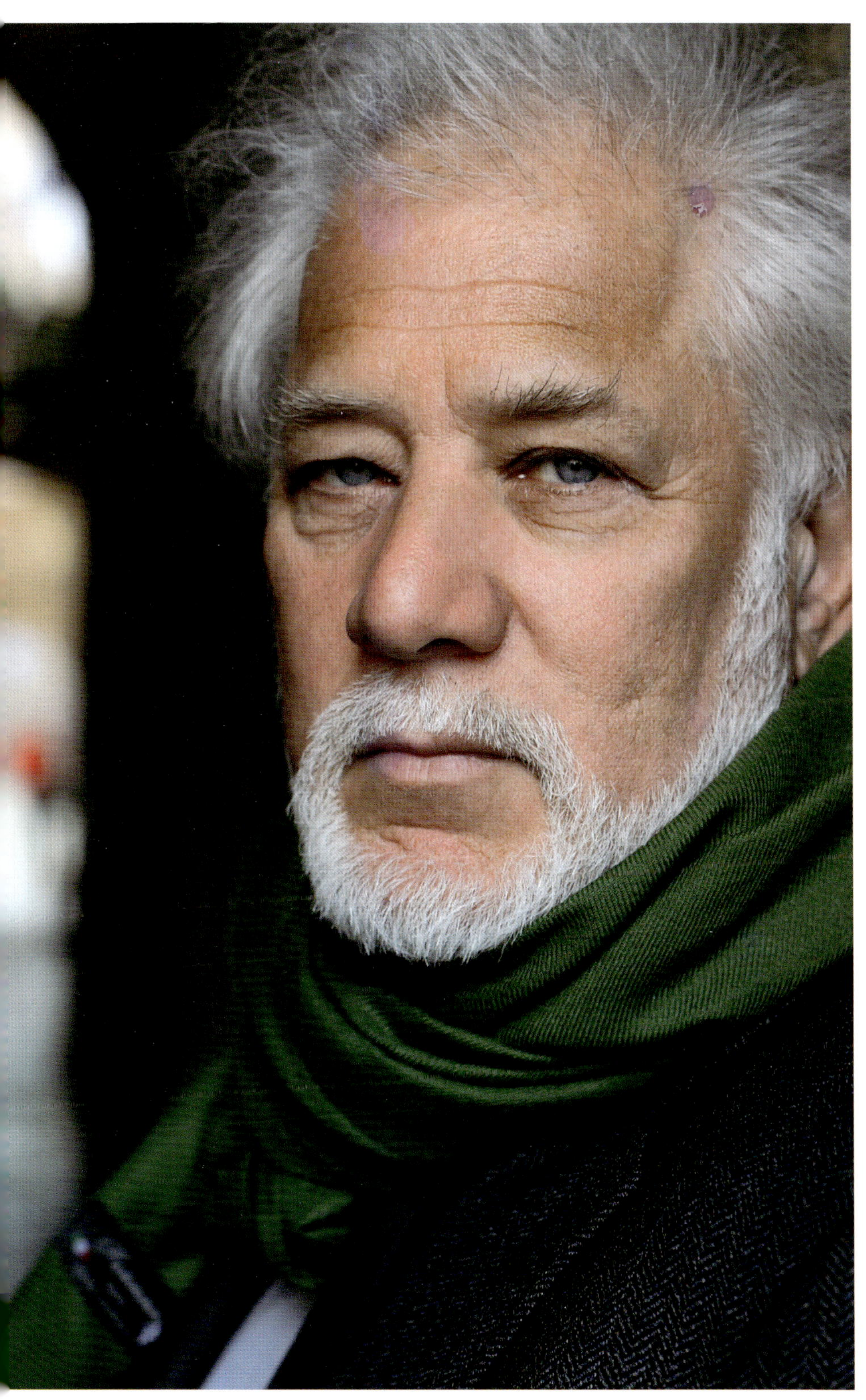

"BEING CANADIAN IS

BEING

—THINK VIMY RIDGE, JUNO BEACH, KIND, CARING, AND ACCEPTING. WE CARING PEOPLE."

ABOUT

TOUGH

AND HOCKEY— BUT ALSO ABOUT BEING ARE A TOUGH PEOPLE, BUT WE ARE A

ERIC WALTERS · YOUNG ADULT AUTHOR

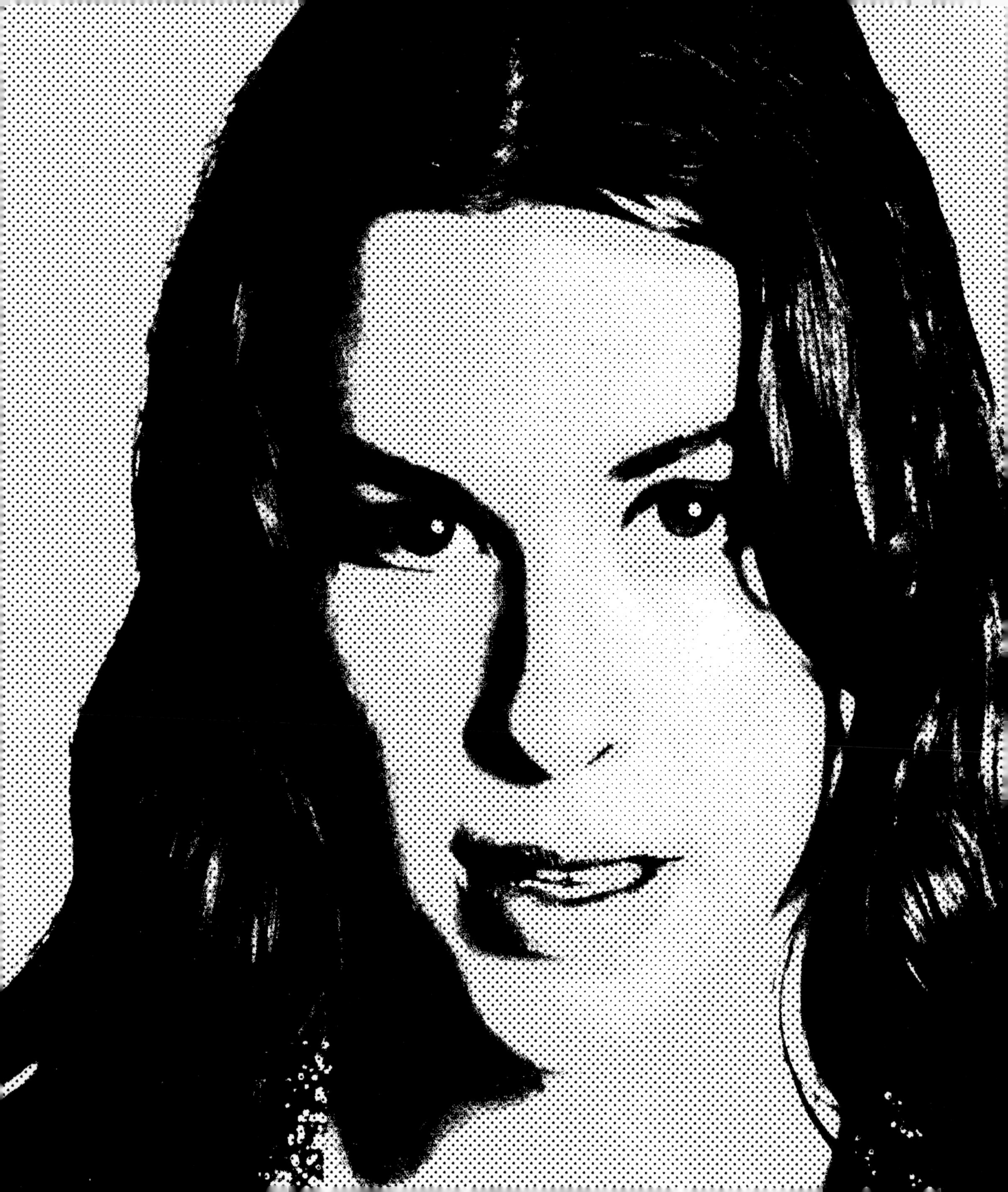

ALANIS MORISSETTE · MUSICIAN · SONGWRITER

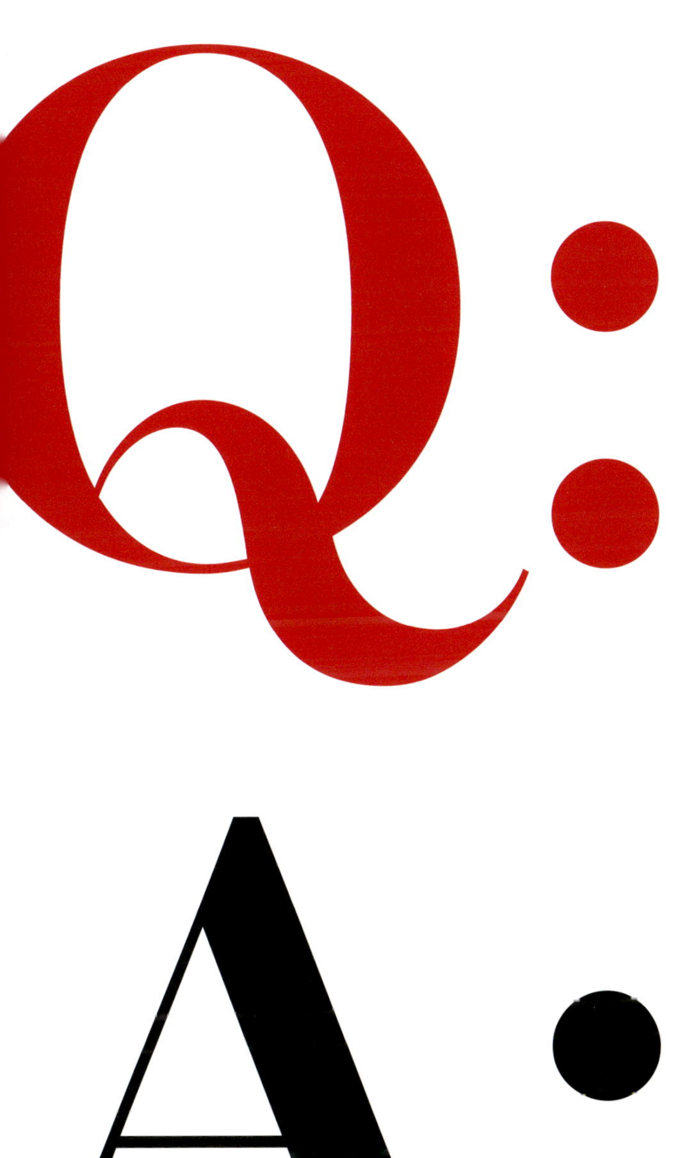

WHAT DOES IT MEAN TO BE CANADIAN?

"It means I am/one is conversational, curious, filled with self-deprecating humour, and internationally minded, if I dare generalize. Polite until we aren't. And yes we say 'sorry' often enough for it to be noticeable… but we truly are an empathic bunch."

WHAT MAKES YOU PROUD TO CALL YOURSELF CANADIAN?

"Health care, midwifery is popular, being known for our friendliness, how breathtaking the country is, a deep affinity for the great outdoors, and the genius idea of melting cheese curd on french fries and then topping it off with gravy."

THE BEST WAY TO ENDEAR YOURSELF TO A CANADIAN IS…

"Never mock the way we say 'about,' don't ask if we know a Jennifer from Canada, and don't use 'eh' wrongly in order to bust our chops. It is a word that helps us stay connected with each other."

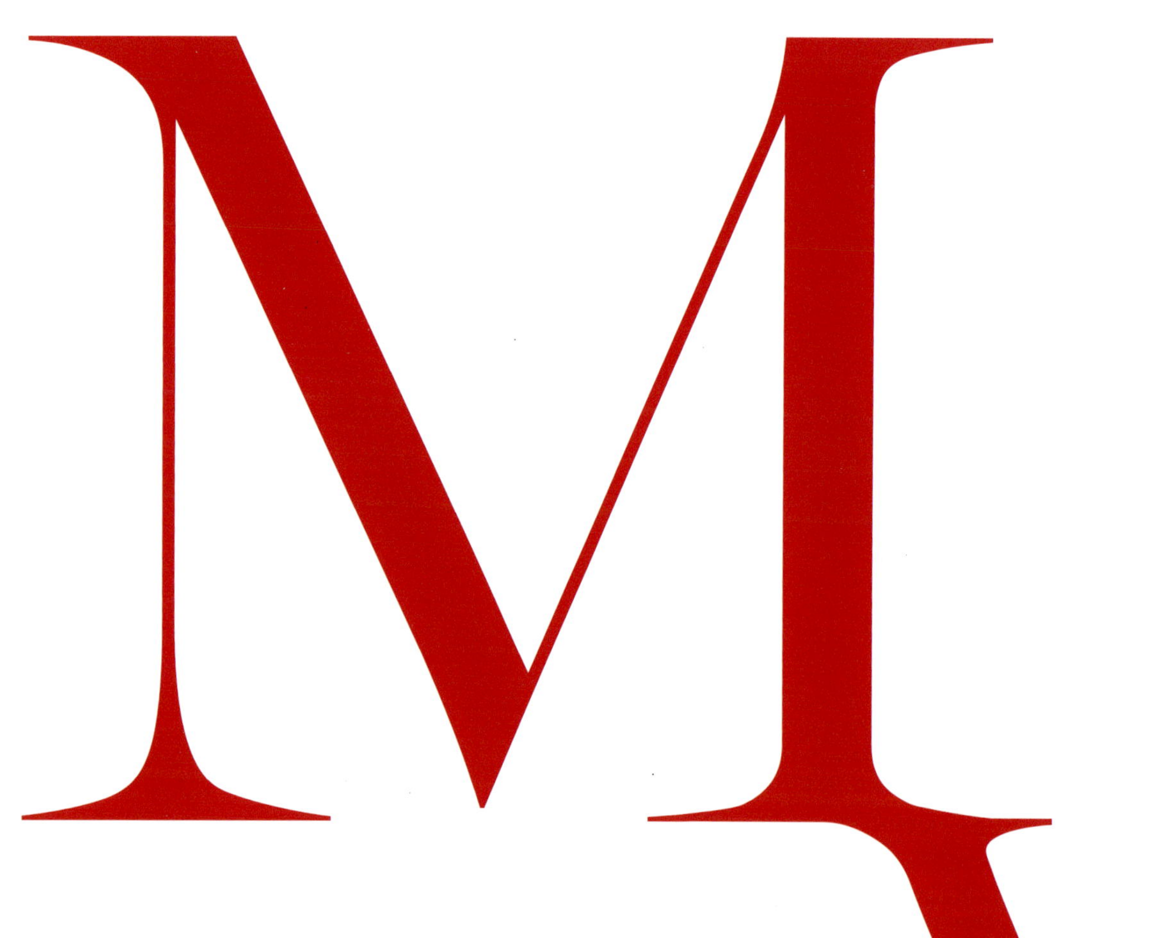

My BIRTHDAY WISH FOR CANADA IS THAT IT HONOURS ITS OBLIGATIONS TO FIRST NATIONS IN THIS LAND, AND FULLY AND PROPERLY RECONCILES WITH ITS TRAGIC PAST IN A TRULY MEANINGFUL WAY.

KATHERENA VERMETTE
AUTHOR · POET

"My most 'Canadian' memory is of travelling to and passing through the Canadian Shield. The endless archipelagos of offshore granite islands scraped clean by the retreating glacial ice is part of who I am."

FRANK VIVA
AUTHOR · ILLUSTRATOR

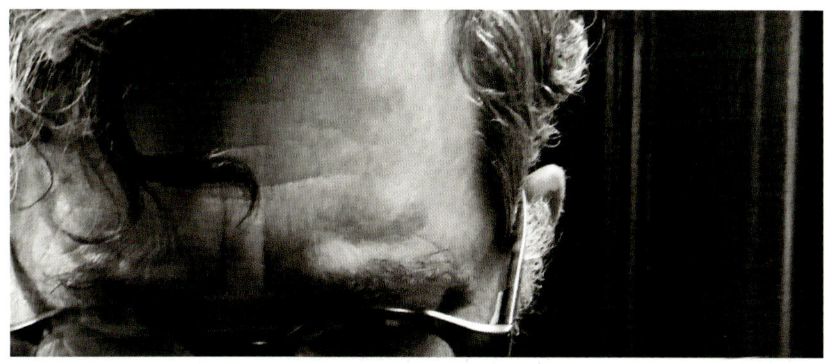

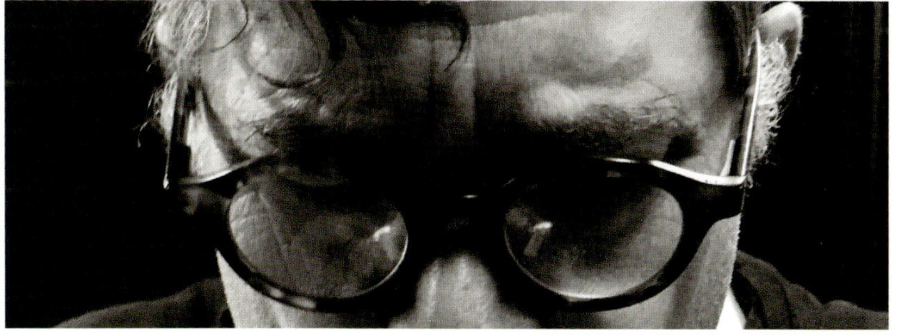

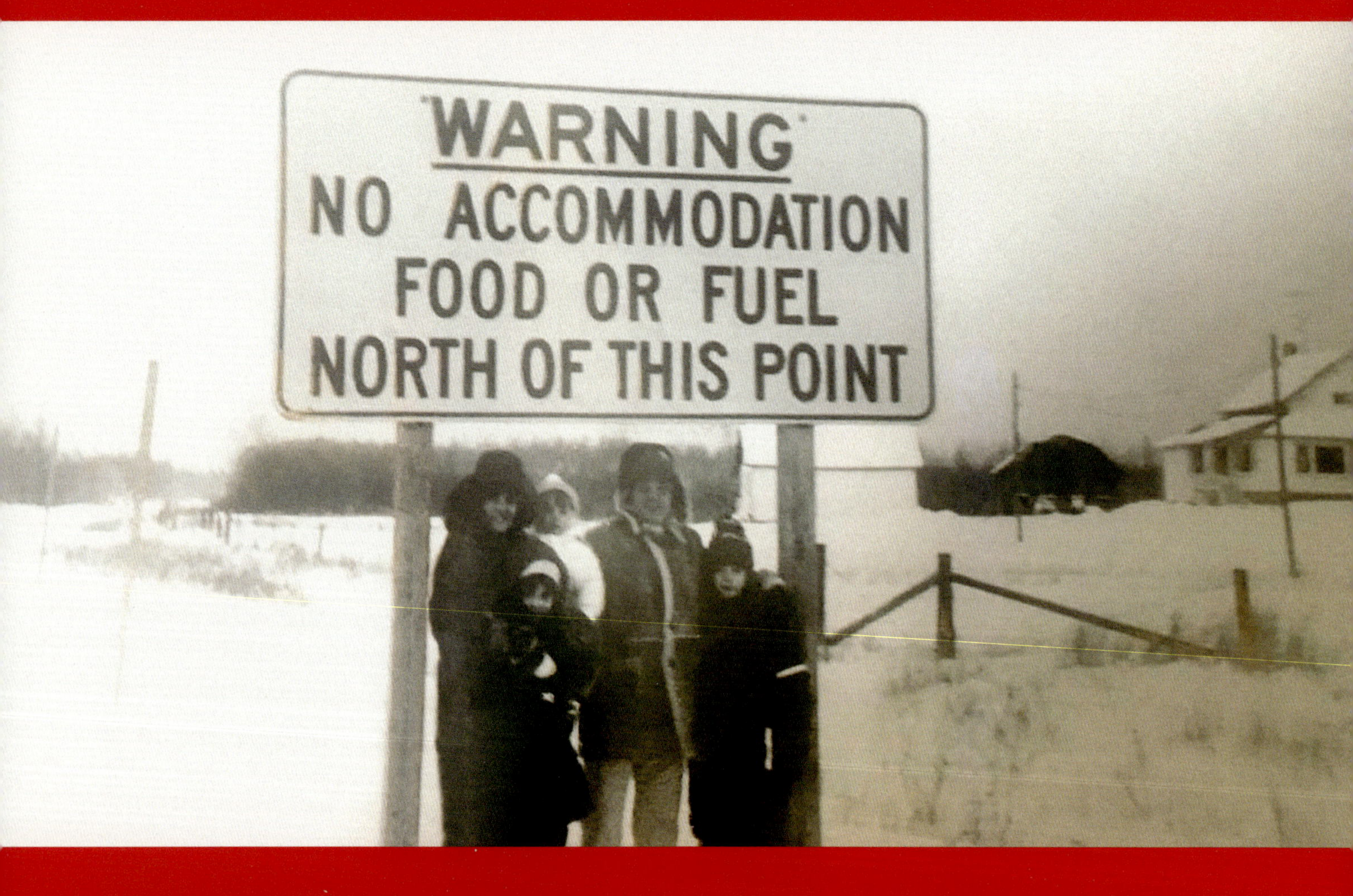
WARNING
NO ACCOMMODATION
FOOD OR FUEL
NORTH OF THIS POINT

"THERE ISN'T A DAY THAT GOES BY THAT I DON'T FEEL THE IMMENSE BENEFITS I HAVE REAPED BY BEING LUCKY ENOUGH TO BE BROUGHT TO CANADA AS A CHILD."

"I was born in New Delhi, India, to American parents who immigrated to Canada in the 1970s. I was just a baby when we arrived, but my brother and sister were older and having some difficulty initially adjusting to a new culture and climate. My parents were teachers who had accepted positions in a very small town about eight hours north of Toronto, so it was quite a contrast to their childhood life in India. As the family legend goes, my brother was being bullied by some tough hockey guys at school, but not for long. my father had an idea of how to resolve the problem. He walked straight into the local arena and signed up to join the curling team. He was a natural at the (highly unusual!) sport, became friends with everyone on the team, and our family was fully embraced by the community as true Canadians at heart. It's just a funny little story, but it has lived on in our family mythology for years, one of many fond memories of our adventures growing up in this incredible place. There isn't a day that goes by that I don't feel the immense benefits I have reaped by being lucky enough to be brought to Canada as a child."

EMILY HAINES
MUSICIAN · SONGWRITER

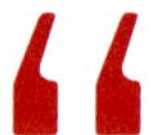

My most 'Canadian' memory was one that I was not present for: the arrival of my parents to Canada in early 1974, with two very small children. They had immigration papers but no jobs lined up. They had come from the eastern edge of the island of Borneo, part of Malaysia. When they landed in Vancouver, I do not know if they had winter coats or umbrellas, or if anyone met them at the airport. It's difficult for me — bittersweet, nostalgic — to imagine what my parents felt when the plane touched the ground. My mother was pregnant, and I would be born two or three months later. They would do their best with three children, they would separate and live very different lives. They would rarely go home again. When my mother passed away too soon, we would put her to rest in a place where, **on a clear day, you can glimpse the Fraser River and imagine the sea.**

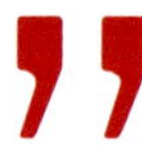

MADELEINE THIEN · AUTHOR

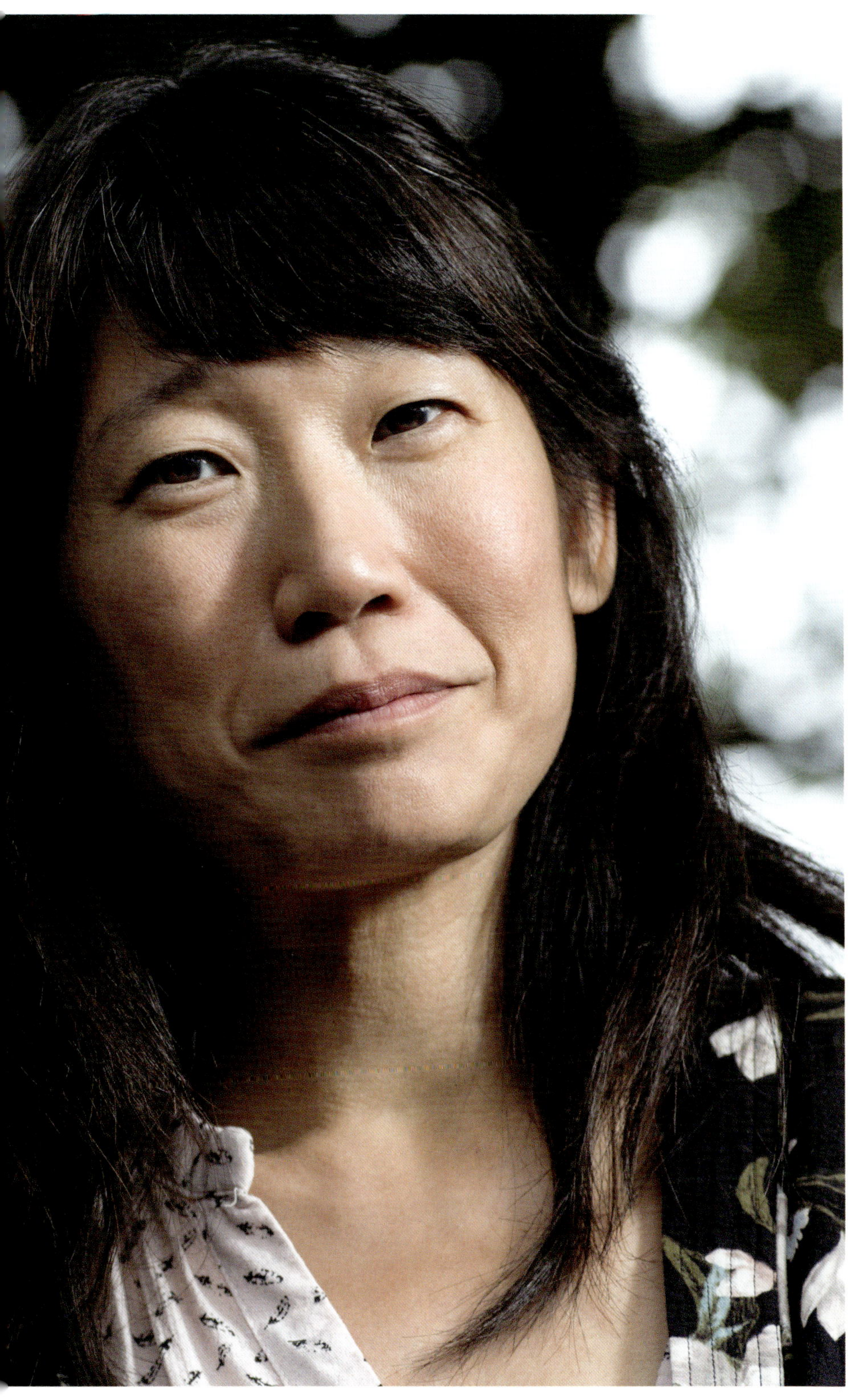

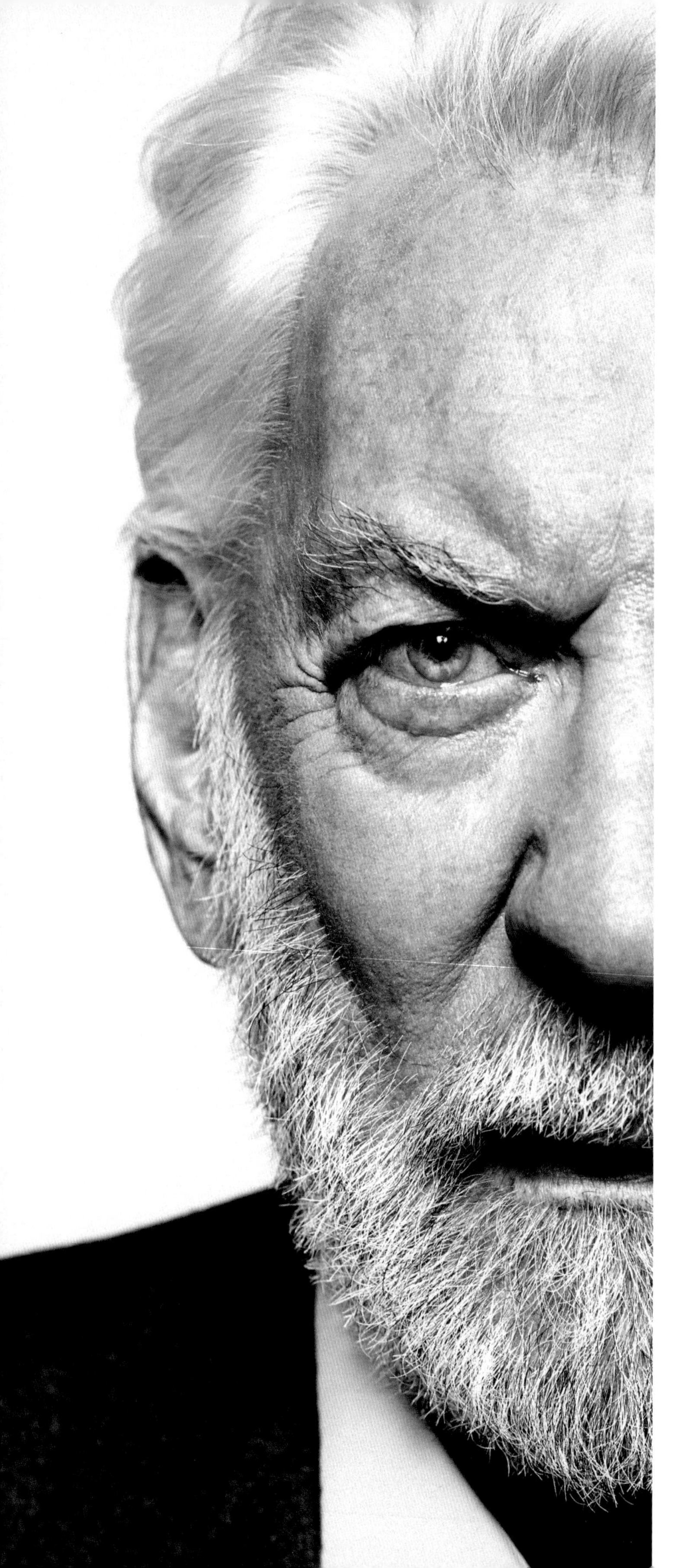

"I'VE NEVER FORGOTTEN SITTING THERE PROUDLY THINKING THIS IS WHAT IT IS TO BE CANADIAN."

DONALD SUTHERLAND · ACTOR

What does it mean to be Canadian?

"To whom? To me? To someone wishing they were Canadian? To someone waiting in line for a doctor? To someone listening to a loon out on the lake. To someone wishing that the flag had blue in it. (That's what the original proposal was. Blue borders, both oceans, a white central ground, and in the middle of that ground there was supposed to be an autumnal maple leaf like the one that used to be on an earlier flag that used the British Ensign. The maple leaf was essentially red but with gold and orange and so on in it. But rumour has it that the liberal government was in power and they decided no blue because that was the conservative party's colour. I have no idea if that's true, but that's what people say. Bottom line, I don't like the flag, there's nothing about it that moves me.) But that doesn't answer your question. Truth be told when you get right down to it, this is what it means to me to be Canadian. In 1954, coming back from Finland on my way home I went through Holland. Through the Netherlands. They thought I was American. They were decent to me. Courteous. But when someone asked what part of the States I was from I said, no, not me, me, I'm Canadian, and they started to cry, the older ones, and they all ran and embraced me and took me inside and fed me and invited neighbours in to see me saying something like 'hij is een Canadees'. I've never forgotten sitting there proudly thinking this is what it is to be Canadian, this is what my cousin Lew, shot by a sniper not far from here two days after D-Day was fighting for. For this, and for me."

What makes you proud to call yourself a Canadian?

"Peacefulness. Climate. Decency. Negotiation. Diplomacy. Stephen Lewis. Tommy Douglas. We had a rough time for a while with Stephen Harper when our values were being shredded as they are now under the new head of government in the United States, but we appear to have survived. We're not perfect, of course, but we're worth being, that's for sure, and we have a wonderful sense of humour."

When you are travelling, what do you miss most about Canada?

"Home."

WHAT DOES IT MEAN
TO BE CANADIAN?

CIVILITY
CIVILITY
CIVILITY

ELISHA CUTHBERT · ACTOR

"When the going gets rough, Canadians don't retreat behind our borders. We reach out to help people, no matter where they are. We understand we are a part of a world that's large, complicated, and not always fair. And we know how important it is to act as global citizens."

KIRSTINE STEWART
MEDIA EXECUTIVE · AUTHOR

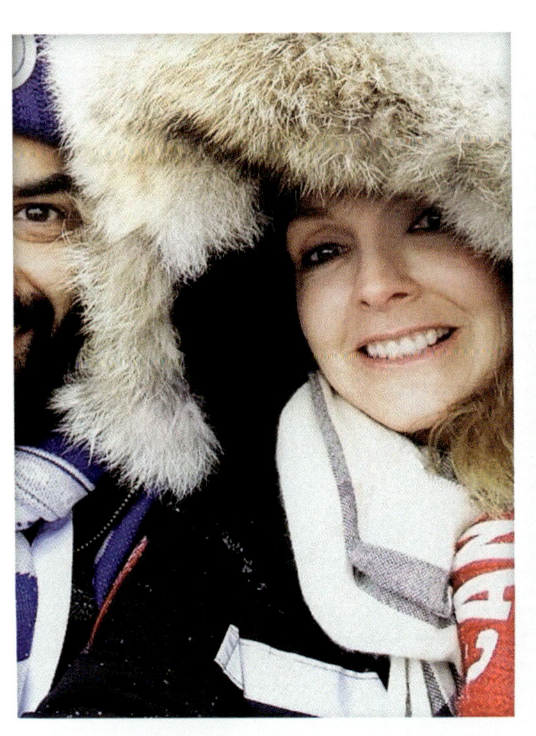

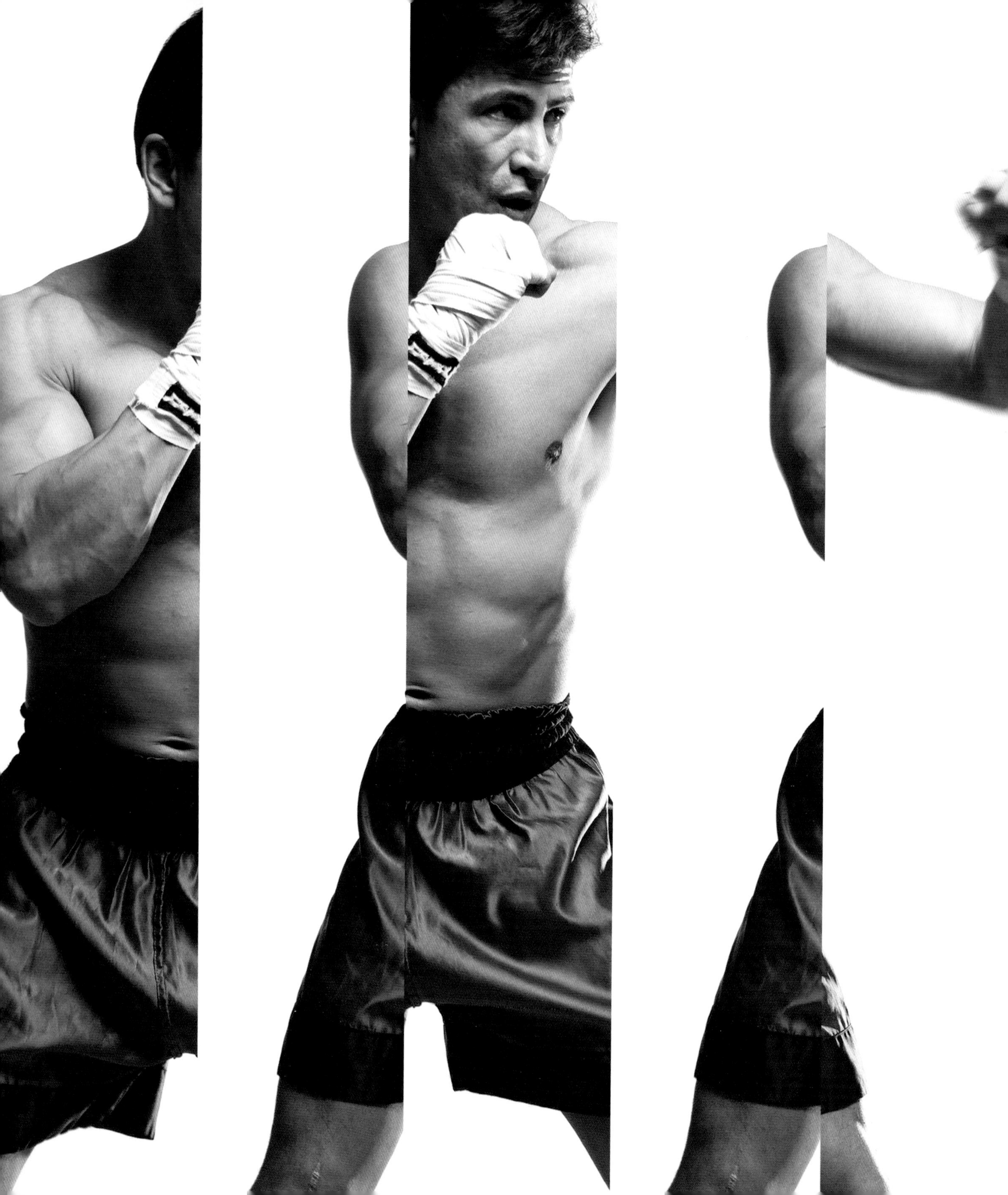

WAYNE BOURQUE · ATHLETE

What does it mean to be Canadian?

"When I think about what it means to be Canadian, one word that comes directly to mind is RESPECT. Canadians are respectful and big-hearted. We respect our land, our wildlife, each other, our elders, their stories and culture. I have tremendous respect for my family, friends, clients, and neighbours, and in turn I feel respected. I believe respect is earned and Canadians know this. We work hard and truly respect and appreciate everyone's contributions: the teacher, the priest, the housekeeper, restaurant owner, waiter, artist, athlete, farmer, doctor, lawyer, journalist, salesperson, mom, etc. To honour all of Creation is to have Respect. I believe this is not only a fundamental attitude of the First Nations and Métis people, but an understanding of all Canadians.

So what makes me proud to call myself Canadian is this respect—this fundamental attitude we all share. And the genuine kind-heartedness of almost everyone. Random acts of kindness are in a Canadian's DNA.

I remember a time I had lost everything. My home burnt down and the fire took all my hopes and dreams of going to the Nationals with it. The year was 1982, I was living in Fort McMurray, and my roommates and I had no insurance and were literally left with the shirts on our backs. The people of Fort McMurray organized a fundraiser that not only got us back in a home with beds to sleep on, but enabled me to go to the Nationals the following week, where I won a bronze medal. I had lost all hope of going, and to this day, I can recall that feeling of love in my heart for what everyone in that city did for me. It was incredible.

The same feeling of gratitude got me just over a year ago. Every Christmas I organize a holiday party for Centre Ring clients and a toy drive for kids who we know won't otherwise have anything under the tree. December 2015 I lost my younger brother Dean very unexpectedly and I was devastated. What did Centre Ring clients do? They did for me what they knew was important and what I could not do myself that year. They organized themselves and raised a ton of money for the Native Friendship Centre here in Toronto in honour of my brother. I was so touched by the kindness and generosity. It is again something I will never forget.

I am very proud to be Canadian. Canadians give their time and money to others in need, and those examples are paid forward. The end result is a nation of people who for the most part feel safe and empowered."

The truth about Canada is...

"It can get cold, but Canadians' hearts are warm."

WHEN YOU ARE TRAVELLING,
WHAT DO YOU MISS MOST ABOUT CANADA?

"POUTINE

I NEVER EAT IT, BUT I LIKE TO KNOW IT'S THERE."

CHARLOTTE GRAY · AUTHOR

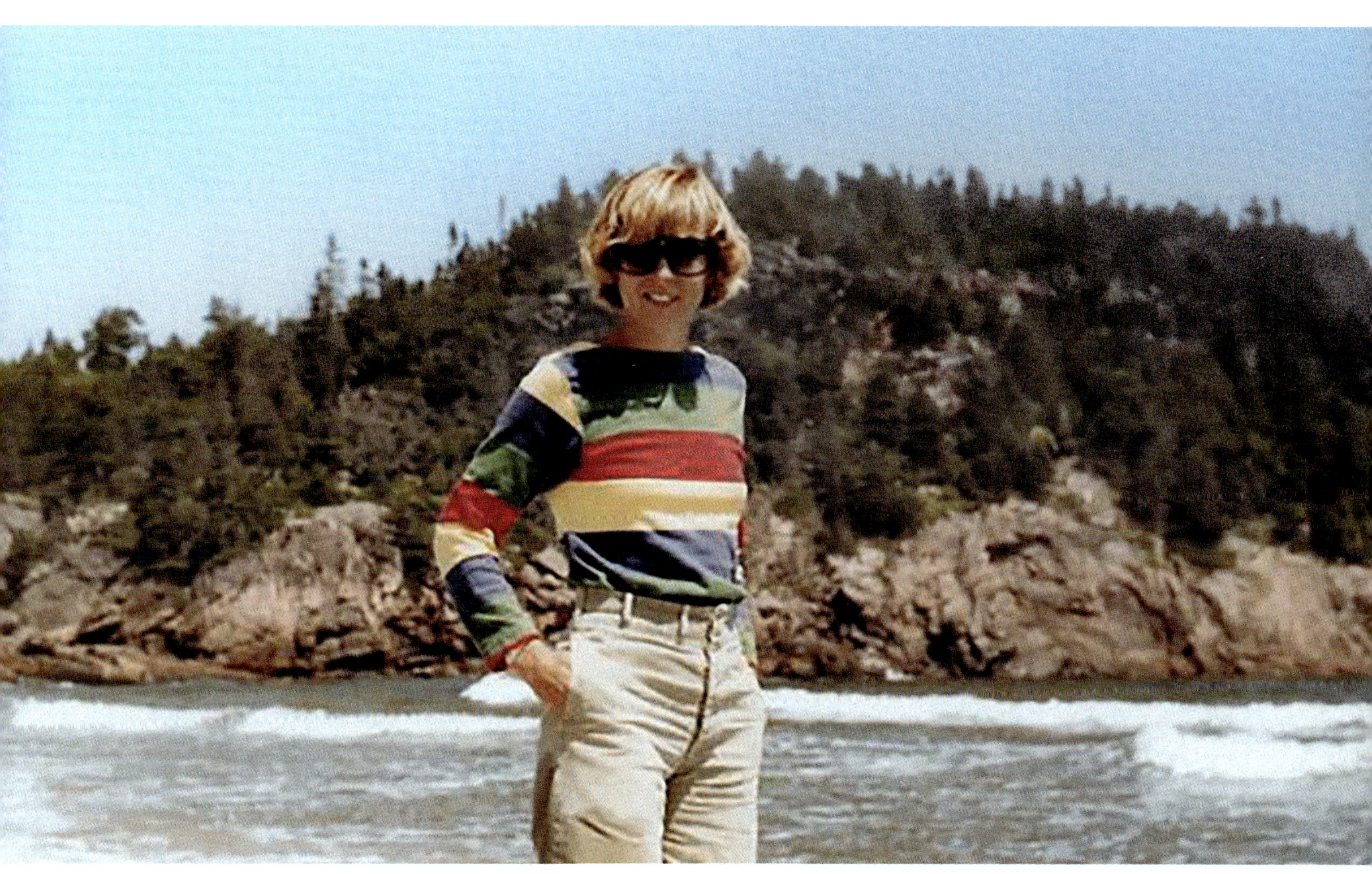

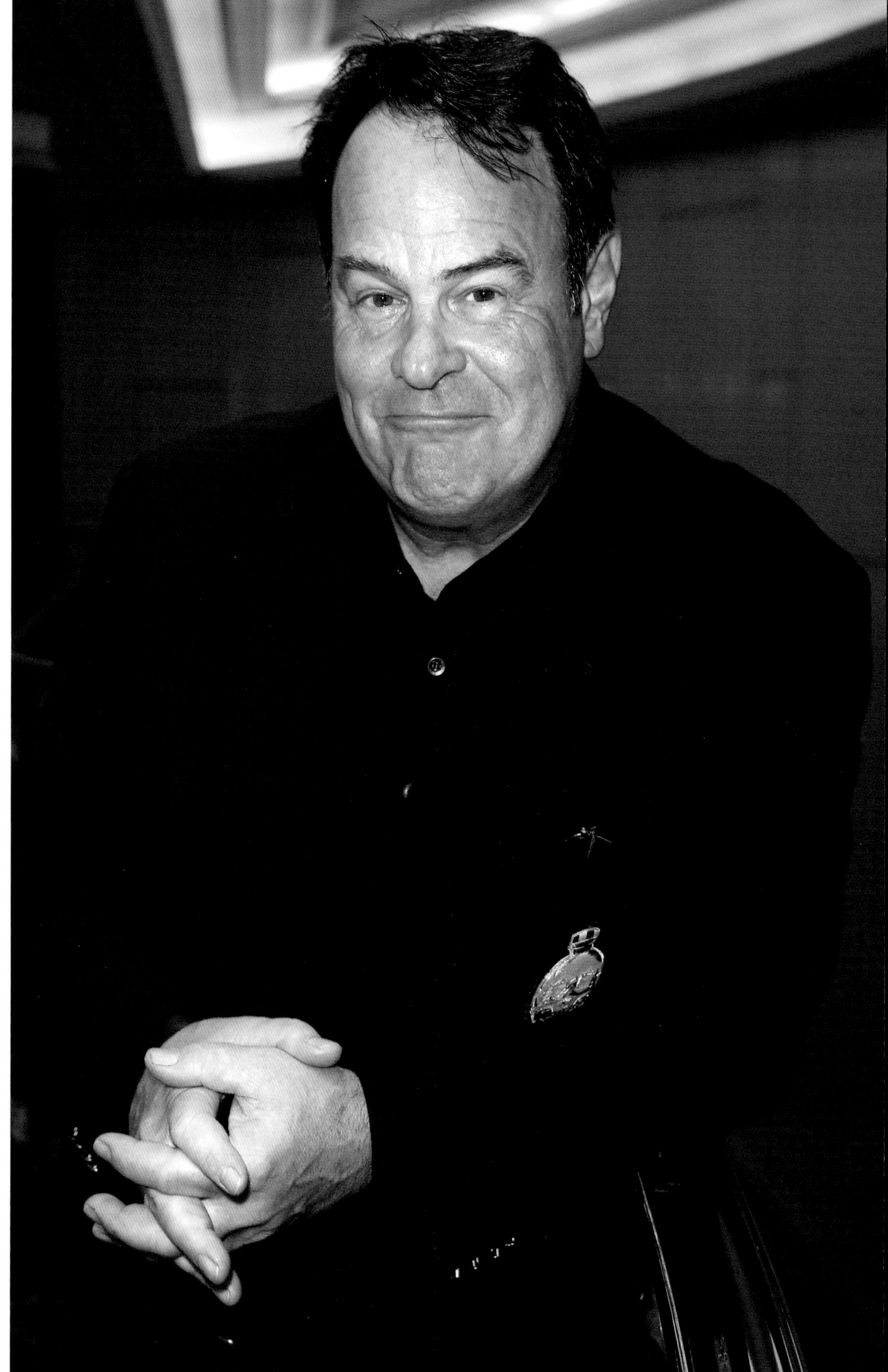

"BEING CANADIAN REALLY DOES MEAN ALWAYS HAVING TO SAY: 'I'M SORRY.' BUT I MYSELF HAVEN'T YET FIGURED OUT WHY WE DO THIS."

What is your birthday wish for Canada?

"My birthday wish for Canada is that its citizens continue to further deepen the sentiments of tolerance and compassion, which have been customarily endemic to our nation and its culture."

What does it mean to be Canadian?

"Being Canadian really does mean always having to say: 'I'm sorry.' But I myself haven't yet figured out why we do this. Perhaps Canadians apologize all the time because we live in a country that has so much more going for it than almost any other place on the planet and it makes us feel a little guilty."

What is your most "Canadian" memory?

"My most vivid Canadian memory was driving a Nodwell flex-track tundra crawler down the cutline of what was to become the Fort Liard oil road at sunset as a white wolf crossed our path between rows of chalk-white birch with shimmering, silvery leaves."

DAN AYKROYD · ACTOR
WRITER · MUSICIAN

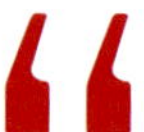

To be Canadian is to be human. And humane. It might mean that you have arrived, only yesterday, from another land. It might mean that your ancestors have been here forever, or for hundreds of years. **It means that you have the right—really, the obligation—to advocate for your own best interests and those of your loved ones, but it also means that you respect the inherent dignity and fundamental rights of every person on this planet,** be that your next-door neighbour or a person living in a country a dozen time zones away. To be Canadian is to be everything that every decent, caring human being aspires to be: successful on your own terms, concerned with individual and collective well-being, and engaged in the betterment of this world.

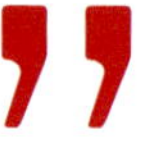

LAWRENCE HILL · AUTHOR

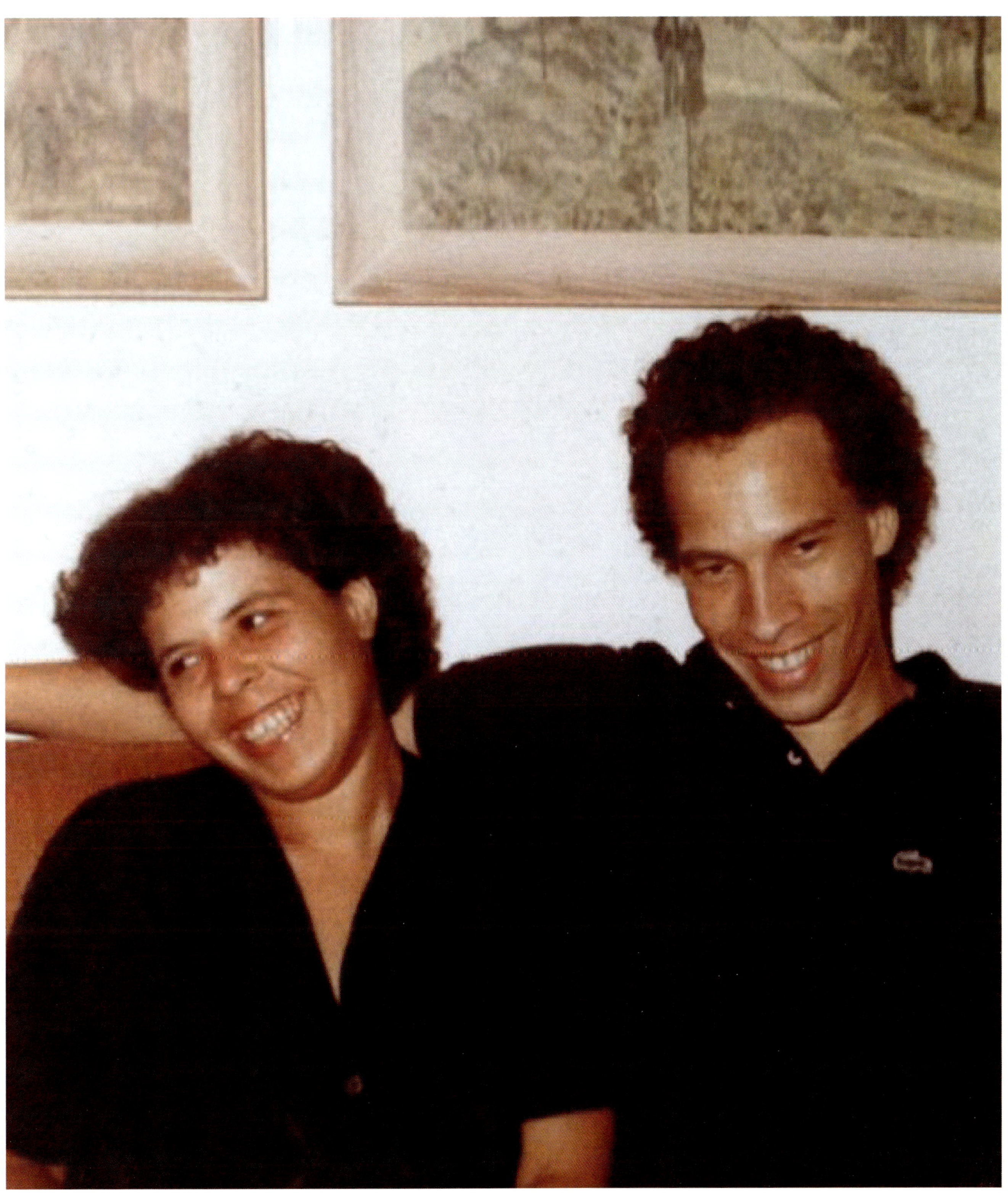

bun·ny·hug
/'bənēhəg/

The common term for a
hooded sweatshirt in Saskatchewan.

tour·tière
/tōōr'tyer/

C'est un plat typiquement canadien-français composé de porc, de veau, de bœuf ou de gibier hachés finement en cubes qui sont ensuite insérés entre deux croûtes.

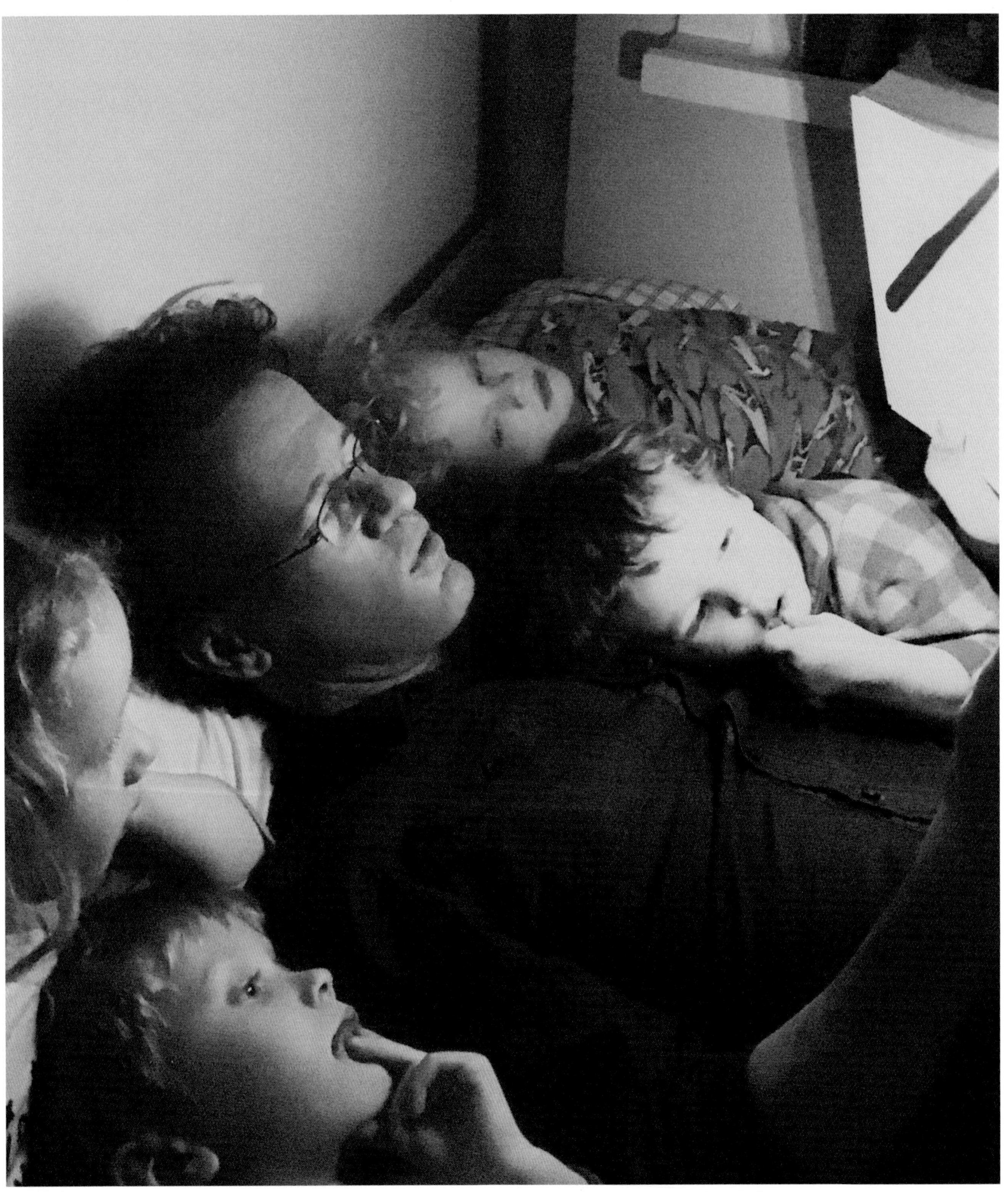

YANN MARTEL · AUTHOR

"I remember once being in the south of India, waiting to make a phone call to Canada from a phone wallah. A couple next to me turned and asked, 'Excuse me, sir, where are you from?' Now, you have to read that with the proper Indian accent and imagine the couple as typically Indian—the woman sari-clad, the two indistinguishable from any other couple on that street 'I'm from Canada,' I said. 'So are we!' they exclaimed with delight. And so they were, from Scarborough. That was a quintessentially Canadian moment for me: meeting strangers, only to find out that they were not, that despite every appearance of distance and difference that they were, essentially, the same as me."

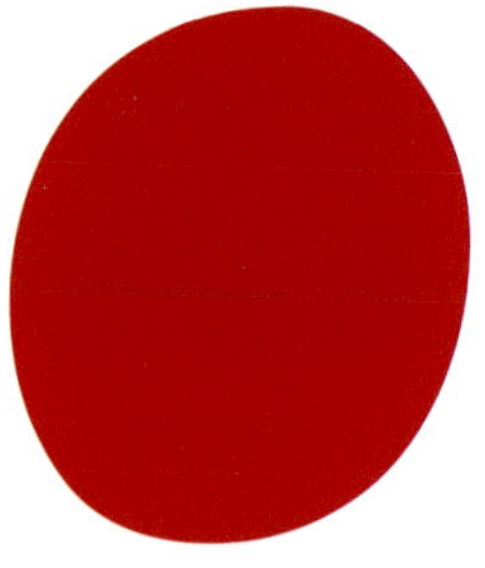

i **have memories of watching the northern lights over frozen lakes growing up in North Bay,** going to Tim Hortons for both lunch and dinner every day for almost a month while working on a record in Niagara Falls, bringing hot chocolates to fans in Winnipeg waiting outside the venue in minus thirty-degree weather, or getting stranded in the middle of a lake one summer with a rock bass I'd just caught flopping around at the bottom of the boat because I didn't have the guts to kill it.

LIGHTS · MUSICIAN
SONGWRITER

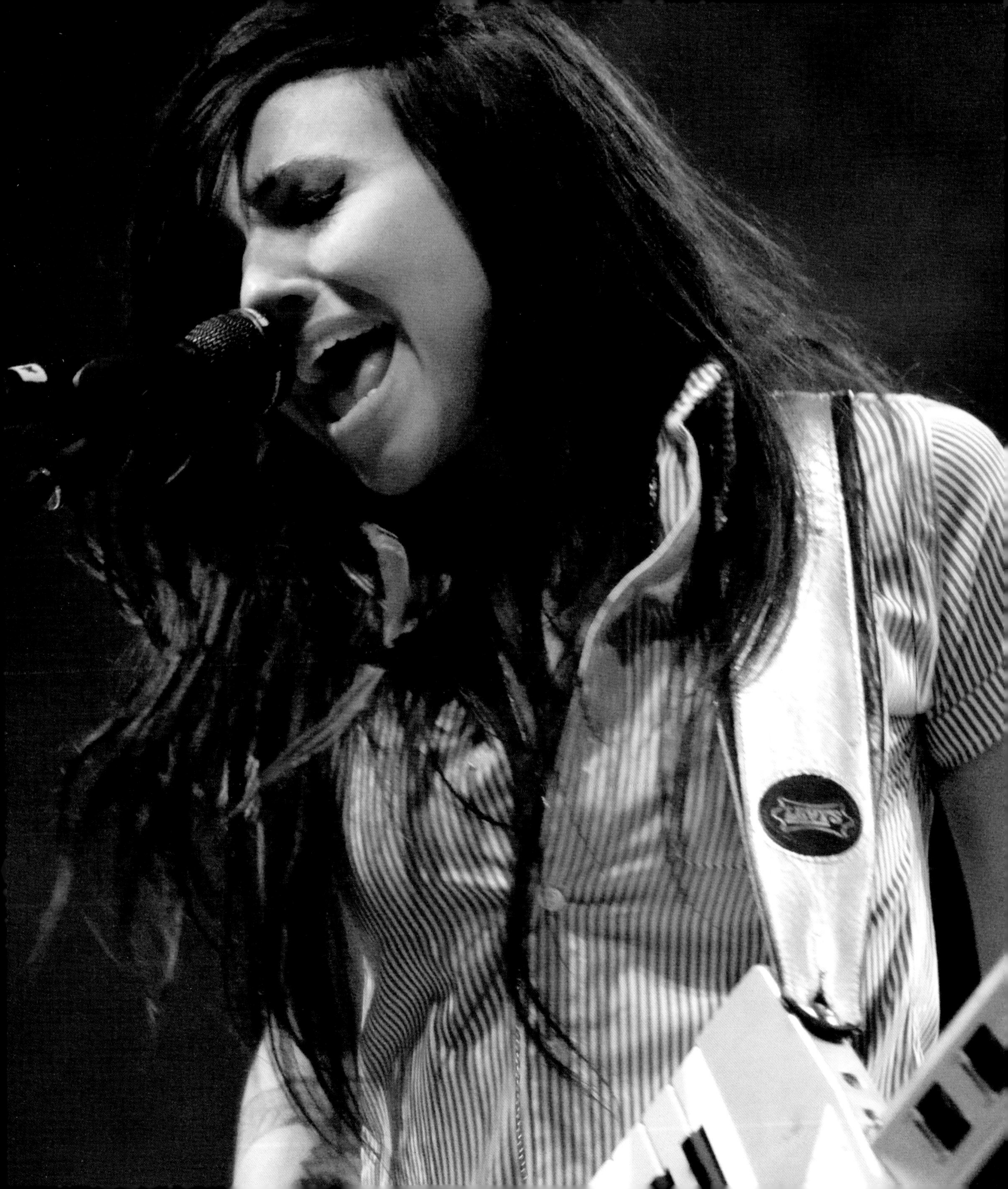

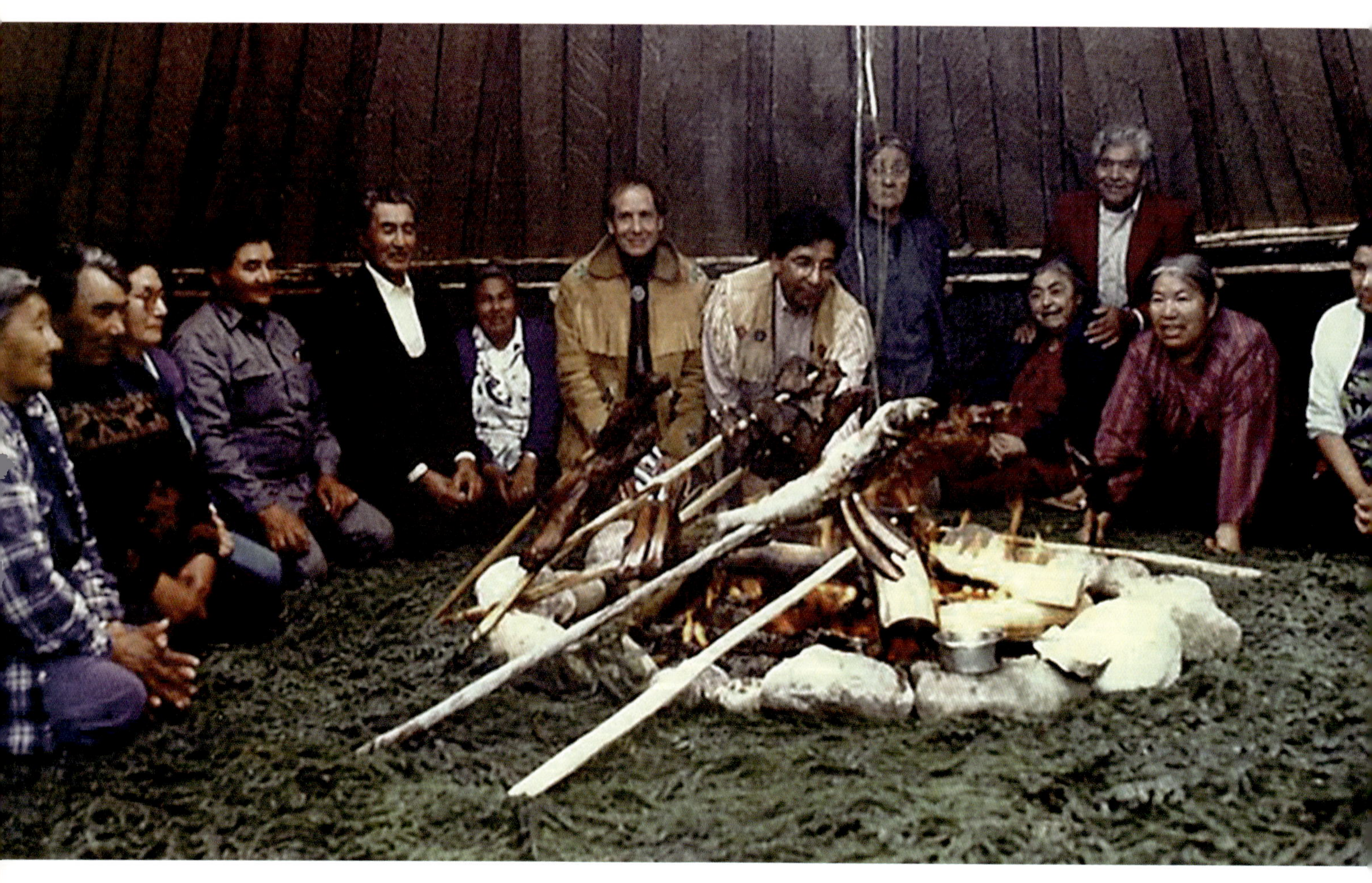

"THE CANADIAN MOMENT THAT STANDS OUT THE MOST TO ME IS WHEN I RECEIVED A HEADDRESS FROM MY KAINAI PEOPLE AND THE ELDERS GAVE ME THE NAME OF MY ANCESTOR, WHO IS THE PEACEMAKER."

DOUGLAS CARDINAL · ARCHITECT

«JE SERAIS UN QUÉBÉCOIS-CANADIEN. JE VIENS DU QUÉBEC, ET JE LE DIS CHAQUE FOIS QUE JE VISITE UN AUTRE PAYS. C'EST MES RACINES, MES ORIGINES, ET LA CHOSE LA PLUS IMPORTANTE POUR MOI.»

CÉLINE DION · MUSICIAN

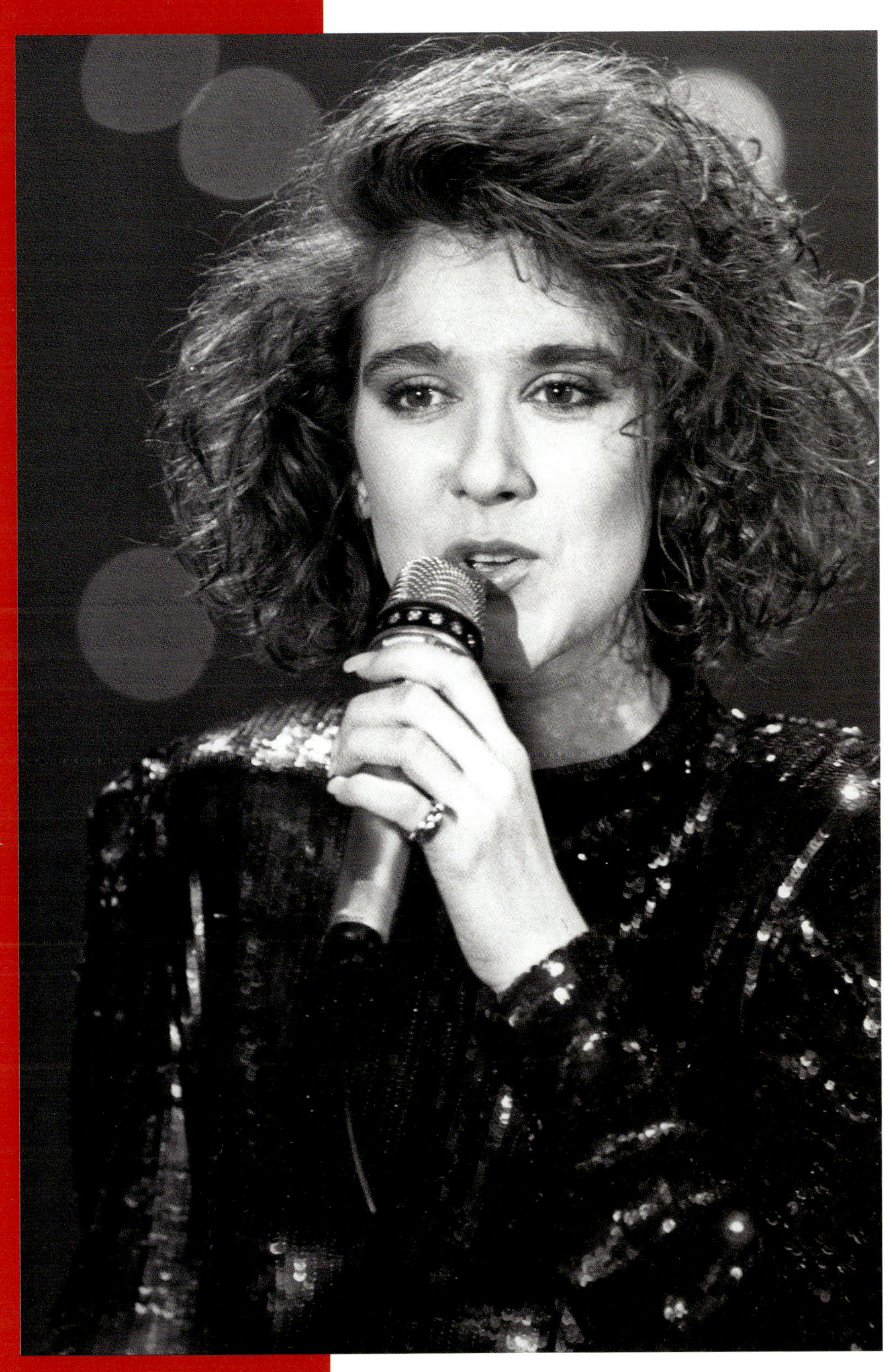

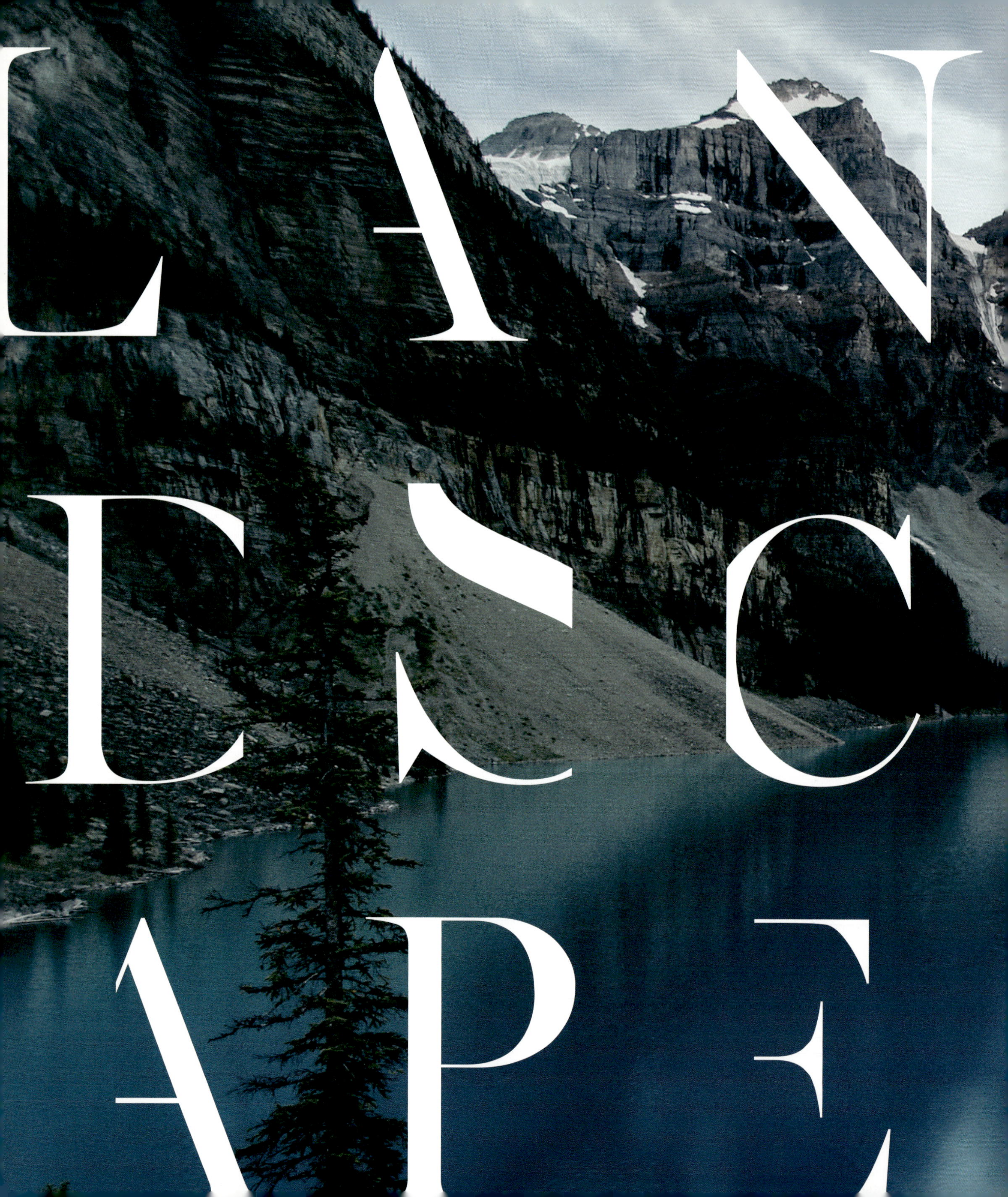

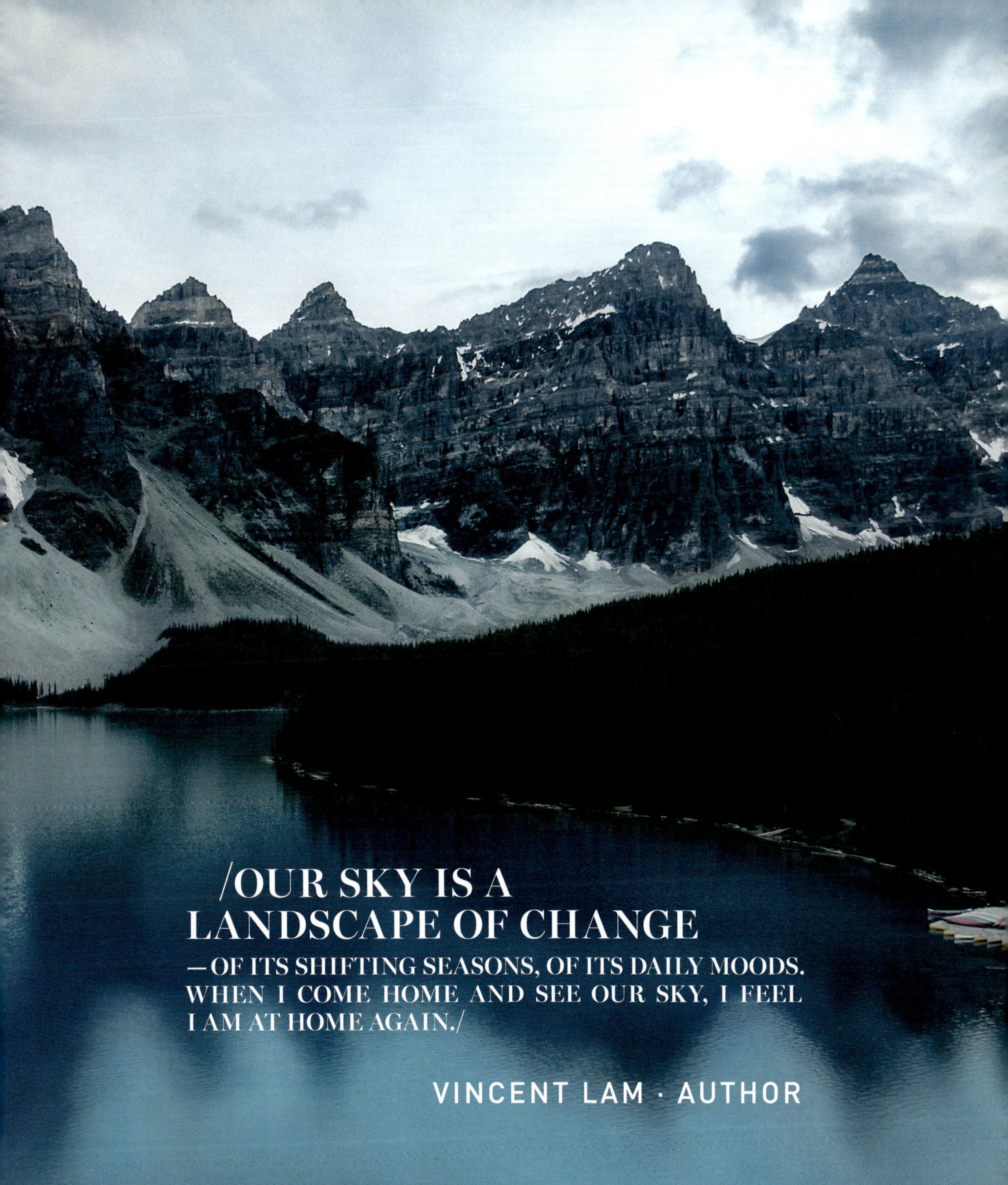
/OUR SKY IS A LANDSCAPE OF CHANGE
—OF ITS SHIFTING SEASONS, OF ITS DAILY MOODS. WHEN I COME HOME AND SEE OUR SKY, I FEEL I AM AT HOME AGAIN./
VINCENT LAM · AUTHOR

MICHAEL BONACINI
CHEF · AUTHOR

"I arrived in Canada in 1985 for my first chef's job at the Windsor Arms Hotel in Toronto. One day, a young pastry chef came down with a stack of blueberry pancakes, warm maple syrup, and three slices of peameal bacon and said, 'Welcome to Canada, Chef.' It was a small gesture, but so representative of how welcoming Canada is. That moment has stuck with me ever since. So much so that my family and I have a tradition of enjoying blueberry pancakes, warm maple syrup, and peameal bacon every Canada Day."

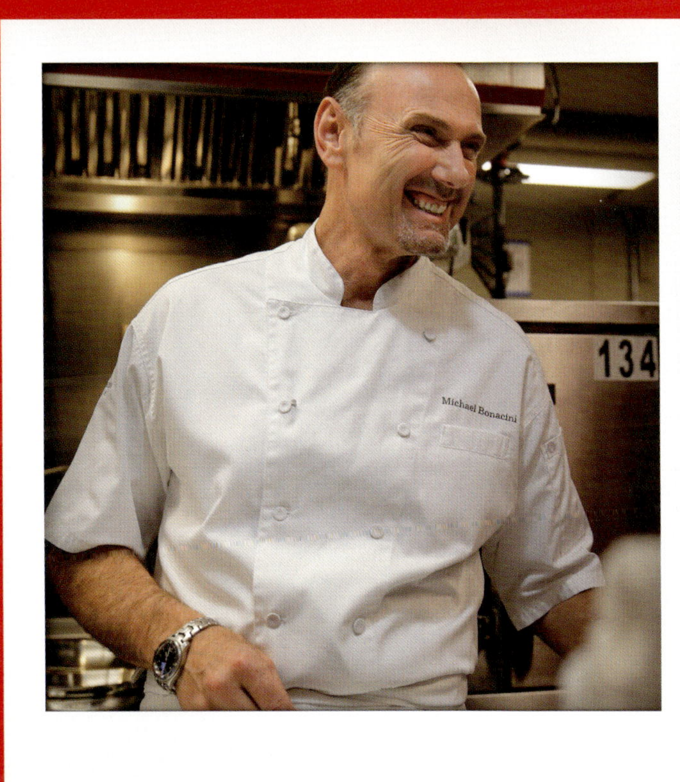
134
Michael Bonacini

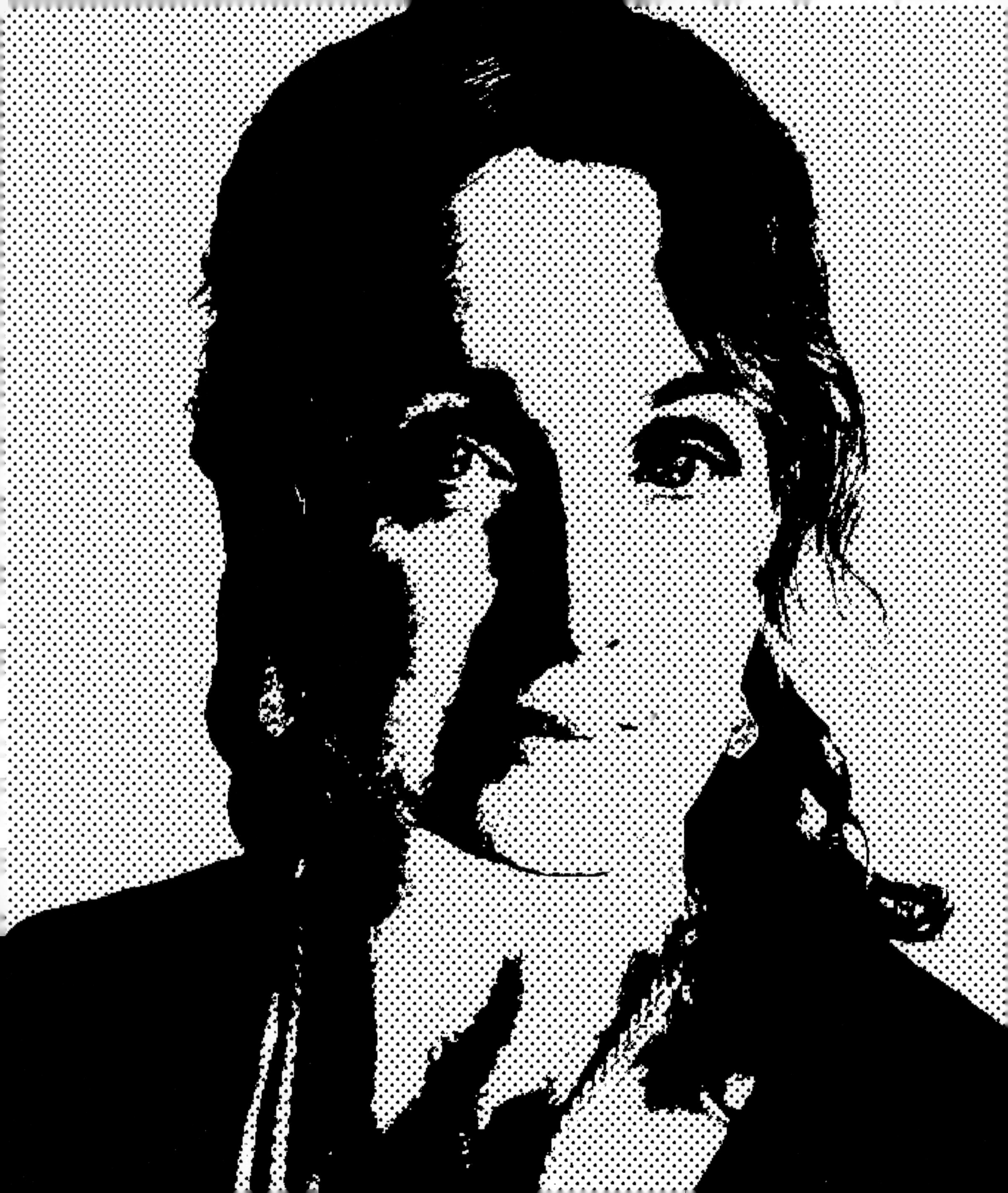

JUDITH THOMPSON · PLAYWRIGHT · AUTHOR

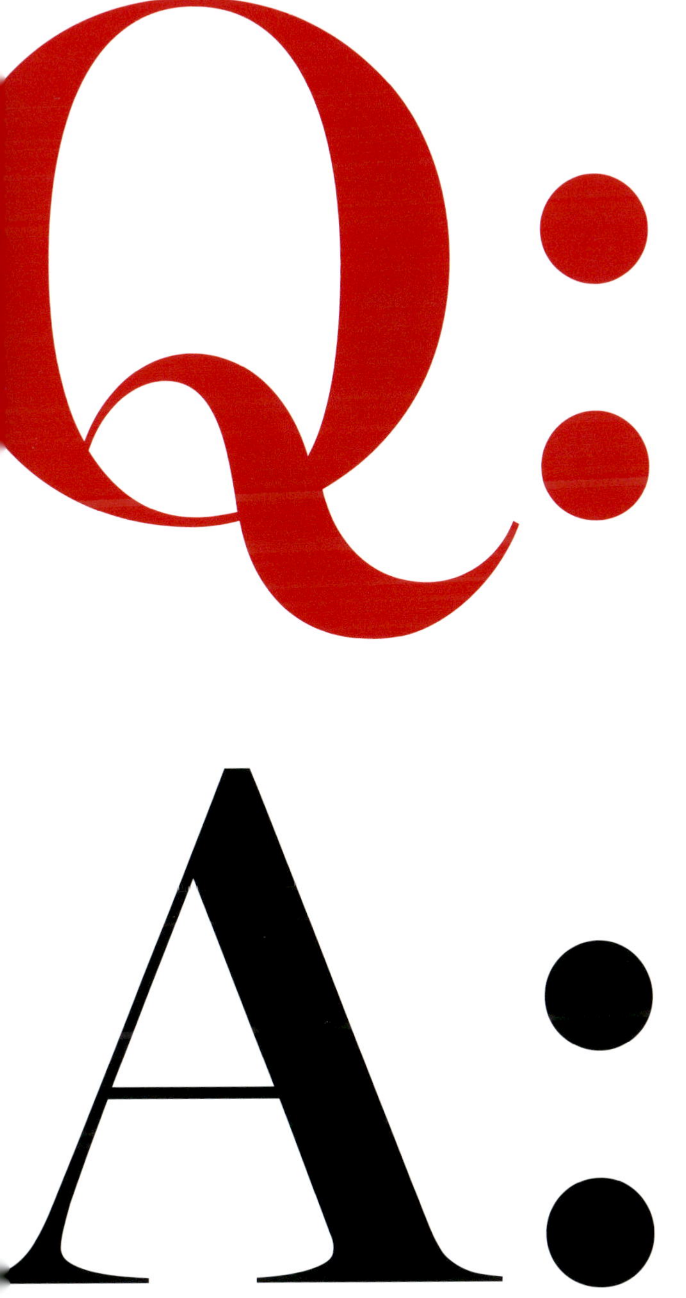

WHAT MAKES YOU PROUD TO CALL YOURSELF CANADIAN?

"Walking the streets of Toronto and hearing myriad languages all around me, somehow in harmony, together creating the unforgettable, penetrating music of Canada."

OK, THIS IS A PRETTY CANADIAN MOMENT...

"My daughters and I skated on the Harbourfront rink overlooking the lake yesterday. As grey afternoon turned to clear evening, I was stunned by the natural beauty, and most of all, I was heartened and amazed by how fluidly, how perfectly we skated around one another—seniors skating for the very first time, tourists and new Canadians, hot-dogging teenagers, hockey players, figure skaters, hand-holding couples, fearless kids, ankles on the ice, falling, getting up, falling again, up again—and I did not see one collision. Not one. We would gracefully miss each other by inches, gliding in and out, around and around, and I thought, yes, that is how most of us are. We can easily, happily live together in harmony with everyone, everyone on this ice, and everyone is welcome, and there is always, always room for more."

“ONE OF MY MOST ‘CANADIAN’ MEMORIES IS CROSSING THE COUNTRY ON VIA RAIL IN THE '80s.”

DANIEL MACIVOR · PLAYWRIGHT

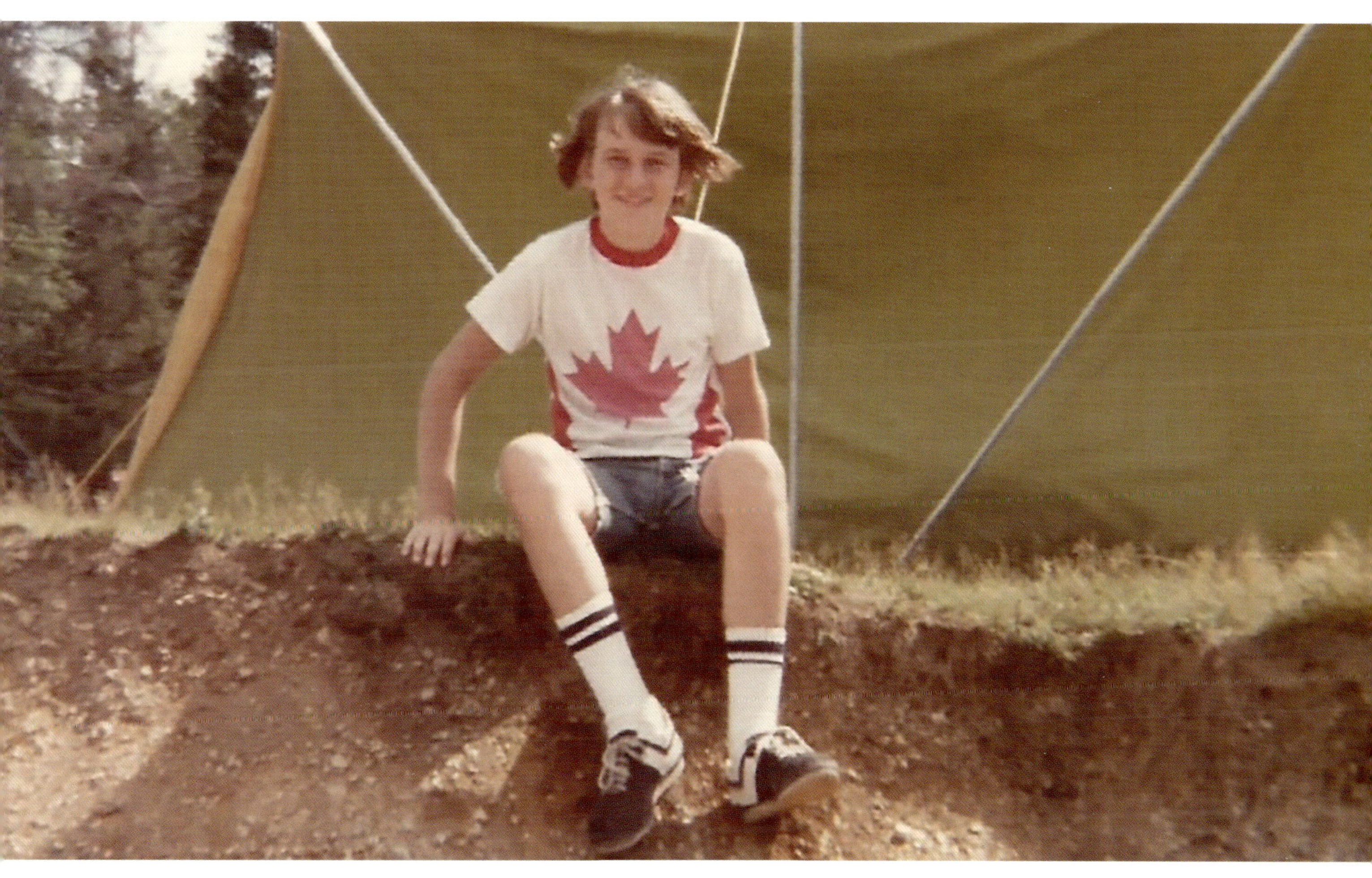

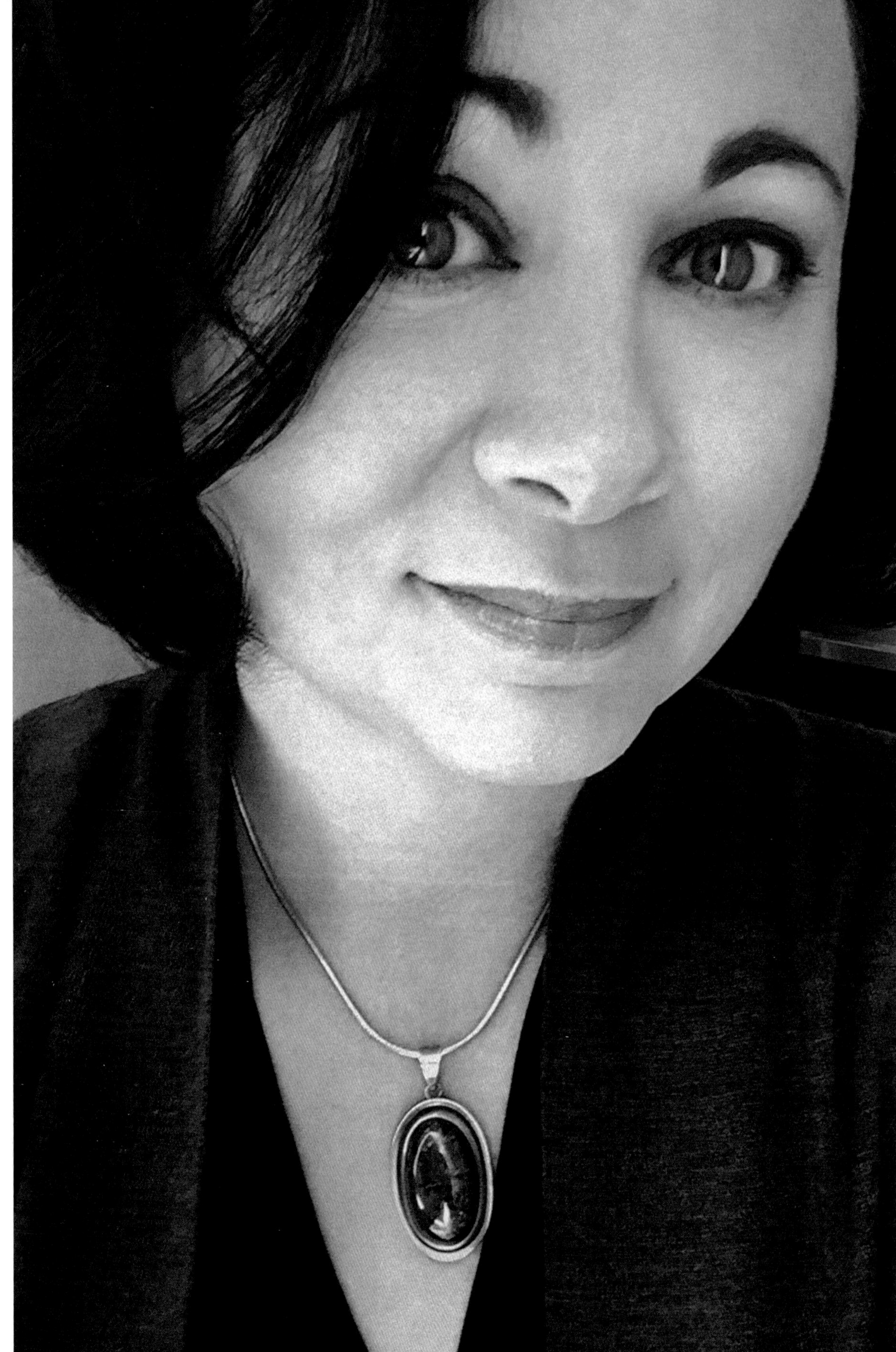

AMI MCKAY · JOURNALIST · AUTHOR

/ONE BY ONE WE TURNED IN OUR TESTS AND WAITED IN SILENCE./

What does it mean to be Canadian?

"Because I'm an immigrant, you might guess it would be the memory of the day I took my Oath of Citizenship. Actually, my most Canadian memory comes from a few months before that. It was the day I took my citizenship test. My eldest son, who was 11 at the time and too young to be required to take the test, had worked hard to help me study, memorizing the sample questions and quizzing me every chance he got. I'd been a good student in school and university and had never suffered from test anxiety in the past, but preparing for this test set my nerves completely on edge. This was a test I had to pass. When I arrived at the assigned building at the appointed time, there was a crowd of equally nervous people already waiting for the proctor to administer the test. As a group we were a lively (if anxious) representation of Canada's diverse population — a true cultural mosaic to say the least. We'd come from all over the world and were of various races, creeds, and ages. For most, English was not a first language. After saying goodbye to our loved ones, we were ushered into a room to take the test. Instructions were given slowly and clearly, and we were informed that no one would be allowed to leave until we'd all finished and the results had been recorded. One by one we turned in our tests and waited in silence. After what felt like an eternity, the person in charge came to the front of the room to make an announcement. In an instant his face went from serious to beaming as he said, 'I'm pleased to inform you, everyone has passed.' A joyful chorus of applause and cheers went up in the room. Next to the laughter of my children or my husband saying 'I love you,' it is the most glorious sound I've ever heard."

"MY CANADIAN-NESS AFFECTS EVERY ASPECT OF MY BEING. MY AMERICAN FRIENDS ONCE ACCUSED ME OF ENJOYING BEING CANADIAN. GUILTY AS CHARGED."

MIKE MYERS · ACTOR · COMEDIAN

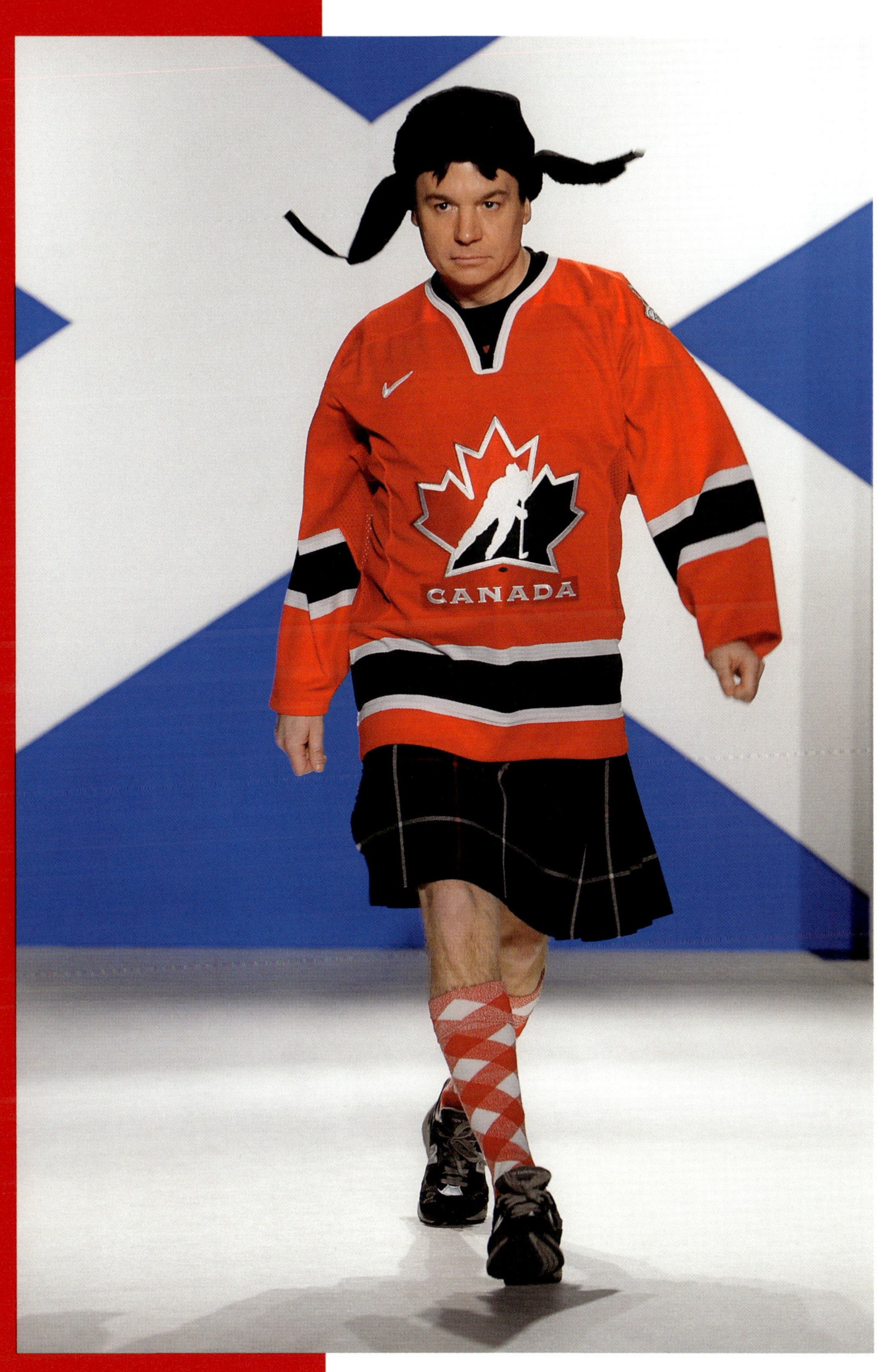
CANADA

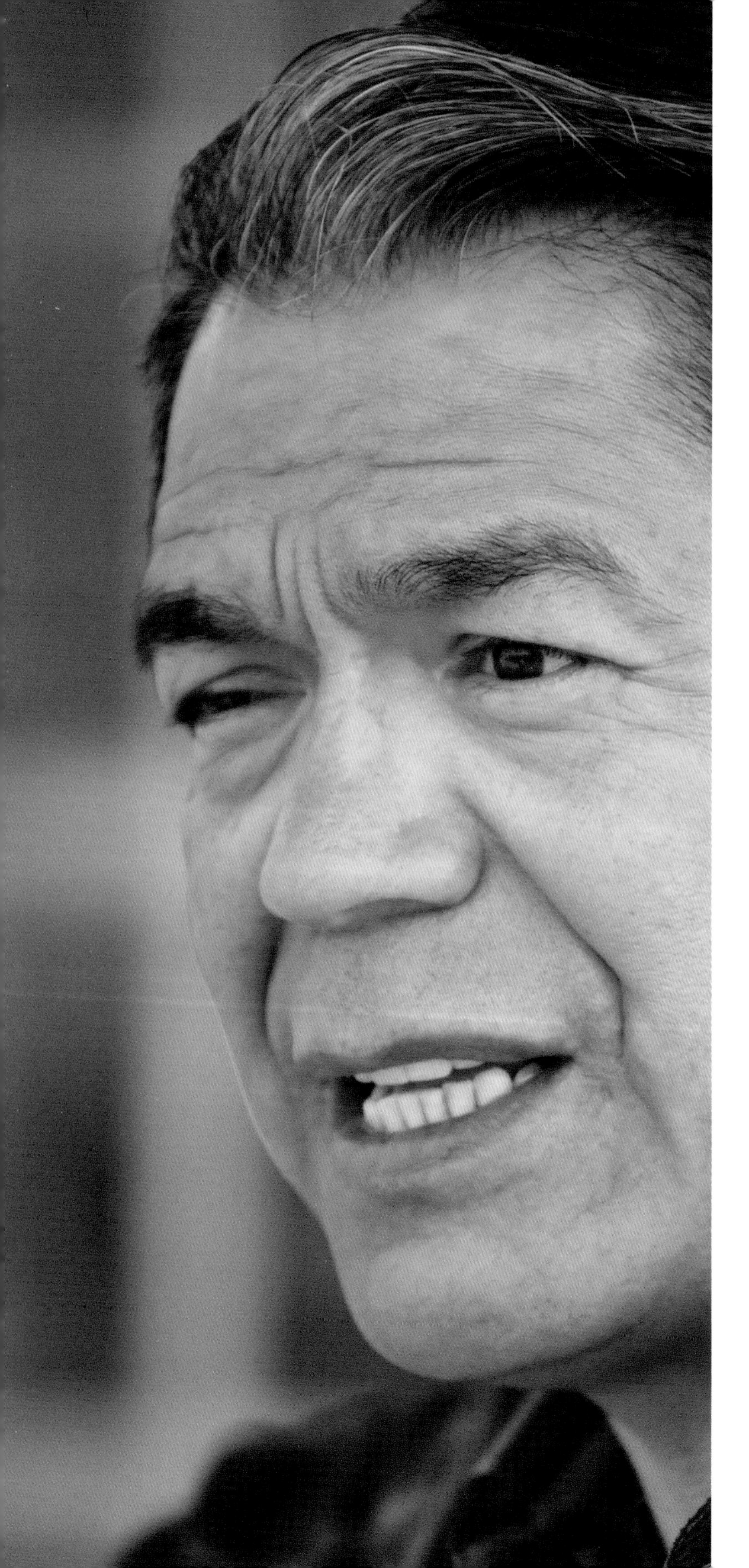

"WHAT AM I DOING TO MAKE AND KEEP RELATIONSHIPS IN GOOD ORDER AND TO MAKE MY PART OF THE WORLD A CLEAN, PURE, SACRED PLACE?"

LORNE CARDINAL · ACTOR

The best way to endear yourself to a Canadian is...

"To not say 'eh!' Or 'aboot.' Instead, compliment or even recognize the achievements we have given to the world in the fields of science, robotics, and engineering. Hollywood wouldn't be the same without our Canadian talents.

Most successful professional and amateur sports teams can boast of Canadian athletes.

Let us not forget our much-coveted policies in regards to health and education that other countries dream of.

Also mention a thanks to the men and women who serve in harm's way who are trying to bring peace and safety to the world.

A mention of any of the above would definitely earn you a 'Welcome to Canada' beverage!"

The truth about Canada is...

"The origin of the word or name of Canada derives from the word *kanatan* that is found in the languages of the Iroquois, the Cree, and the Algonquin-speaking peoples of North America. *Kanatan* means 'it is pure, clean, sacred,' which denotes a place. When the word is shortened to *kanata* it comes to mean 'to make pure, clean, sacred'—it becomes an action.

By understanding the word *kanata* in this way is to see the name of our country as a verb and not a noun. From which we are reminded every day, to seek ways in which to make *kanata* into *kanatan*. In order to achieve this goal, we must ensure that our relationships are in order. We, therefore, must look first into ourselves to ensure that we are in balance. Then we must look out to our family, our community, our nation, the Earth, the cosmos, and the spirit world with this one directive: 'What am I doing to make and keep relationships in good order and to make my part of the world a Clean, Pure, Sacred place?'

This is a teaching shared with me from my brother, Lewis Cardinal."

"THE MOST CANADIAN THING IS A GAME OF SHINNY ON A FROZEN LAKE UP AT THE COTTAGE, FOLLOWED BY HOT COCOA, HOT DOGS, AND HOT SEX

NOT NECESSARILY IN THAT ORDER."

TYLER STEWART · MUSICIAN

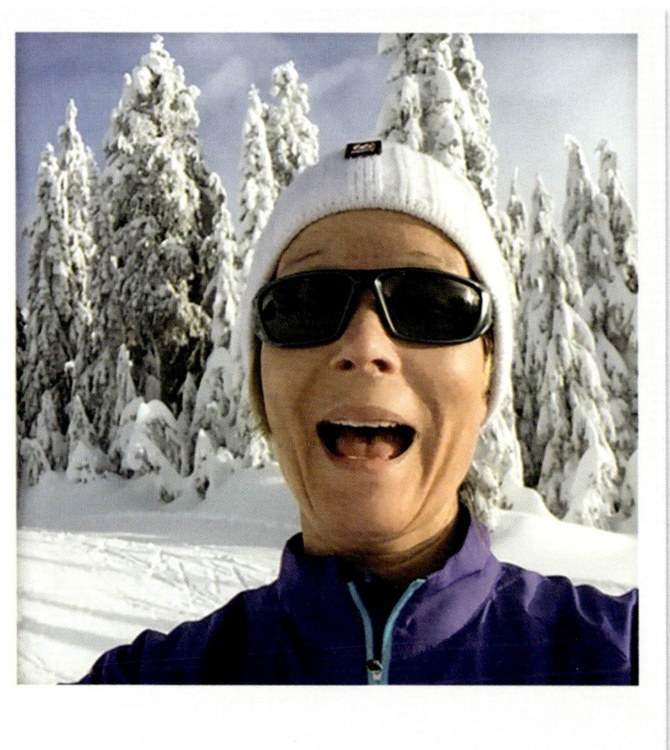

"I love to travel, especially for my books, but I get homesick sometimes for our outdoors. I live in Vancouver and I'm used to being in the woods, or on my bike, or on cross-country skis, or swimming in the ocean. I miss our wide open spaces."

SUSIN NIELSEN · AUTHOR

"FOR ME, THE VERY WORD 'CANADIAN' CONJURES A WELCOMING STANCE: POWERFUL, PLANTED, WITH ARMS STRETCHED WIDE. THIS IS A STANCE OF COURAGE AND COMPASSION."

ANN-MARIE MACDONALD
AUTHOR · PLAYWRIGHT

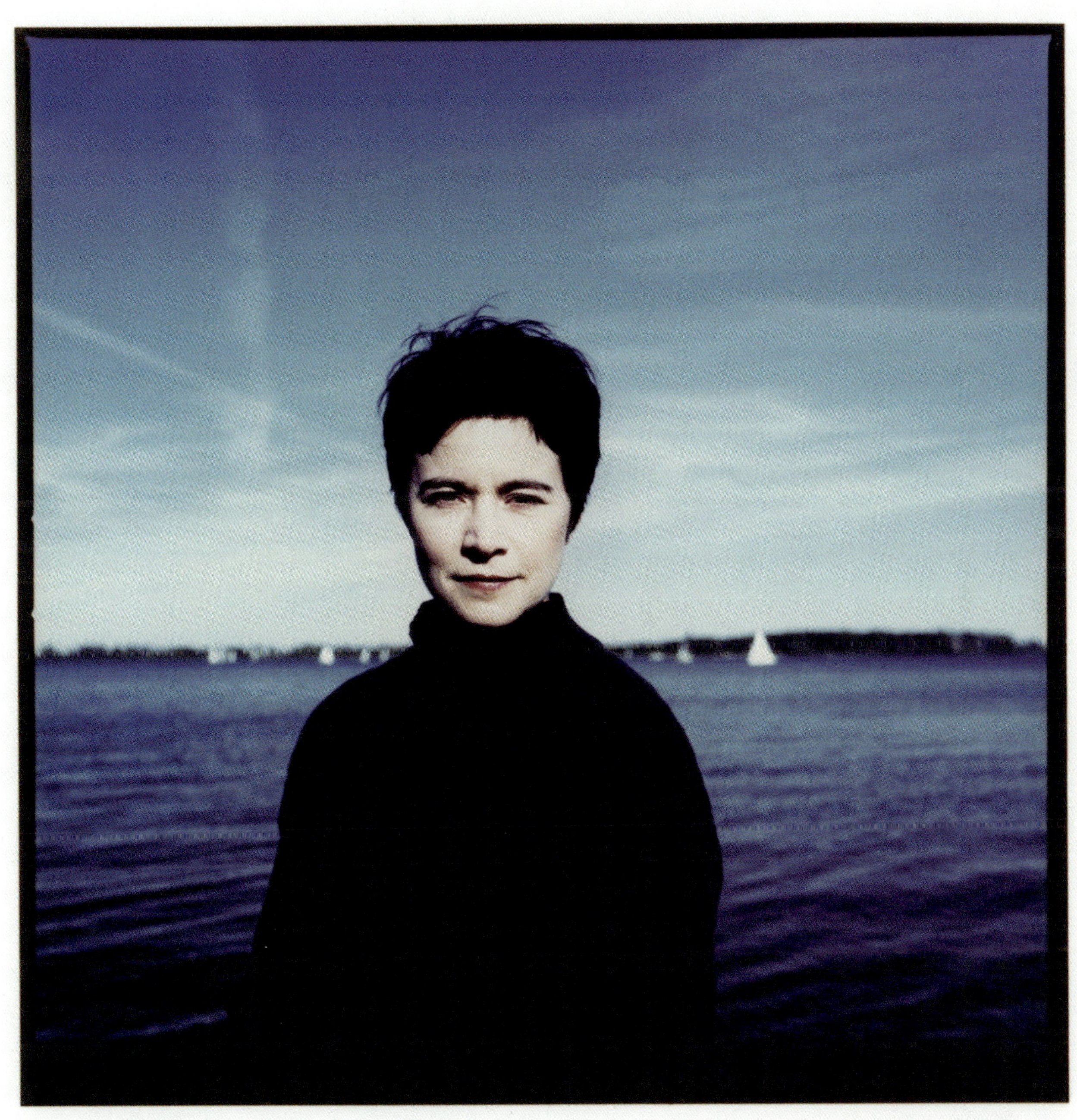

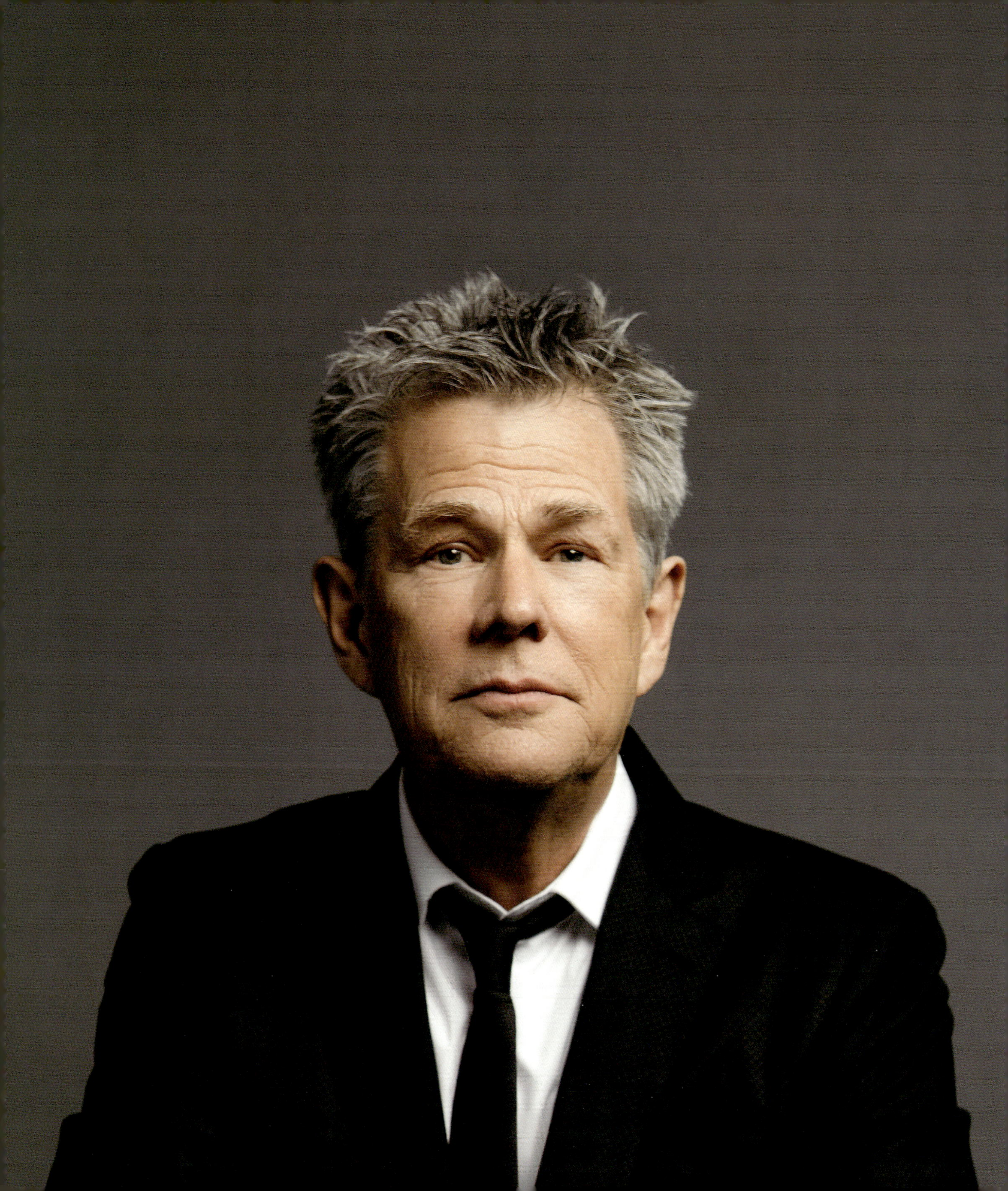

“HAPPY BIRTHDAY
TO THE MOST BEAUTIFUL
COUNTRY IN THE WORLD.
BEING CANADIAN HAS
BEEN A SECRET WEAPON
FOR ME MY ENTIRE LIFE.
I’M THE BIGGEST
FLAG-WAVER YOU WILL
EVER MEET—ALWAYS HAVE
BEEN—ALWAYS WILL BE.
THANK YOU, CANADA,
FOR BEING MY
LIFELONG SOULMATE!!”

DAVID FOSTER · PRODUCER

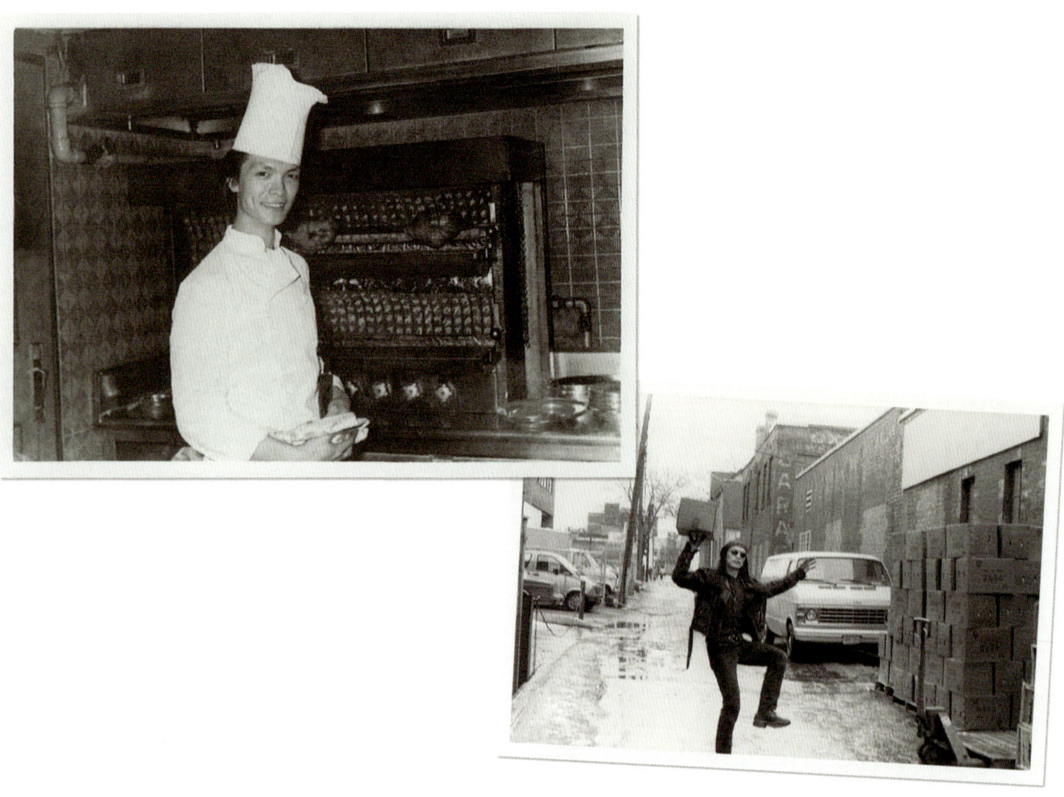

What does it mean to be Canadian?

"Being an immigrant, Canada holds a special place in my heart. I call it home now. **I'm grateful that the Canadian people welcomed me with open arms and gave me the opportunity to live and work with other cultures.** Canadians are a proud nation, and for great reasons. There is a rich Canadian history and the land is so fertile and diverse from coast to coast. As a chef, I appreciate the power of the land and sea. As a father, I'm proud to be able to raise my sons within our family business as the next generation of restaurateurs in Toronto."

SUSUR LEE · CHEF

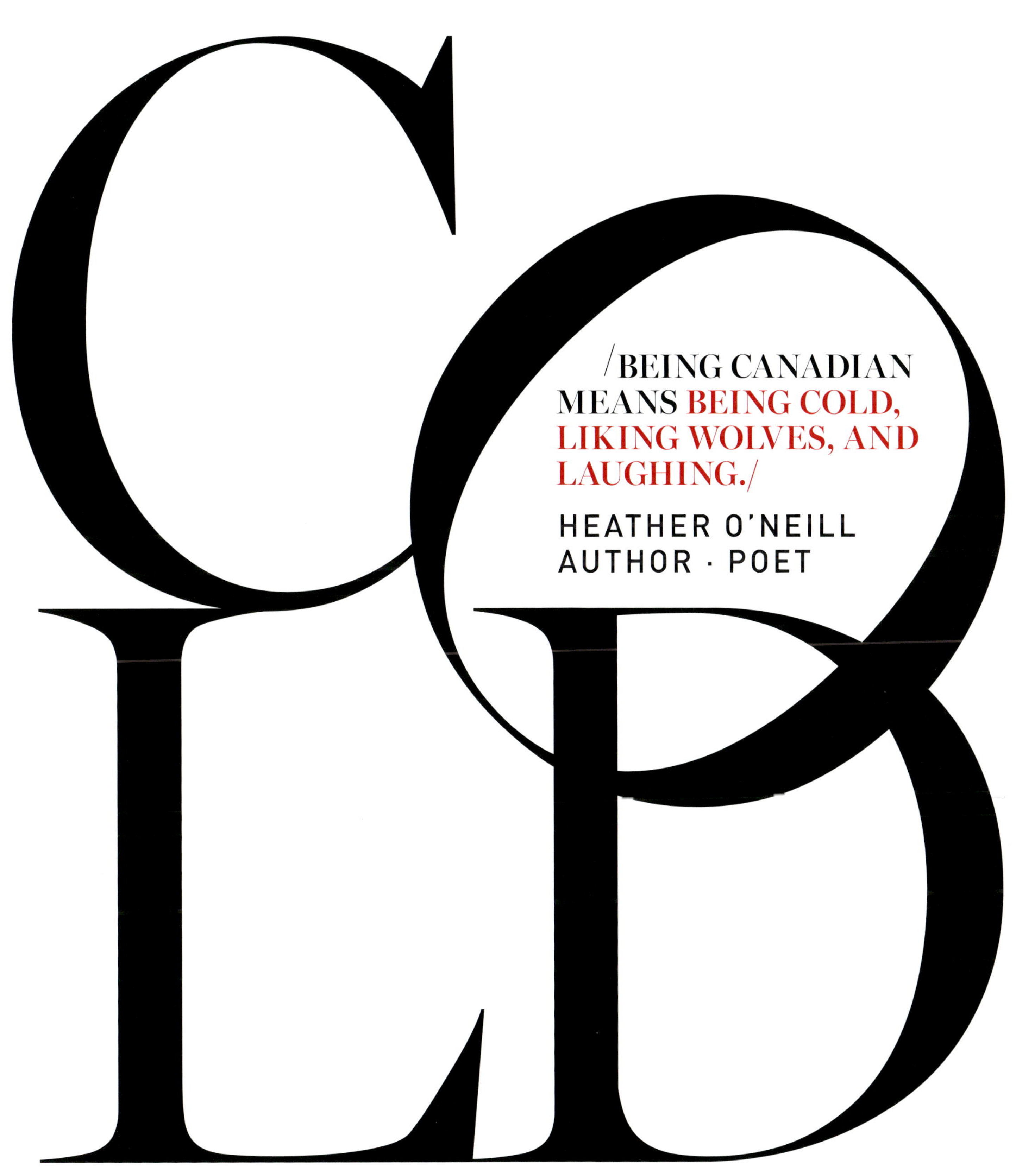

/BEING CANADIAN MEANS BEING COLD, LIKING WOLVES, AND LAUGHING./

HEATHER O'NEILL
AUTHOR · POET

"In Canada, we're happy to provide a safe haven for next-door neighbours in the middle of a marital dispute. And if anyone trips while crossing the border, we're happy to set their broken bones for free."

DOUGLAS COUPLAND
ARTIST · AUTHOR · FUTURIST

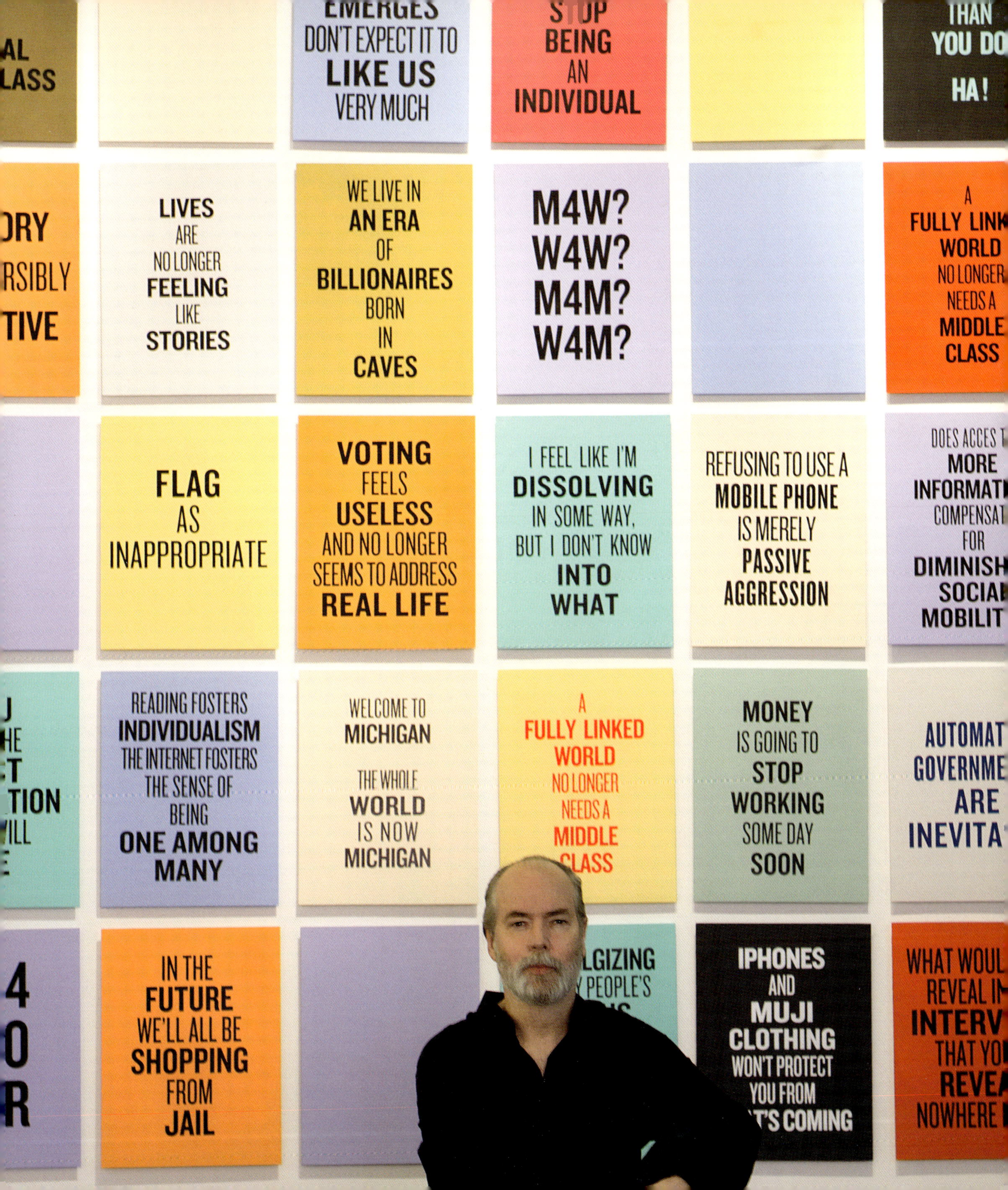

STOP BEING AN INDIVIDUAL

LIVES ARE NO LONGER FEELING LIKE STORIES

WE LIVE IN AN ERA OF BILLIONAIRES BORN IN CAVES

M4W? W4W? M4M? W4M?

A FULLY LINKED WORLD NO LONGER NEEDS A MIDDLE CLASS

FLAG AS INAPPROPRIATE

VOTING FEELS USELESS AND NO LONGER SEEMS TO ADDRESS REAL LIFE

I FEEL LIKE I'M DISSOLVING IN SOME WAY, BUT I DON'T KNOW INTO WHAT

REFUSING TO USE A MOBILE PHONE IS MERELY PASSIVE AGGRESSION

READING FOSTERS INDIVIDUALISM THE INTERNET FOSTERS THE SENSE OF BEING ONE AMONG MANY

WELCOME TO MICHIGAN

THE WHOLE WORLD IS NOW MICHIGAN

A FULLY LINKED WORLD NO LONGER NEEDS A MIDDLE CLASS

MONEY IS GOING TO STOP WORKING SOME DAY SOON

IN THE FUTURE WE'LL ALL BE SHOPPING FROM JAIL

in·su·lin
/'insələn/

The life-saving peptide hormone discovered by Sir Frederick Banting, Charles Best, and others at the University of Toronto in 1921.

to·bog·gan
/tə'bägən/

The name for a long, narrow sled derived from the French word *tabaganne*, which is rooted in the Mi'kmaq word *topaĝan*.

MALCOLM GLADWELL
AUTHOR

"When I was in my teens, at the tail end of the Vietnam War, my parents were part of a small group in our hometown who sponsored three Vietnamese refugees. They were all in their teens as well. They spoke no English. They stayed at our house for a time, and I remember us buying them winter coats. They wandered around our high school in a daze. Today, one is a successful local businessman, and the other two went on to get graduate degrees—and jobs—in computer science. Everything I love about Canada and what I think it means to be Canadian is contained in that story. Canadians are people who open their hearts to others. Canada is a place that provides opportunities. My birthday wish for Canada is that it never change."

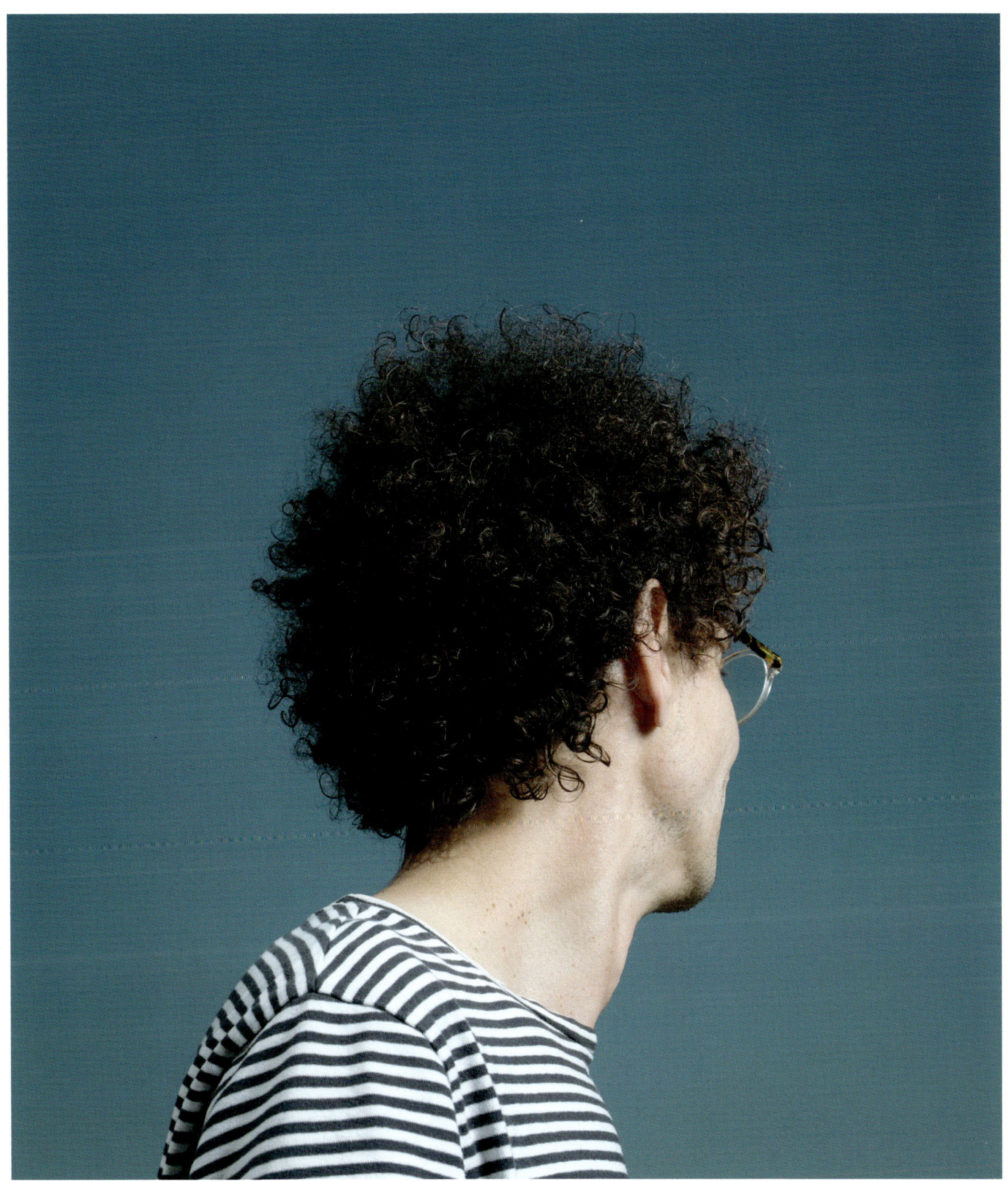

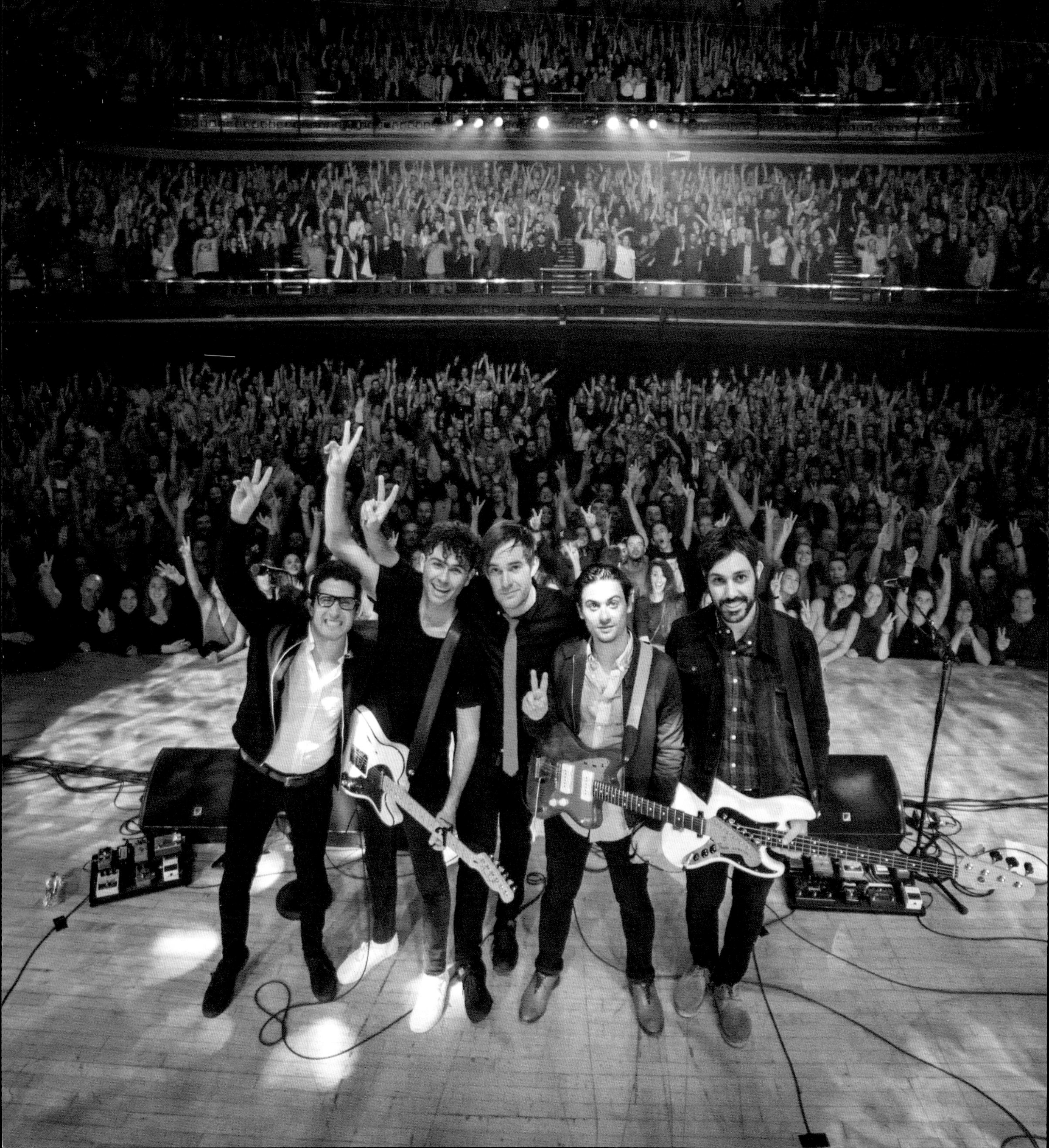

"IF YOU CAN TELL A STORY WITH HUMOUR AND COMPASSION, YOU'LL WIN OVER ANY CANADIAN."

ARKELLS · MUSICIANS

"I FELL IN LOVE WITH A LITTLE RCMP MOUNTIE DOLL THAT I WANTED MORE THAN ANYTHING ELSE."

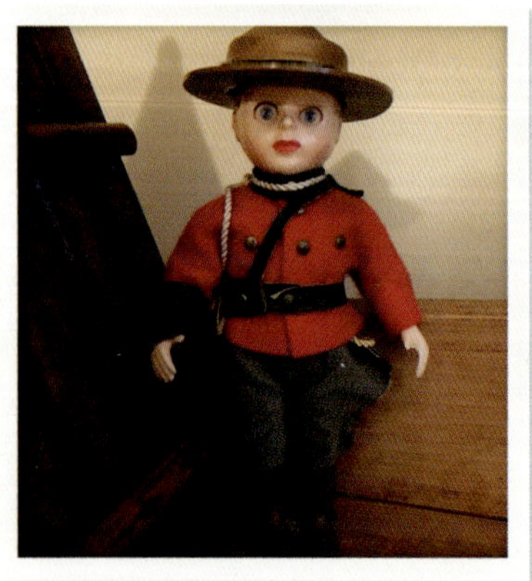

"My most 'Canadian' memory is visiting Ottawa on a motor trip with my parents as a little girl, and falling in love with a little RCMP Mountie doll that I wanted more than anything else. My parents didn't have all that much money, so I guess my mom thought the little doll was too expensive, and she didn't want to indulge me. I was so disappointed that I cried myself to sleep in the back seat of the car. A few miles outside of Ottawa, my mom was feeling sorry for me and had a change of heart. She asked my dad to drive back to the shop so she could get me the doll. I awoke to find myself back in Ottawa and was dumbfounded when my mom presented me with that amazing little doll. I loved it so, so much! All these years later, the little Mountie doll stands proudly at my country home, reminding me of the pride I felt as a young Canadian visiting Ottawa for the first time."

JEANNE BEKER
TV PERSONALITY
FASHION EDITOR

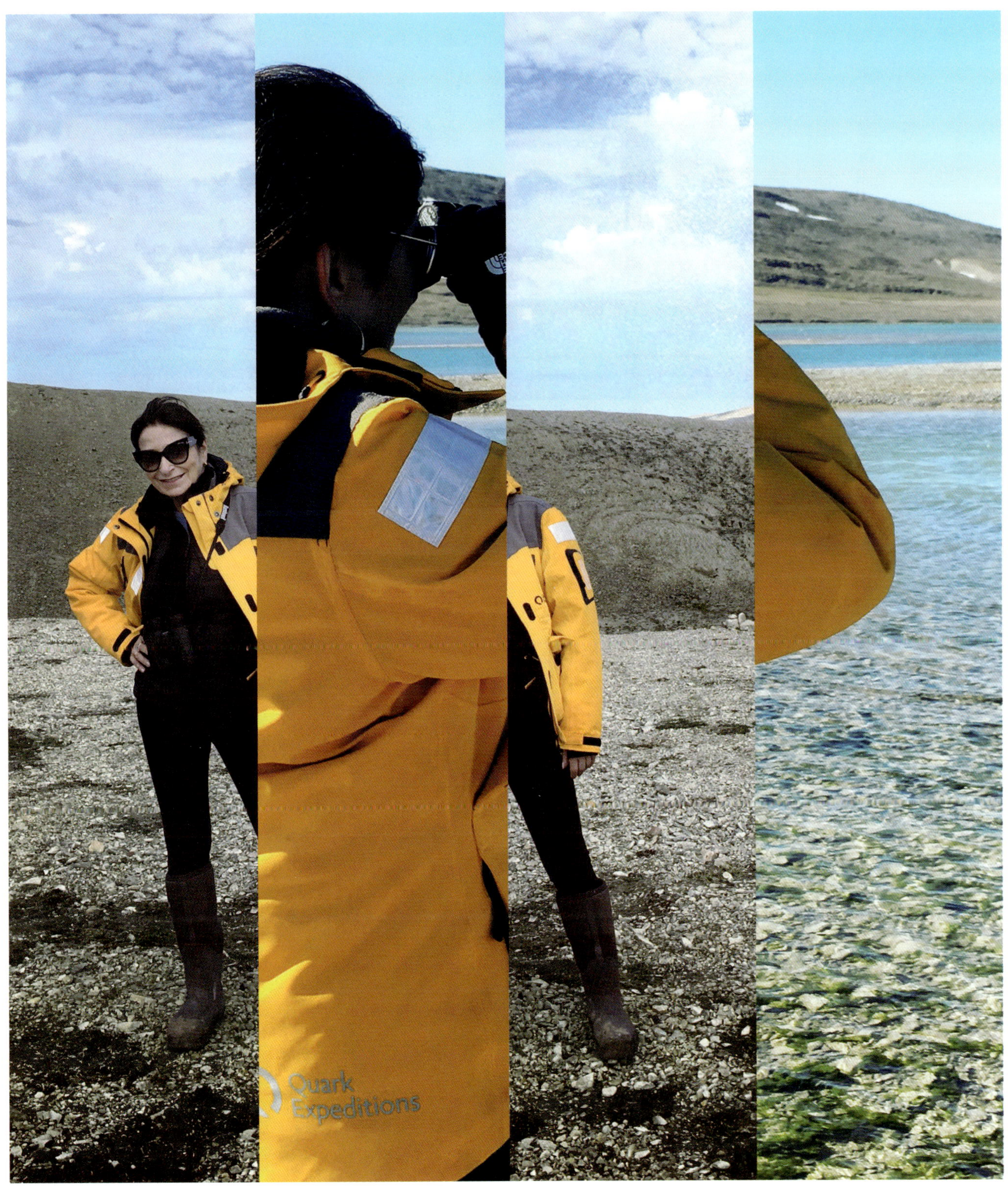
Quark
Expeditions

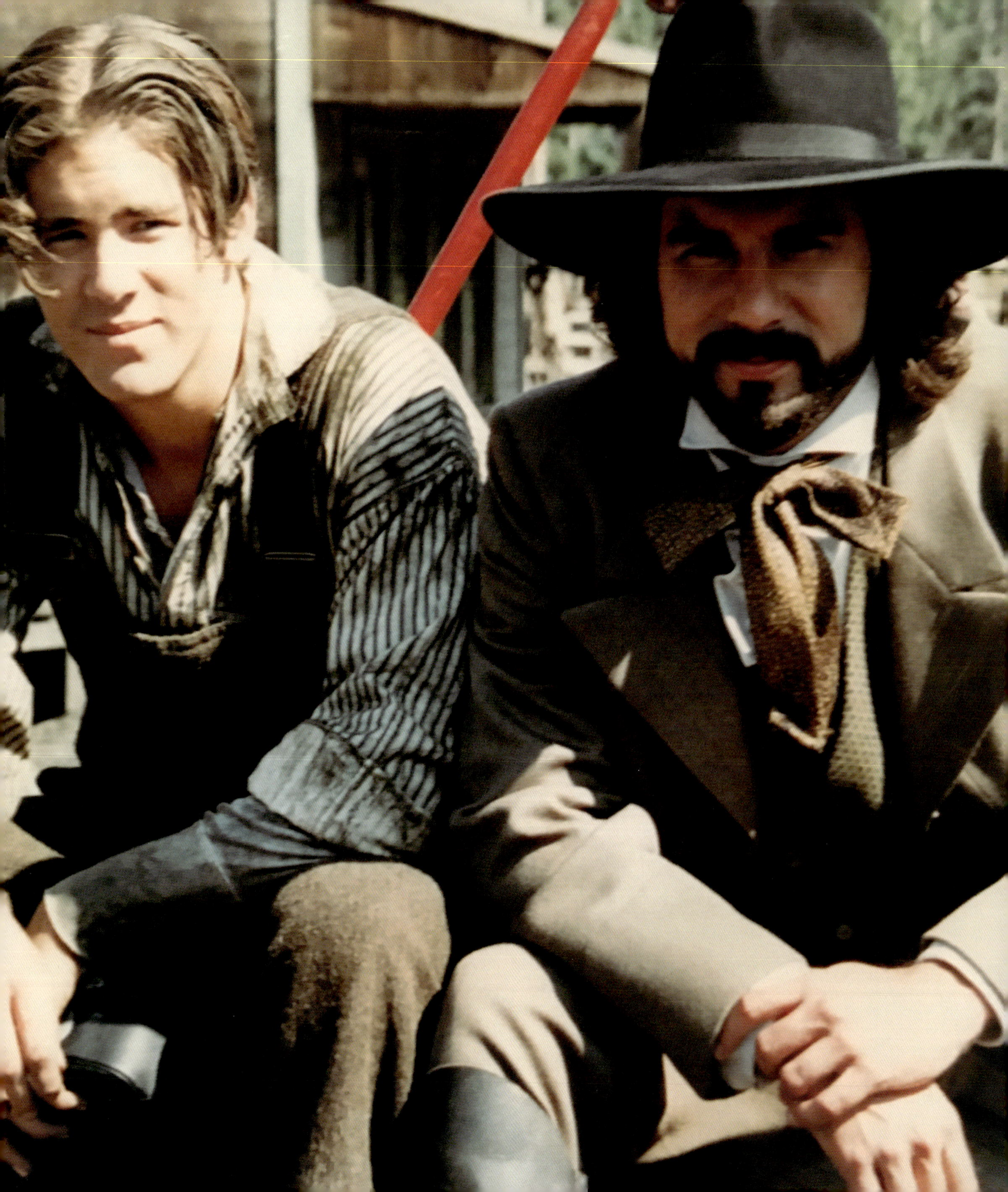

ERIC MCCORMACK · ACTOR

"I received a star on Canada's Walk of Fame in 2010. At the ceremony, moments before I got up to accept my (incredible) honour (notice I spelled it with an *ou*), they had a surprise for me: one of my heroes, Burton Cummings, sitting at a piano, played my favourite Guess Who song, *Sour Suite*. It was a quintessential Canadian moment... and yet *not*, because in my youth, Canadians would never have celebrated themselves like that. It struck me that night, as Sarah Polley and Clara Hughes and Nelly Furtado and David Clayton-Thomas took the stage, that Canada has finally given itself permission to feel genuine pride, without losing any of the humility that makes us who we are."

“The truth about Canada is that it exists on stolen land. Some First Nations have treaty agreements with Canada, but there are broken treaties and much unceded land. What does this mean for us as we celebrate Canada's 150th anniversary? Well, for me, as a settler in this country, **Canada 150 is a moment to respond to the calls to action in the Truth and Reconciliation Commission's report.** Have you read them?”

FARZANA DOCTOR
AUTHOR

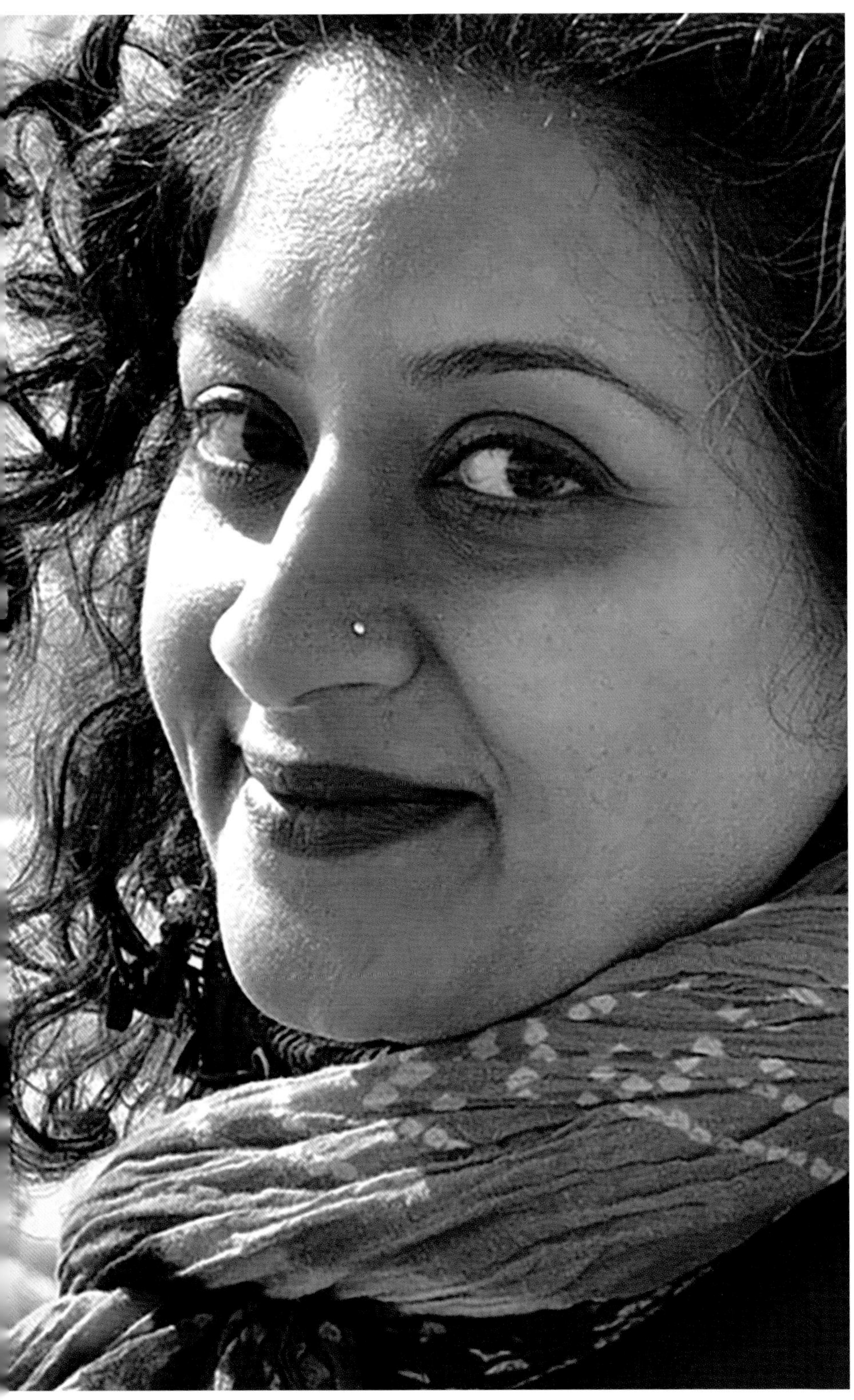

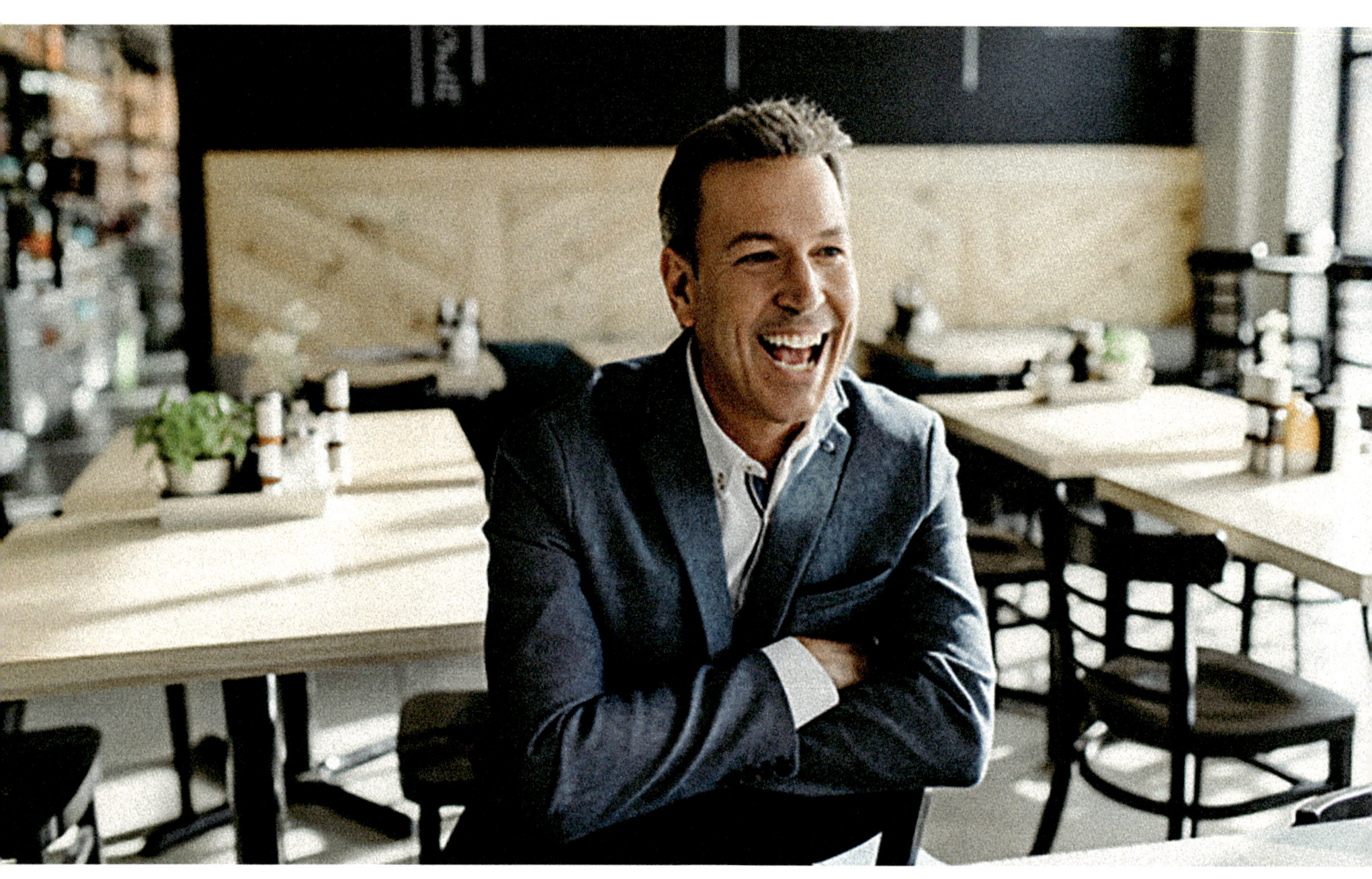

«JE SAIS QUE MON PAYS EST UNE MULTITUDE DE RÉALITÉ, QUI PARFOIS SEMBLE BIEN LOIN LES UNES DES AUTRES ET QUI POURTANT S'UNISSENT COMME NULLE PART AILLEURS AU MONDE.»

«Nous sommes les fiers descendants d'immigrants, épris de liberté et d'un rêve plus grand et plus fort que tout : nourrir sa famille, la protéger, la voir s'épanouir en paix. Nous sommes façonnés par notre climat et par la grandeur de notre territoire.

Nous sommes aussi toutes ces premières nations de qui nous nous sommes trop longtemps coupés et sans qui le rêve ne sera jamais complet.

La mer, comme les plaines, mettent au monde des hommes et des femmes aux horizons infinis. Notre terre nous a sculptés, nous a définis.

Il y a près de 30 ans, je me suis arrêté à l'église pour prier, pour que ma famille soit protégée. J'ai fermé la portière et je suis parti sans jamais regarder derrière.

J'ai pleuré longtemps, presque jusqu'au Manitoba. Je devais pourtant partir vers l'ouest, c'était plus fort que moi. Ce départ était ma première conquête, la certitude que ma vie m'appartenait et que malgré la peur de laisser derrière moi ceux que j'aimais, mon destin était ailleurs. Je suis arrivé à Saint-Boniface le 1er juillet en fin de journée. J'y ai fêté ma première fête du Canada en français, au son des groupes de musique franco-manitobains. C'était la première fois que je ressentais ce sentiment de grandeur nationale. Quand le soleil s'est levé, j'ai repris la route vers ma nouvelle patrie, la Saskatchewan. Je n'avais jamais vu autant de ciel, et si bleu. J'ai senti la liberté, celle qui allait me définir comme homme, comme Canadien. Je me suis dit que cette terre allait me rendre heureux. Et je le suis.

Mes ancêtres ont sûrement eu peur de cette traversée vers l'inconnu, comme les immigrants qui arrivent aujourd'hui ont sûrement peur de ce nouveau départ, mais rien n'est plus enivrant que le sentiment qu'ici, c'est maintenant chez moi. Se dire qu'ici, je peux respirer à pleins poumons et être moi-même. Savoir qu'ici, mes idées seront encouragées plutôt que sacrifiées. Mon envie du dépassement me vient en partie des plaines sans fin. Lorsque je suis revenu au Québec, je n'étais plus le même.

Chacun d'entre nous traversera ses propres plaines, montagnes et océans. Je sais que mon pays est une multitude de réalité, qui parfois semble bien loin les unes des autres et qui pourtant s'unissent comme nulle part ailleurs au monde. Grâce à mon métier, j'ai visité chaque province, chaque territoire de cette grandiose nation. Je suis privilégié d'avoir partagé des repas avec des familles toutes différentes les unes des autres, mais toutes unies dans leurs valeurs de respect et d'écoute.»

RICARDO LARRIVÉE
CHEF · AUTHOR

"My most 'Canadian' memory would without a doubt be watching the Canadian men's hockey team win the gold medal at the 2014 Olympics in Gord Downie's hotel room in Timmins with him while drinking Tim Hortons coffee.

I'M NOT MAKING THAT UP."

JEFF LEMIRE
ILLUSTRATOR · AUTHOR

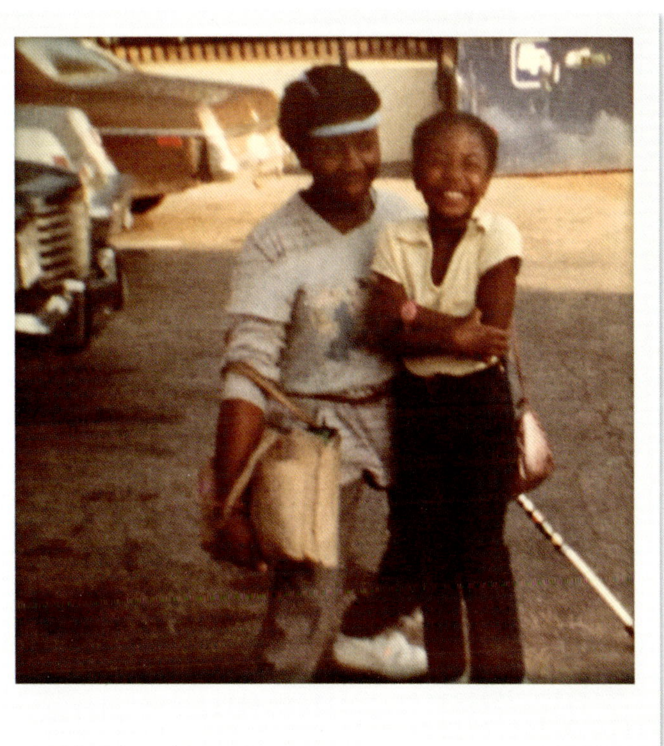

"I'm most proud to call myself Canadian because only in Canada can one go from being raised in an at-risk community to becoming, according to the CBC, one of Canada's greatest singers of all time. All without compromising who I am, my values, morals, ethics, or self-respect. Canada celebrates and encourages diversity, and I see it as a blessing to have been born in this generation, because we build bridges from one heart to the next—not walls! We are Canada!"

JULLY BLACK · MUSICIAN

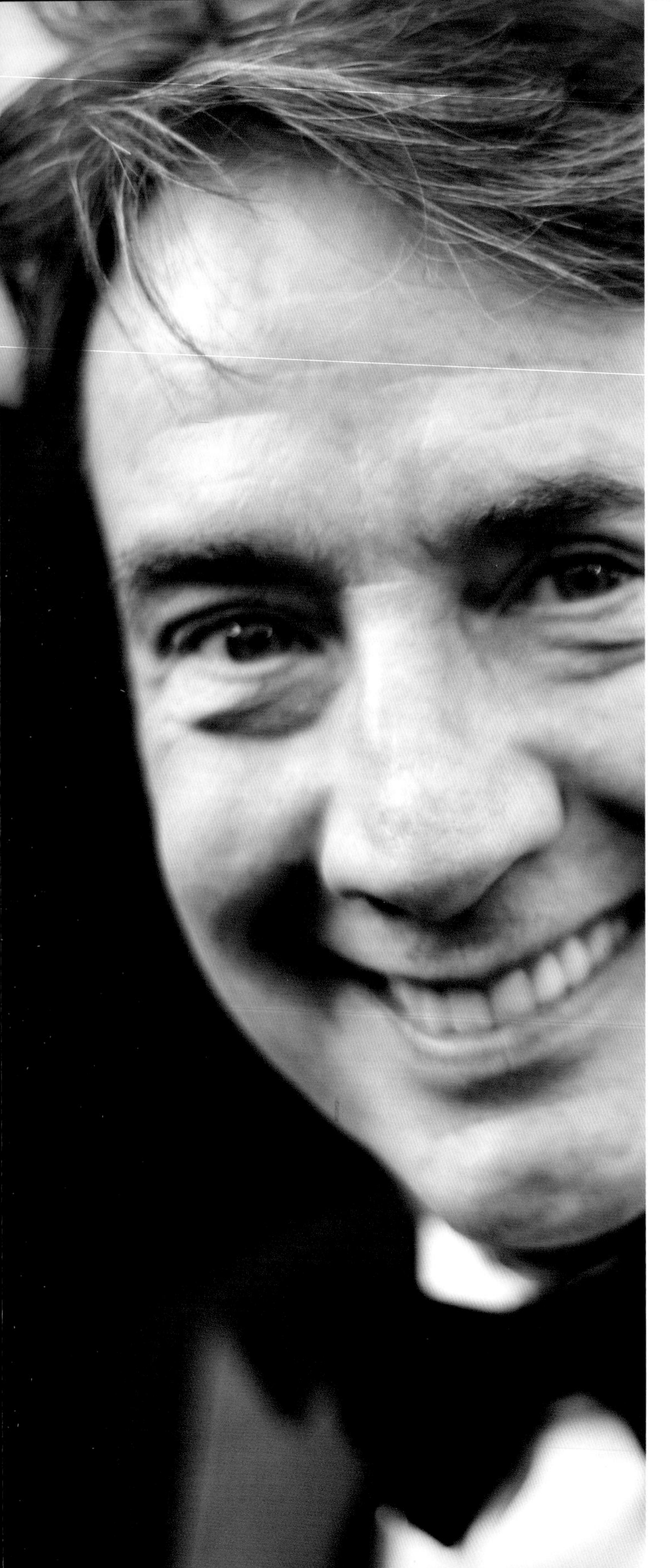

“WHAT
I ADORE
MOST ABOUT
CANADA IS
THE UTTER
PRIDE I
FEEL WHEN I
GET TO TELL
PEOPLE THAT
I AM INDEED
A CANADIAN.”

MARTIN SHORT · ACTOR · COMEDIAN

"I have adored Canada my entire life. And let's not forget (although I would like to) that I'm now 67 years of age, so that's a pretty impressive statement. And what I adore most about Canada is the utter pride I feel when I get to tell people that I am indeed a Canadian.

As a Canadian who has lived primarily in the United States since the mid-'80s, I can honestly say that I've never met an American who wasn't just a tad bit envious.

Multicultural harmony? We established that long ago, becoming one of the models for the world. Universal health care? We did that long ago. Sensible gun control policy? Again, long ago. Inspiring some of the most influential and funniest people in comedy? We're still doing that.

Yes, when this little Hamiltonian sees that gorgeous red maple leaf flapping in the wind, my heart still skips a beat, and if I happened to be wearing a vest, the buttons would most certainly pop off.

So Happy 150th Birthday, Canada. There's no country on the planet more magnificent than you... but surely you know that."

DAVID SUZUKI · ENVIRONMENTALIST · ACTIVIST

What is your birthday wish for Canada?

"My birthday wish for Canada is that 2017 begins a fundamental shift in the path we are on. Modern Canada was founded on the takeover of lands occupied by Indigenous people since the end of the last ice age. For more than 150 years, newcomers were drawn to Canada by the vast natural riches of the country that were exploited without regard for sustainability of their actions.

Despite the terrible impacts of disease and programs imposed to eliminate Indigenous people and their cultures, they have survived, and now we are beginning to realize the wisdom of Indigenous perspectives that 'Mother Earth' is the source of earth, air, fire, and water — the critical elements that give us life and health. In songs, prayers, and rituals, Indigenous people constantly express gratitude for Mother Earth's generosity, and, in giving thanks accept a reciprocal responsibility to protect and care for her. On this birthday, Canada could abandon the ecologically destructive path we are on and begin to act through the Indigenous perspective."

What does it mean to be Canadian?

"I have never been more aware of what it means than when I was living and studying in the United States from 1954 to 1962. Sputnik was launched by the Soviet Union in 1957 and triggered a space race between the two superpowers. The U.S. poured massive amounts of money and effort into NASA, universities, and research facilities, and even as a foreigner, I was offered several university positions without even applying. It was a golden time for budding scientists.

Nevertheless, I decided to decline all American offers and returned to Canada, because Canada was different from the U.S., and for me, that difference was preferable. Canada to me meant the CCF, later called the NDP, could be a legitimate and respected political party. To me, Tommy Douglas, an idealistic politician, was a hero and role model. Canada meant equalization payments whereby the good fortunes of the wealthy provinces were shared with those less fortunate.

Canada meant medicare and a society that tried to care for all instead of allowing Darwinian competition and survival of the fittest. Quebec, the National Film Board, and the Canadian Broadcasting Corporation were also critical differences that appealed to me, and I have never regretted committing to Canada as my home."

What is your most "Canadian" memory?

"In 1957, at the end of my third year at Amherst College in Massachusetts, I invited three of my fellow students to spend two weeks canoeing in Algonquin Park. They came from different cities in the United States and we set forth in a howling rainstorm. The rain made us appreciate all the more when perfect weather settled in for the rest of the journey. We spent the most carefree time swimming, paddling, fishing, and sitting around campfires regaling each other with stories and jokes before slipping into our tents. The days swept by as we marvelled at the loons, a bear, deer, and plentiful trout. I even hooked a bat one evening as I was fishing. We spent days without encountering another human being, totally immersed in nature and so grateful for her beauty and bounty. It was the company and exuberant response of my American friends that made me acutely aware of how lucky Canadians are to live in a place so rich in nature."

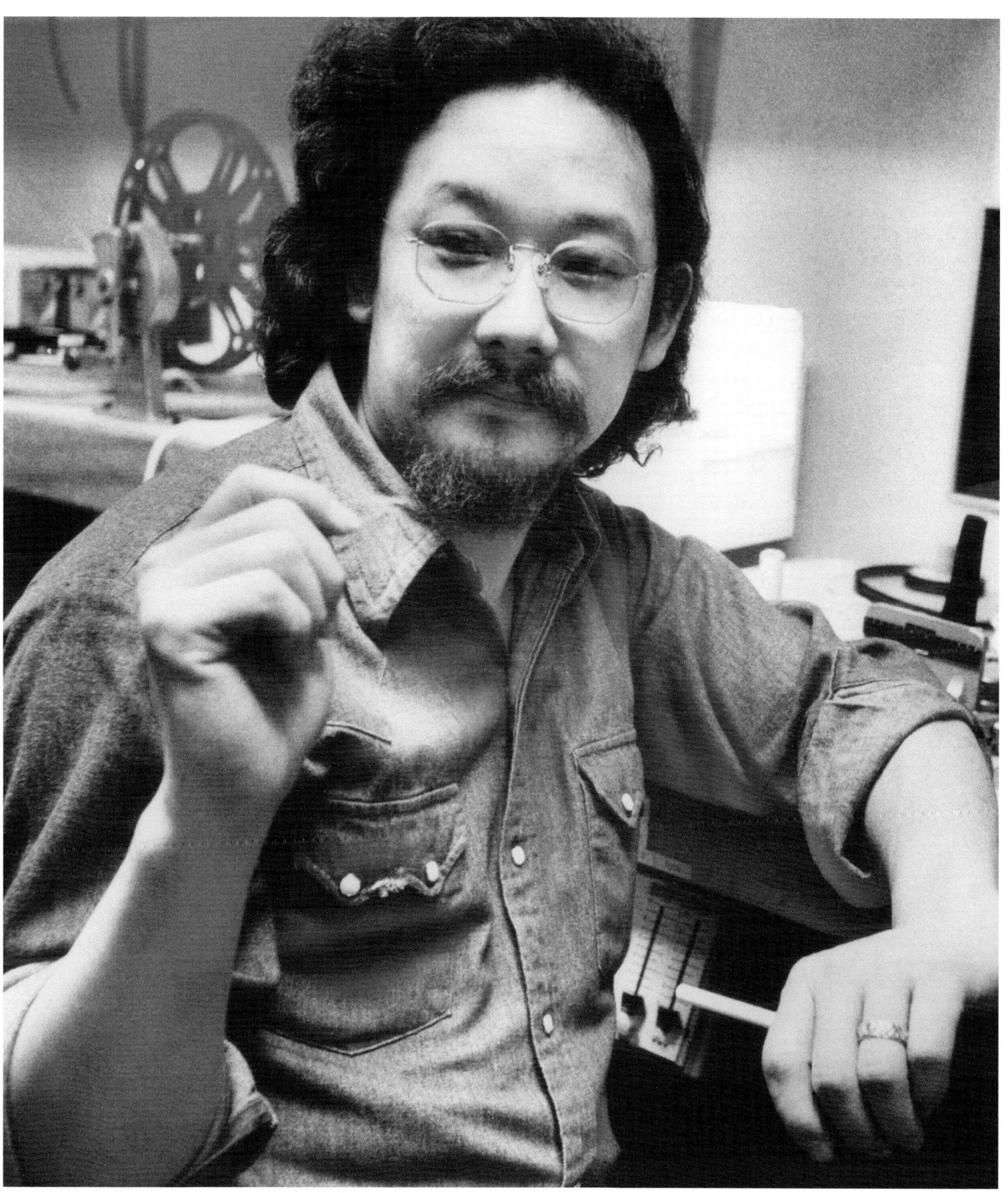

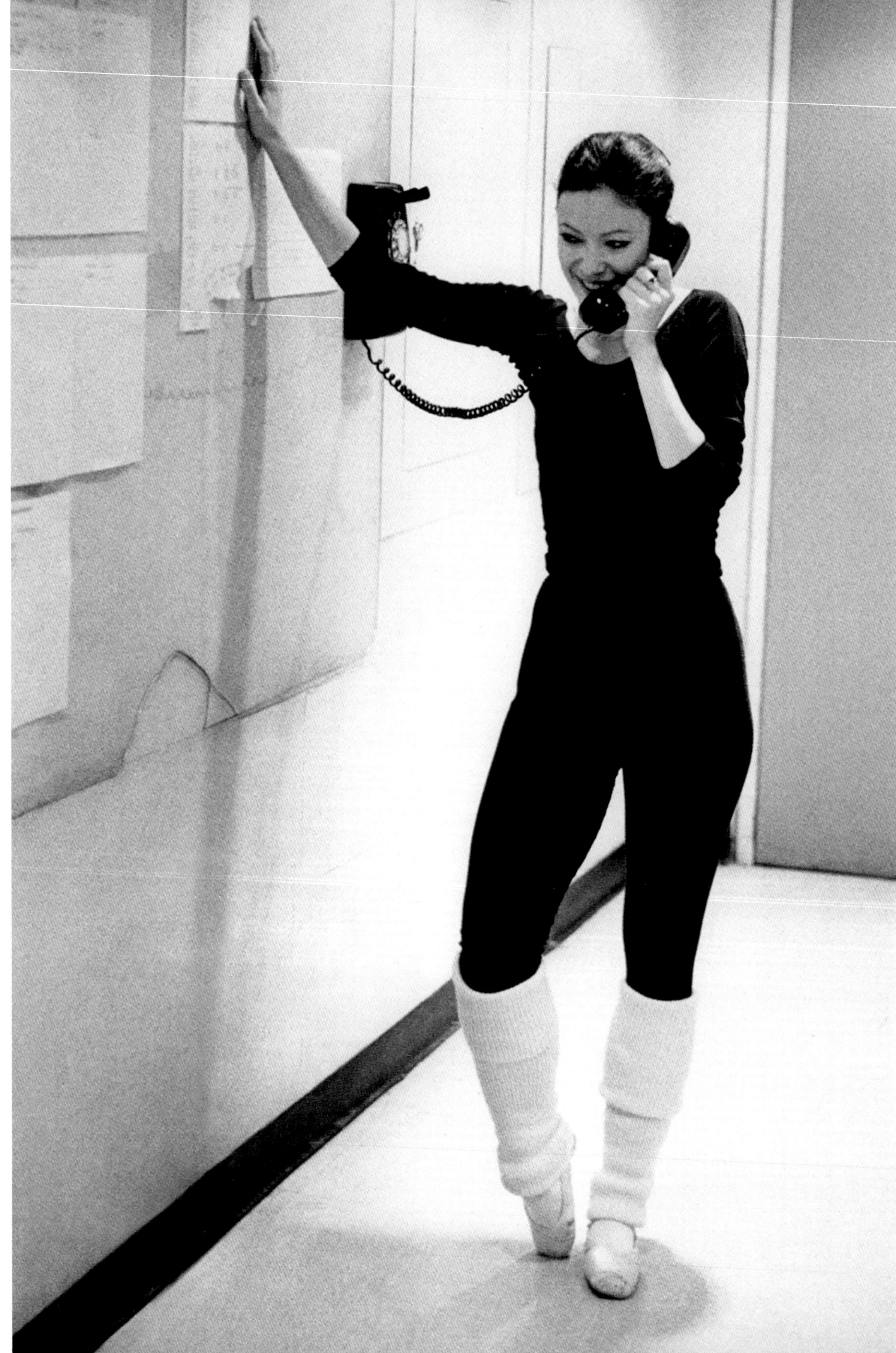

"I FELT TINY AND INSIGNIFICANT IN THE FACE OF NATURE, YET CONNECTED TO EVERY LIVING CREATURE."

"My most 'Canadian' memory was my father's birthday and, as it was a milestone one, we decided to make a voyage together with other nature lovers in a 68-foot ketch that circumnavigated Haida Gwaii. Part of the adventure was the opportunity to band ancient murrelets, an endangered seabird, for scientific study. We were standing in the midnight cold surrounded by chicks racing to the sea to join their parents in the majestic, lush Canadian landscape. I felt tiny and insignificant in the face of nature, yet connected to every living creature, especially to my aging father, who is no longer with me. It was a truly humbling experience that has stayed with me all these years."

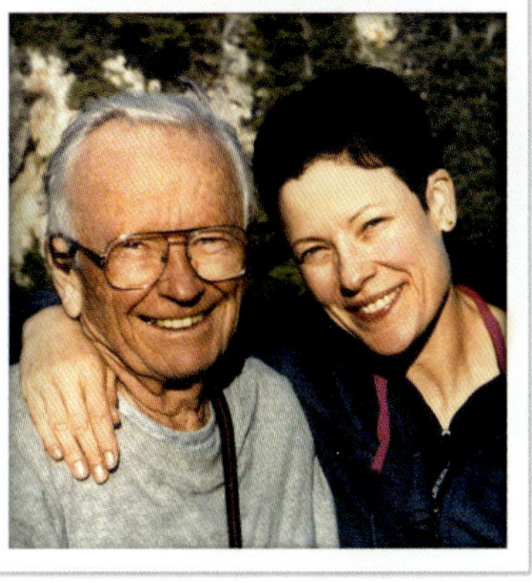

KAREN KAIN
ARTISTIC DIRECTOR OF THE NATIONAL BALLET OF CANADA

"ODDLY ENOUGH, MY MOST 'CANADIAN' MEMORY HAPPENED OUTSIDE OF CANADA. OUR LADY PEACE PLAYED A CONCERT IN TRAFALGAR SQUARE IN LONDON, ENGLAND, ON CANADA DAY IN 2012.

I'VE NEVER SEEN SO MANY CANADIAN FLAGS. SO MUCH RED AND WHITE. THE CROWD SANG LOUDER THAN I'VE EVER HEARD AT A CONCERT, BUT IT WAS A DIFFERENT KIND OF SINGING; IT HAD A DISTINCT PRIDE THAT GAVE ME CHILLS. IF YOU WERE IN THE CROWD AND NOT CANADIAN, YOU WISHED YOU WERE THAT EVENING."

RAINE MAIDA
MUSICIAN · SONGWRITER

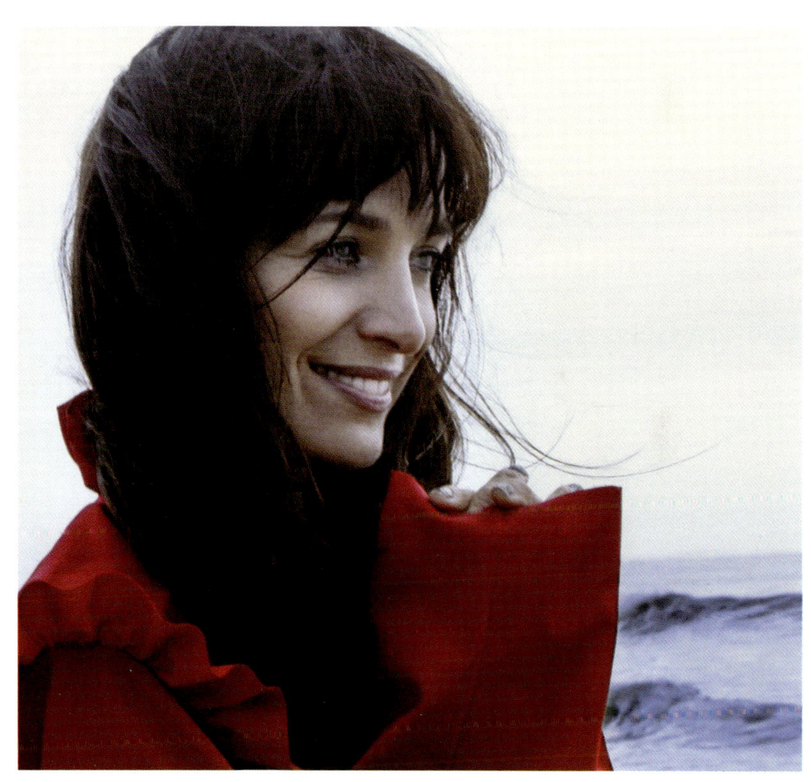

/WHAT I MISS MOST ABOUT CANADA WHEN I'M TRAVELLING IS THE RECIPROCAL KINDNESS OF STRANGERS. I LOVE THAT WE SEE AND KNOW OUR COMMONNESS AS CANADIANS IMMEDIATELY./

CHANTAL KREVIAZUK
MUSICIAN · SONGWRITER

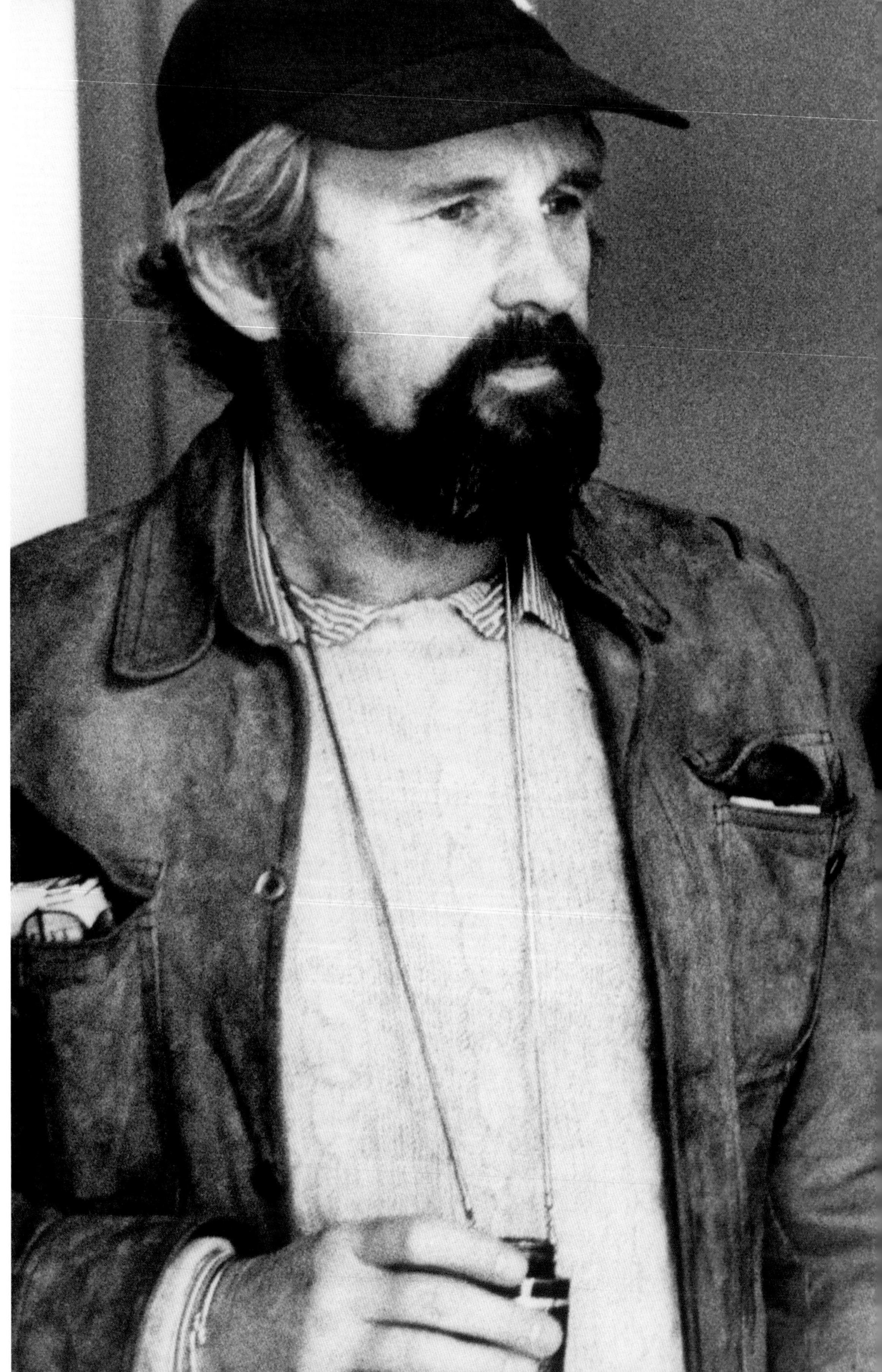

"THE ROMANCE OF MAPLE SYRUP PRODUCTION IS UNIQUELY CANADIAN, AND I'LL ALWAYS REMEMBER SITTING ALONE IN THE SUGAR SHACK ON A COLD SPRING NIGHT."

What is your birthday wish for Canada?

"My birthday wish for Canada for this year and years to come is that we may be an inspiration to the rest of the world for peace and understanding, and international support for climate change."

What does it mean to be Canadian?

"I treasure and I'm filled with gratitude for the good fortune of my birth in this wonderful land of Canada."

What is your most "Canadian" memory?

"My favourite memory is from the spring of 1978, when I tapped my first sugar maple and we began a tradition of making our own maple syrup from our own trees.

The romance of maple syrup production is uniquely Canadian, and I'll always remember sitting alone in the sugar shack on a cold spring night, listening to the hockey game on the radio and waiting with great anticipation for my first draw."

NORMAN JEWISON
FILMMAKER

“My most 'Canadian' (and painful) memory happened during my first winter in Canada. I had come from South Africa to study at McGill University and had parked my third-hand jalopy in an open parkade while grocery shopping at Steinberg's. It was so cold that when I returned laden with groceries, my car key would not turn in the door lock. **It does not get this cold in South Africa, so I was at a complete loss as to what to do.** However, my innate resourcefulness took over, and I decided to put my mouth over the keyhole and use my breath to thaw the lock. My lips instantly froze and stuck to the door handle and, as I recoiled in fright, the skin of my lips stayed with the car.

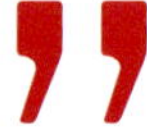

PETER OLIVER
RESTAURATEUR

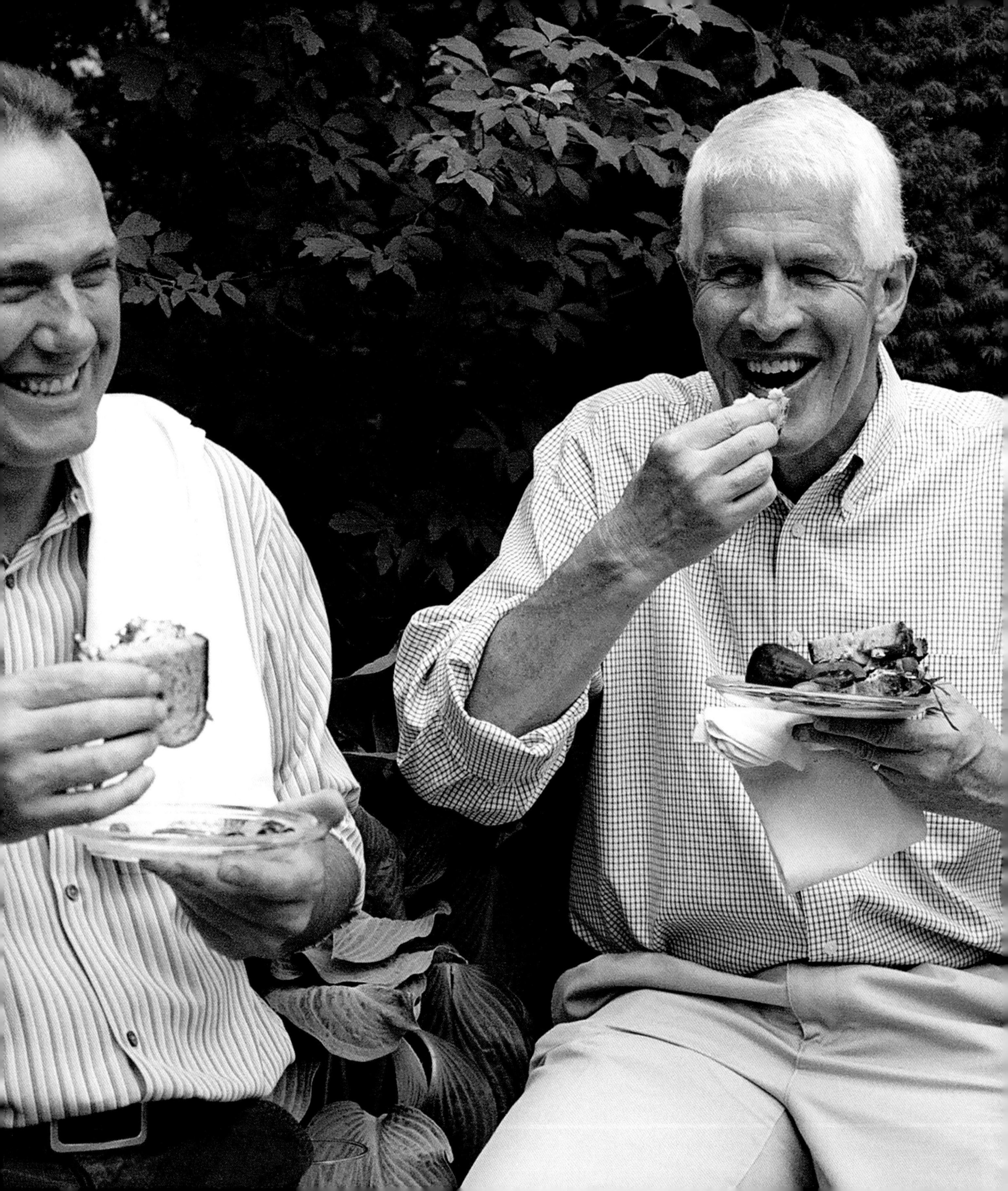

ODE AU CANADA

J'adore que notre croyance dans l'égalité se trouve non seulement dans la Charte canadienne des droits et libertés, mais aussi dans notre ADN.

J'adore que les soins de la santé soient un droit et non un privilège.

J'adore que les auteurs, musiciens, artistes et autres créateurs canadiens de tous les domaines se distinguent sur la scène internationale.

J'adore que nous comptions parmi les nôtres les fondateurs de Right to Play, de We Day et d'Enfants Entraide, et que tant de Canadiens personnifient l'esprit de la générosité, tant dans leurs communautés que dans le monde entier.

J'adore que notre richesse culturelle comprenne deux langues officielles.

Bien que cela ait pris un certain temps, j'adore que nous adoptions les recommandations de la Commission de vérité et de réconciliation.

J'adore que nous nous souciions tant du changement climatique et que nous soyons de plus en plus sérieux au sujet de la protection de l'environnement.

J'adore que notre marque, le CANADA, soit respectée dans le monde entier, et ce, pour toutes les bonnes raisons.

J'adore (et j'apprécie) que je sois inspirée par des Canadiens tous les jours.

Et...

J'adorerais le Canada davantage si...

Nous célébrions encore plus audacieusement nos réussites ainsi que les choses qui nous rendent si spéciaux.

Parce que nous le sommes véritablement.

Joyeux 150e anniversaire, Canada!

ODE TO CANADA

"I love that our belief in equality is not only in our Charter but deep in our DNA.

I love that health care is a right and not a privilege.

I love that Canadian writers, musicians, artists, and creatives from all fields punch so above their weight on the world stage.

I love that we can claim as 'ours' the founders of Right To Play, WE Day, and War Child – and that so many Canadians embody the spirit of giving back, both at home and around the world.

I love that part of our riches includes two official languages.

I love that we embrace multiculturalism.

I love that, though it took time, we are beginning to embrace the recommendations of the Truth and Reconciliation Commission.

I love that we care about climate change and are getting serious about doing our part to protect the environment.

I love that our brand – Canada – is respected for all the right reasons, all over the world.

I love (and appreciate) that I am inspired by Canadians every single day.

And...

I would love Canada just a little bit more if...

we would more boldly celebrate our achievements and the things that make us so special.

For that we are.

Happy 150th Birthday, Canada!"

HEATHER REISMAN
ENTREPRENEUR · BOOKLOVER

1 IN 3 CANADI

WATCHED THE TRAGICALLY

IT WAS THE SECOND MOST-WATCHED CANADIAN EVENT EVER.

ANS

HIP'S LAST SHOW IN 2016.

WHAT DOES IT MEAN TO BE CANADIAN?

"CURIOSITY. OPENNESS. RESPECT. SPACES. FREEDOM. AMBIGUITY."

PIERS HANDLING
DIRECTOR AND CEO OF TIFF

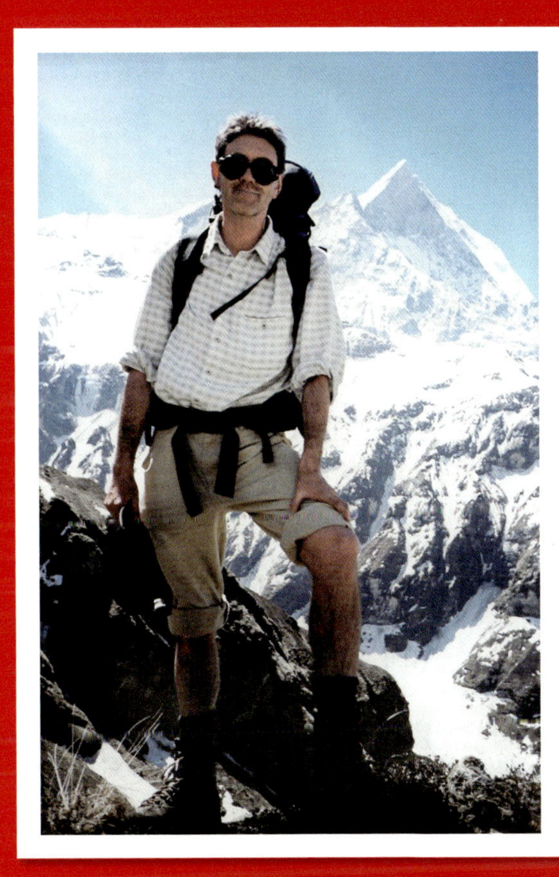

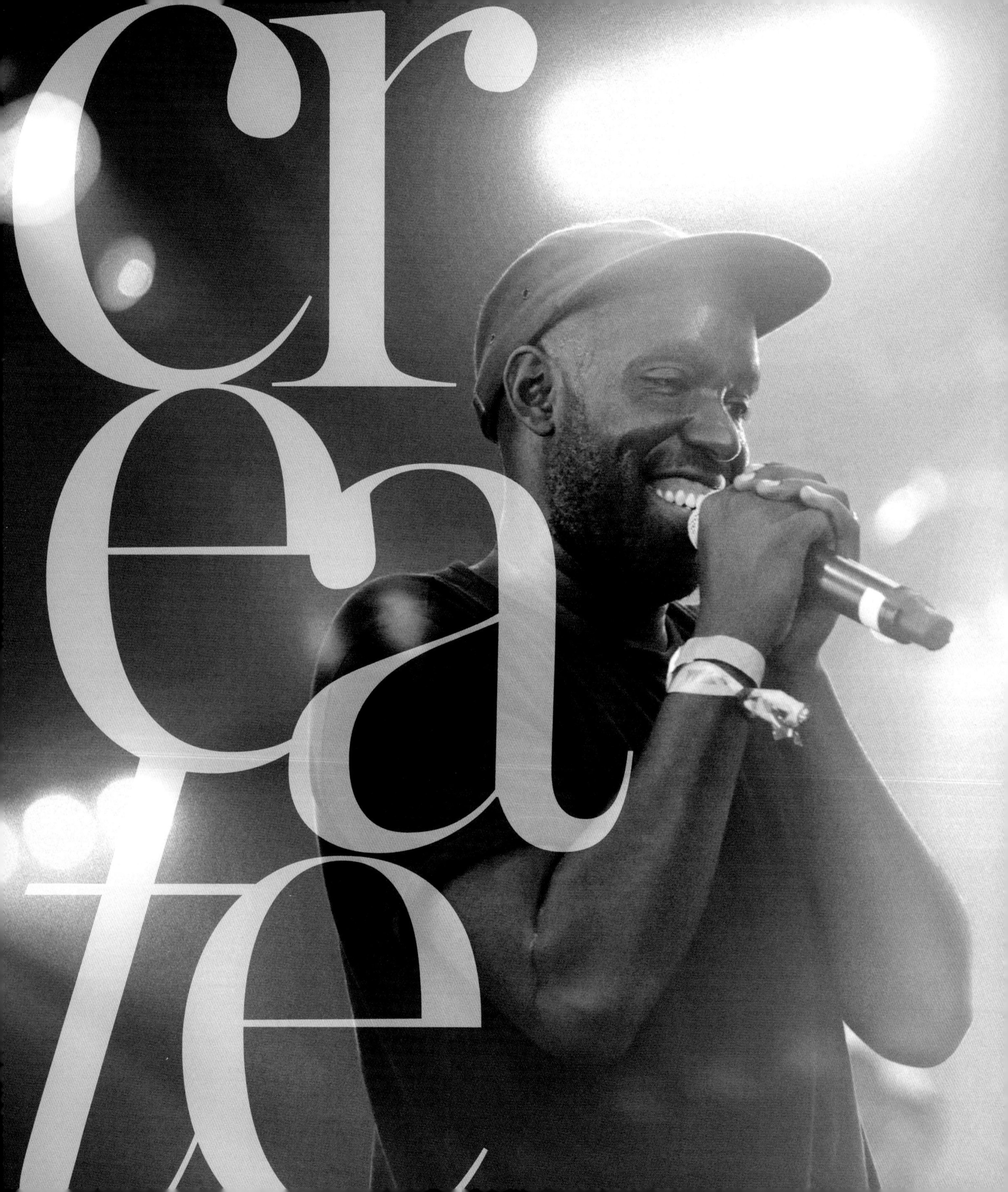
create

SHAD
MUSICIAN · SONGWRITER

"The truth about Canada—and we're becoming increasingly aware of the full gravity of this—is that this nation was founded on the genocide of Indigenous people. Our sesquicentennial happens to fall at a time when many of us feel not quite celebratory, but more motivated than ever to reckon properly with the past and create a better future."

SUGAR SAMMY · COMEDIAN

/J'ÉTAIS L'ENFANT LE PLUS HEUREUX DU MONDE, PAS SEULEMENT PARCE QUE MON ÉQUIPE AVAIT GAGNÉ, MAIS AUSSI PARCE QUE MON PÈRE ÉTAIT HEUREUX./

Qu'est-ce qui vous rend fier d'être Canadien?

«J'aime notre ouverture aux cultures et aux langues différentes. J'ai fait des tournées dans le monde entier, surtout dernièrement, et je crois que c'est un trait propre aux Canadiens. Nous sommes fiers d'apprendre à nous connaître les uns les autres et à nous célébrer. Nous considérons notre diversité culturelle comme une force et non pas comme un facteur de division. La diversité au sein du gouvernement, dans les médias et dans les professions de haut niveau a des années-lumière d'avance sur la plupart des endroits que j'ai visités.»

Quel est votre souvenir le plus « canadien »?

«Je me souviens d'avoir commencé à regarder les parties des Canadiens de Montréal à la télévision à l'âge de 8 ans. Je les aimais parce que mon père les aimait. J'étais tout aussi passionné par les parties que lui. Je me souviens d'avoir été devant le téléviseur avec mon père lorsque Montréal a remporté la coupe Stanley en 1986. J'étais l'enfant le plus heureux du monde, pas seulement parce que mon équipe avait gagné, mais aussi parce que mon père était heureux. Le hockey est une tradition canadienne qui est transmise de génération en génération et bien que nous soyons d'origine indienne, nous nous sommes toujours considérés comme des Canadiens.»

Lorsque vous voyagez, qu'est-ce qui vous manque le plus du Canada?

«Je m'ennuie toujours des grands espaces et de la verdure de notre pays. Nous avons une vaste et belle nation et nous avons tendance à l'oublier, jusqu'à ce que nous voyagions à l'étranger. En tant que Montréalais, j'adore qu'il y ait des parcs, des lacs et même une montagne au milieu de notre paysage urbain. Chaque fois que je reviens au Canada, je profite du plein air un peu plus que la fois précédente.»

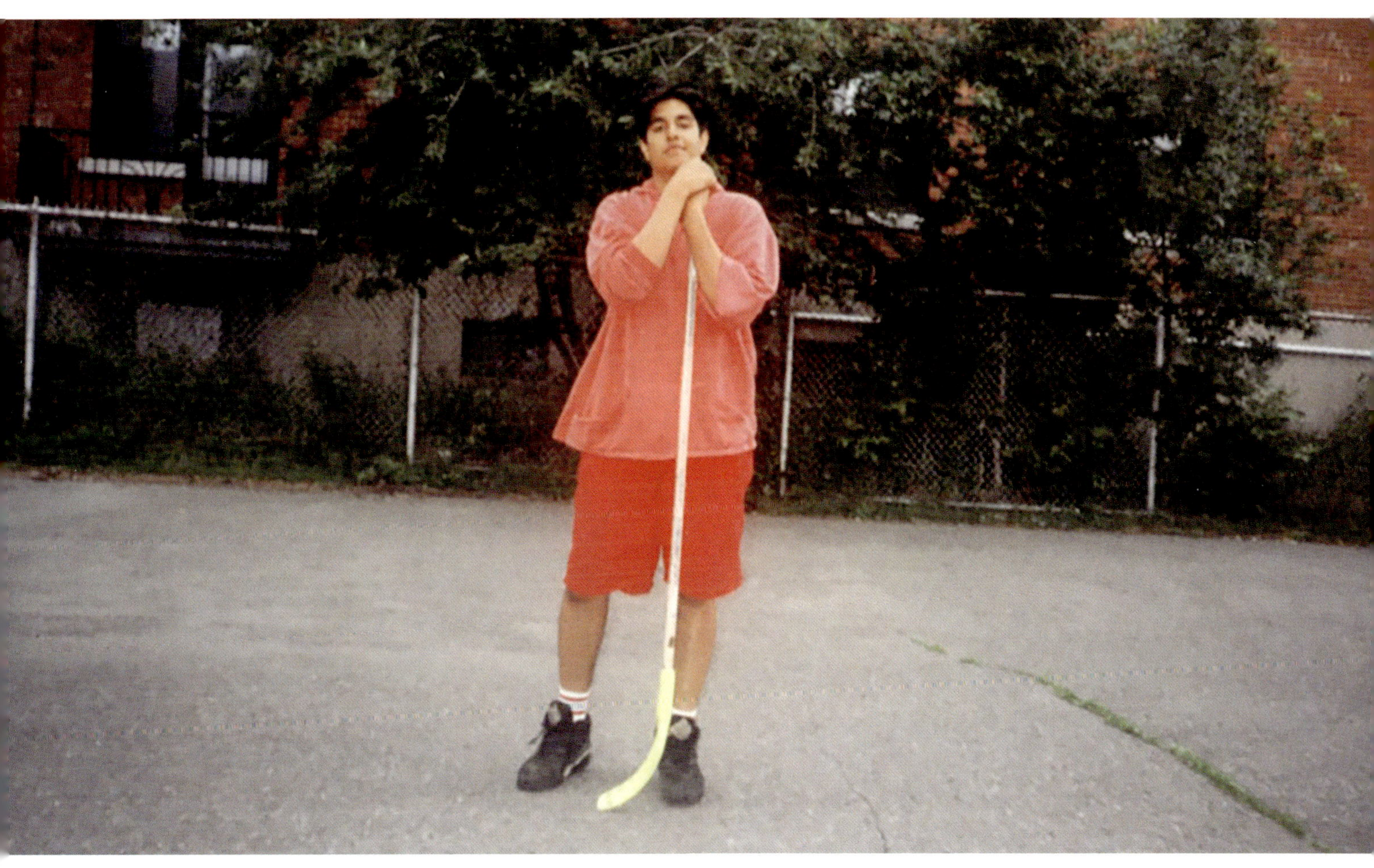

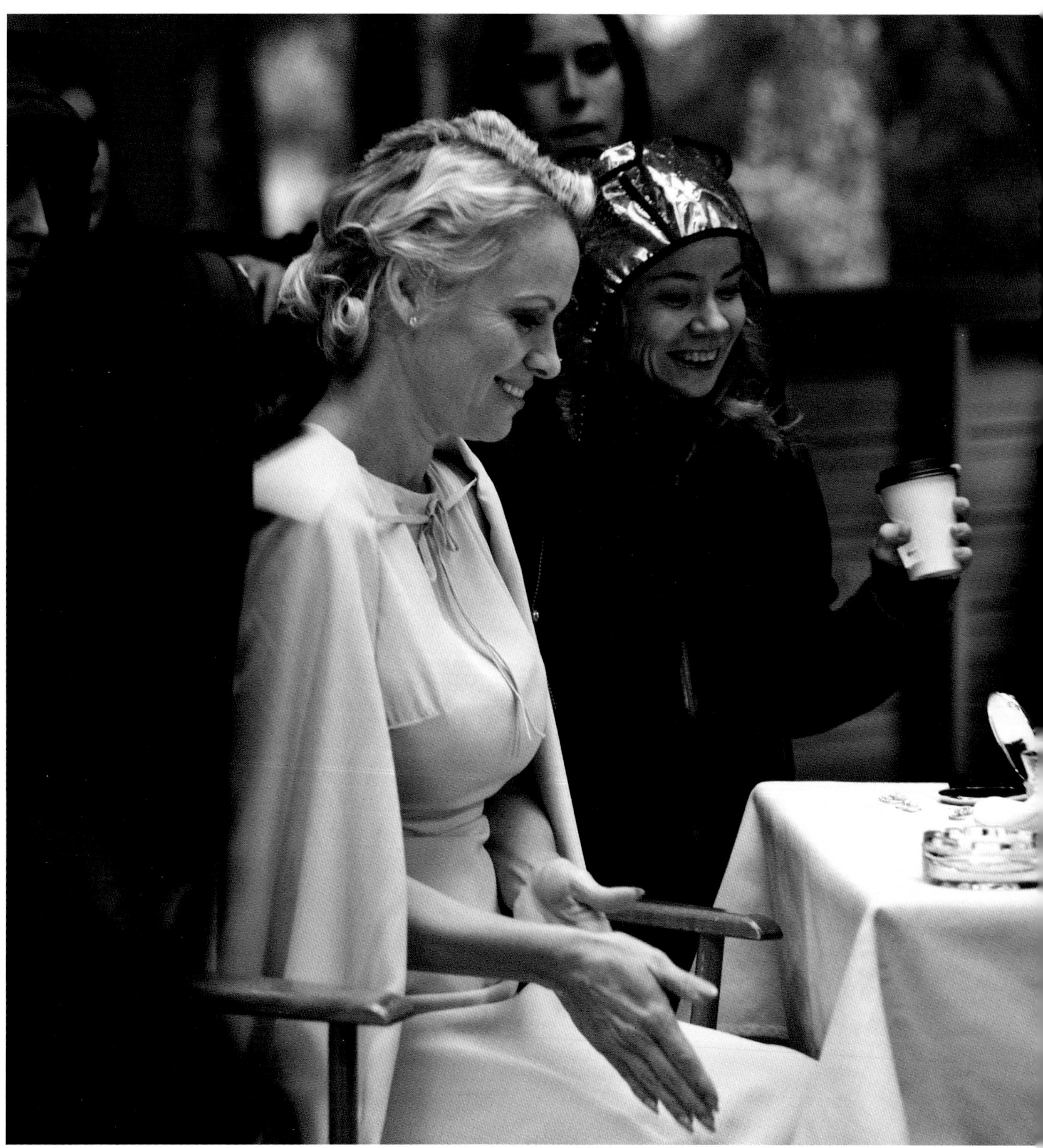

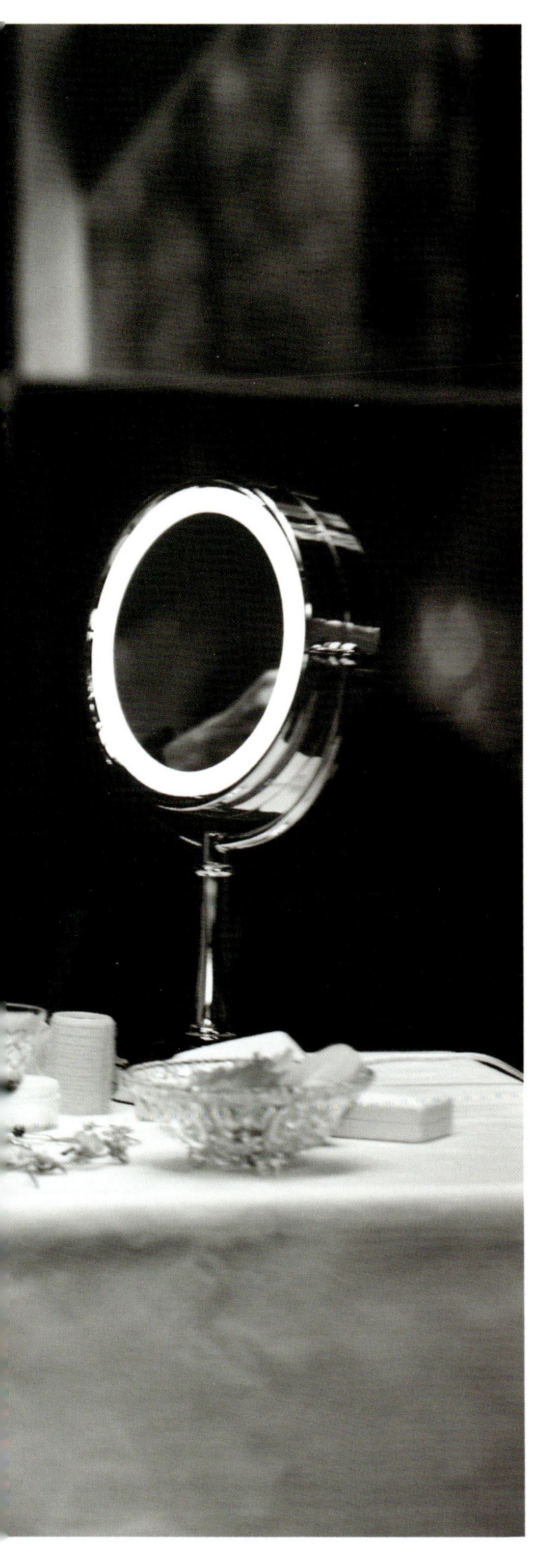

"I FEEL MOST PROUD TO BE A CANADIAN WHEN I SEE CITIZENS ACT WITH BRAVERY AND GRACE UNDER EXTREME PRESSURES."

"My pride for being a Canadian hits me in small moments, like being in the National Gallery and seeing an immersive retrospective on artist Alex Janvier, whose work explores residential schools and the effects of colonization; or when I read Imam Hassan Guillet's preternaturally humane eulogy for victims of the Quebec mosque shooting. I feel most proud to be a Canadian when I see citizens act with bravery and grace under extreme pressures and, in doing so, create and inform Canada's *real* history—one that is flawed but forever trying."

NADIA LITZ
ACTOR · DIRECTOR

“When I am travelling, I miss my homeland in the Canadian Arctic the most. I miss my family, the sense of community where everyone knows one another, and what we call 'country food'—traditional dishes like Arctic char, seal, whale, and caribou, which nourish me physically, emotionally, and spiritually. **There is something very special about coming home to the Arctic after I have been to far-off places to 're-ground' myself to the realities of what inspired me to do the work I do.** Coming home to an Arctic view where the vista in itself is healing, and to bond with my cultural heritage through the sharing and eating of our country food is very special and necessary to carry on with this global work in a world that barely knows who we are, much less appreciates the challenges globalization throws in our way every day.”

SHEILA WATT-CLOUTIER
ACTIVIST · AUTHOR

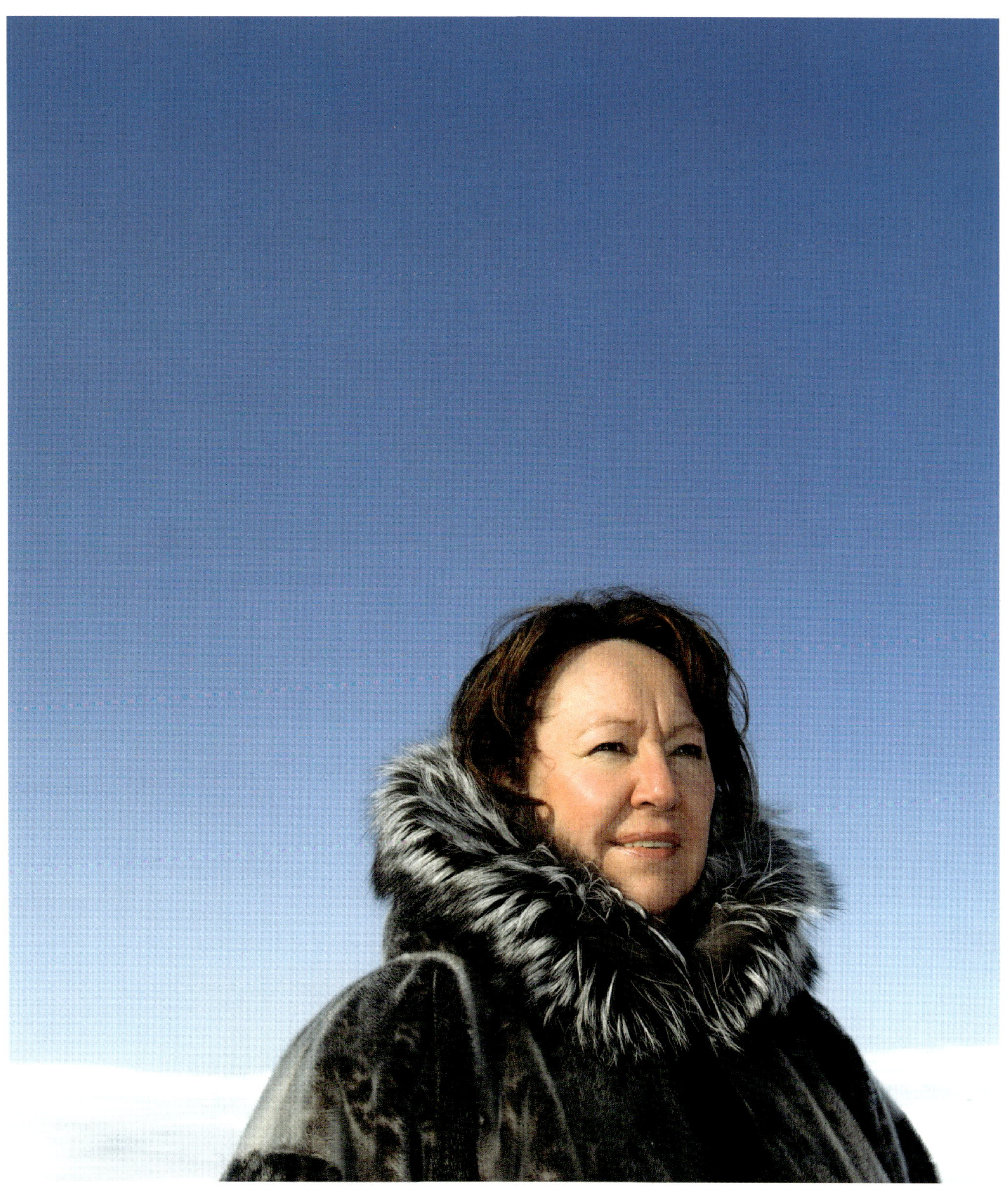

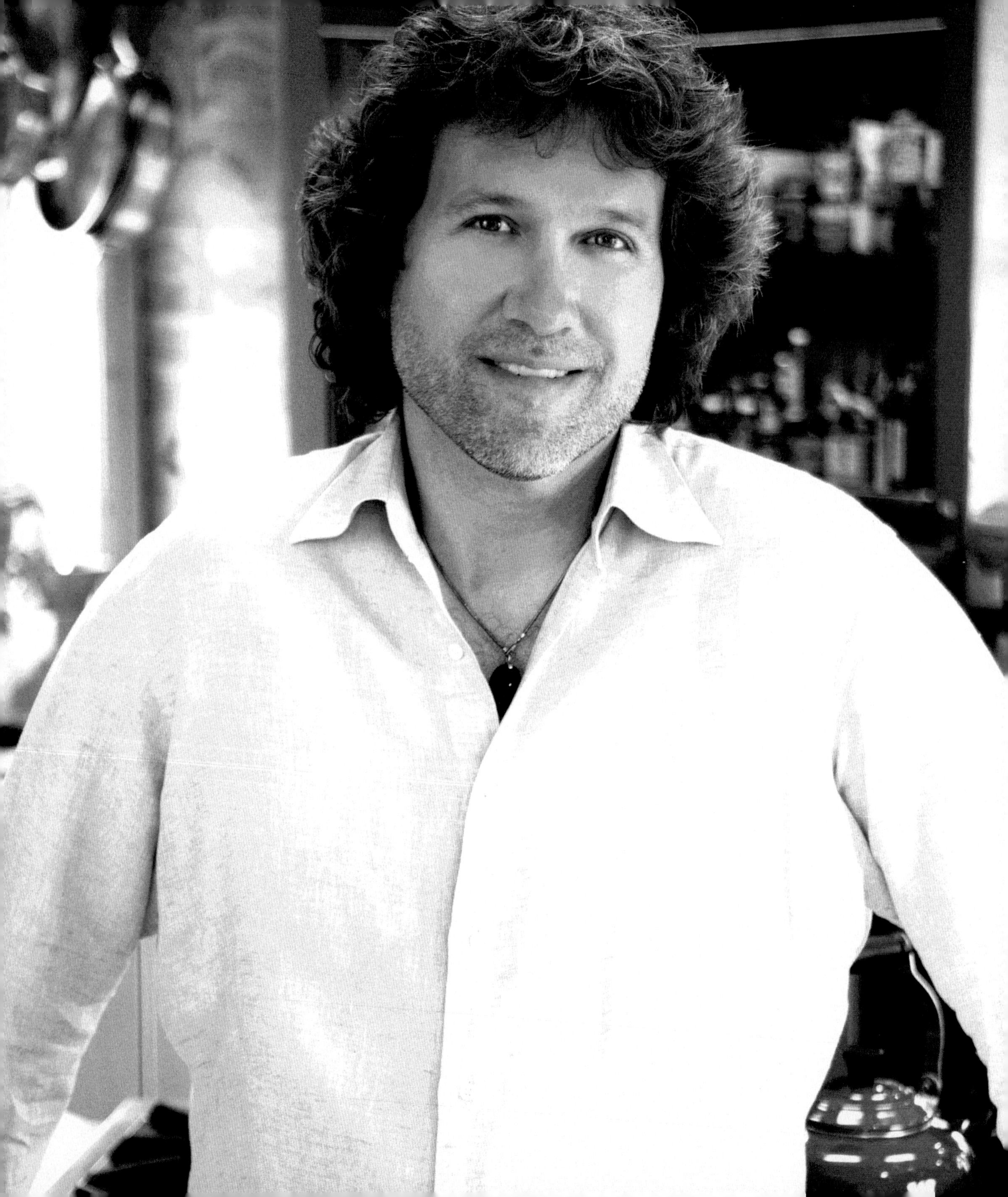

MICHAEL SMITH · CHEF · AUTHOR

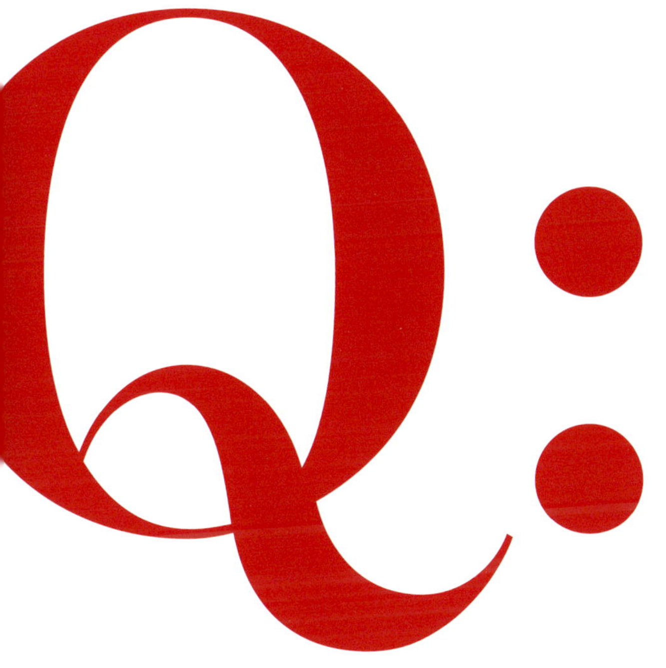

WHAT DOES IT MEAN TO BE CANADIAN?

"To be Canadian is to be filled with respect and love for each other and our environment."

WHAT MAKES YOU PROUD TO CALL YOURSELF CANADIAN?

"I am most proud of our innate willingness to accept immigrants from every corner of the globe with open arms."

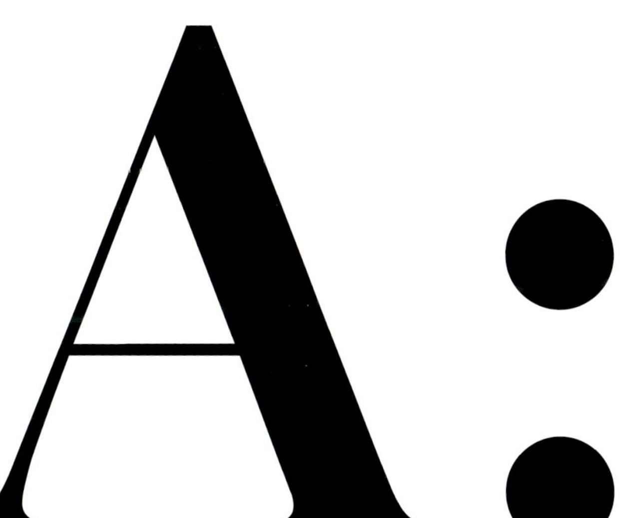

WHAT IS YOUR MOST "CANADIAN" MEMORY?

"My most 'Canadian' memory is my annual skating pilgrimage down the moonlit Rideau Canal."

THE TRUTH ABOUT CANADA IS...

"That we're fiercely proud to be the best country in the world but too humble to shout about it."

“I AM PROUD TO BE CANADIAN, I AM PROUD TO BE FROM TORONTO, AND I HOPE TO CONTINUE TO REPRESENT.”

DRAKE · MUSICIAN · SONGWRITER

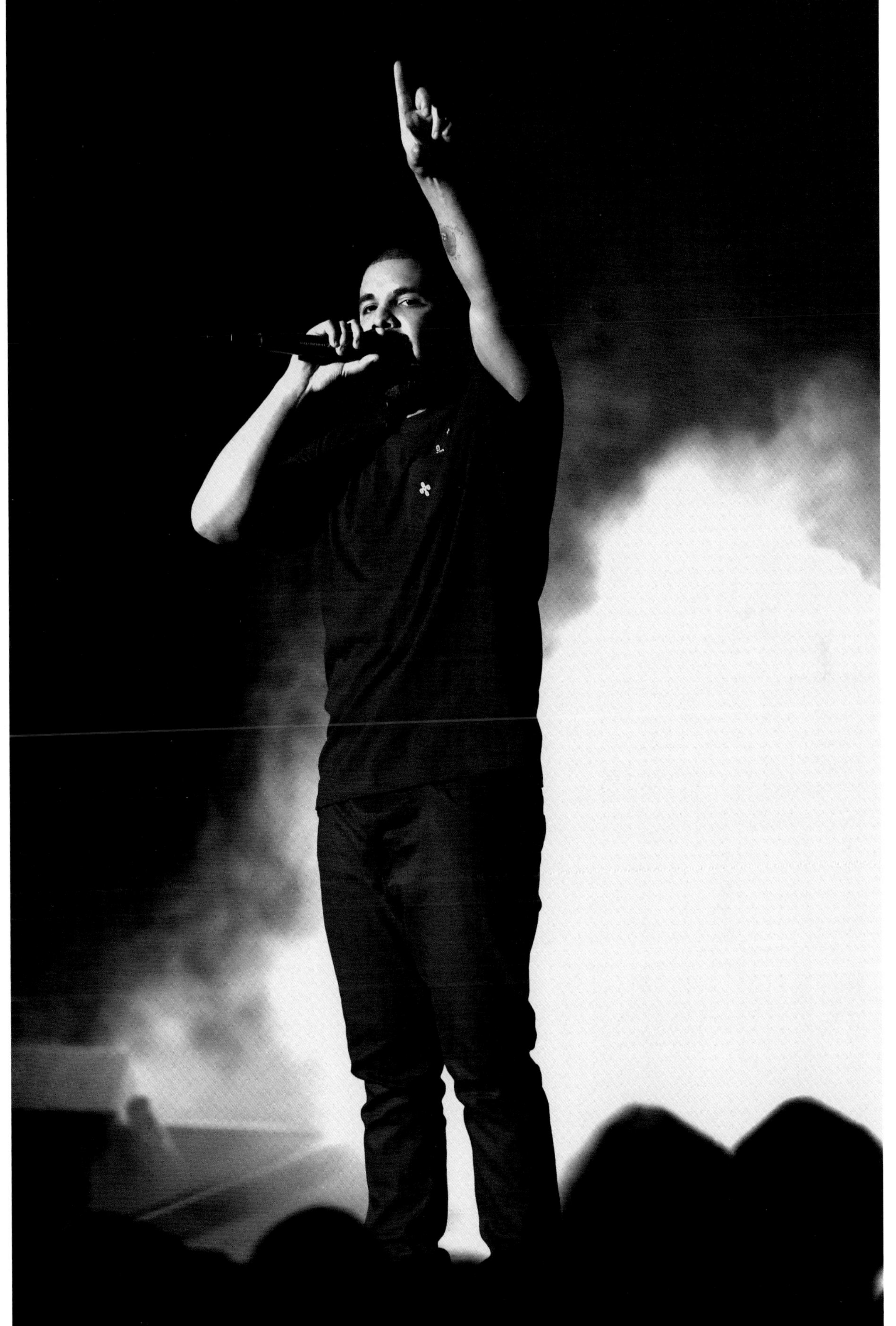

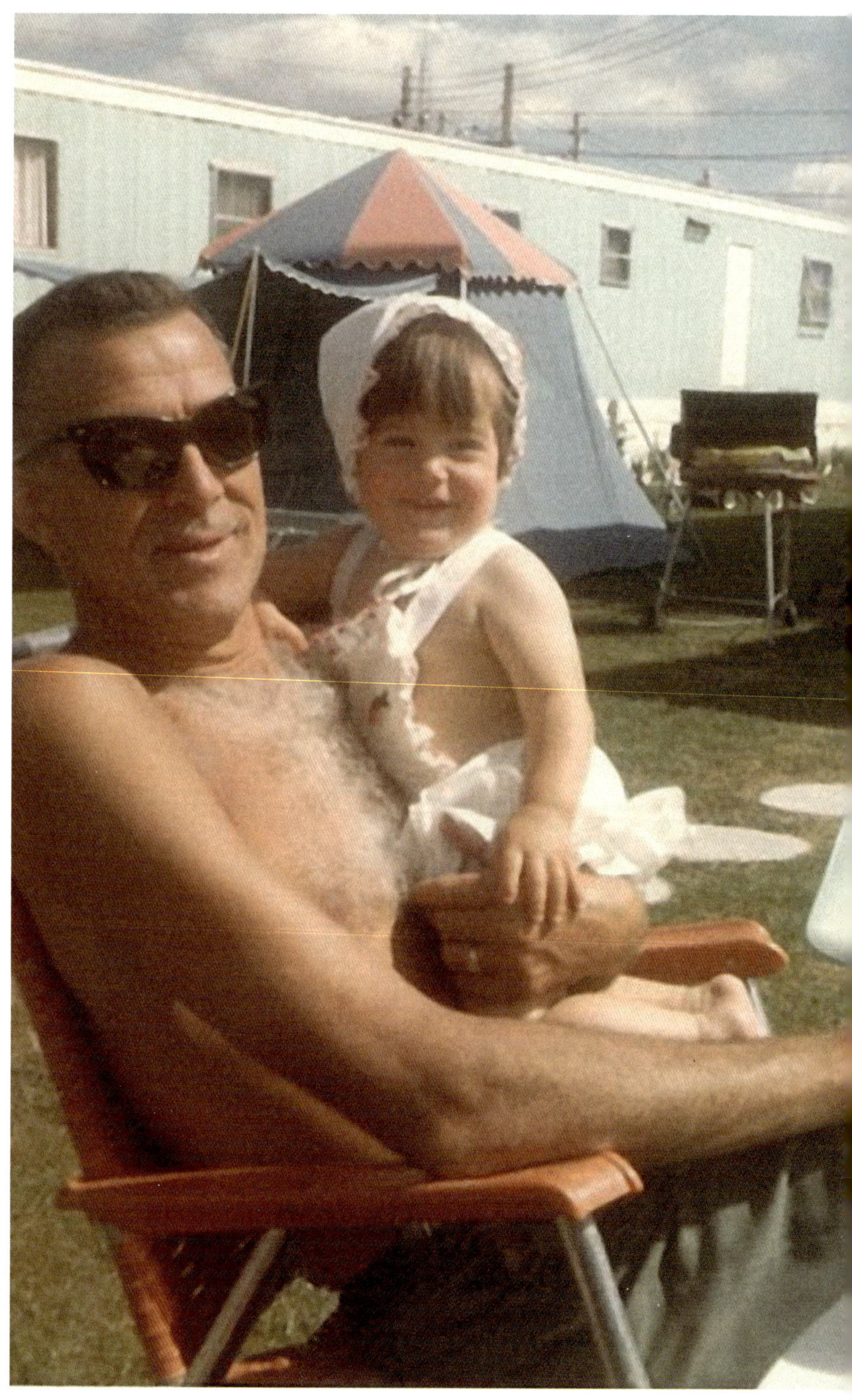

/BEING CANADIAN MEANS GROWING UP IN AN ENERGY OF INNOCENCE AND GOODNESS. IT MEANS CARING ABOUT NATURE AND THE GOODNESS OF HUMANITY./

CARRIE-ANNE MOSS · ACTOR

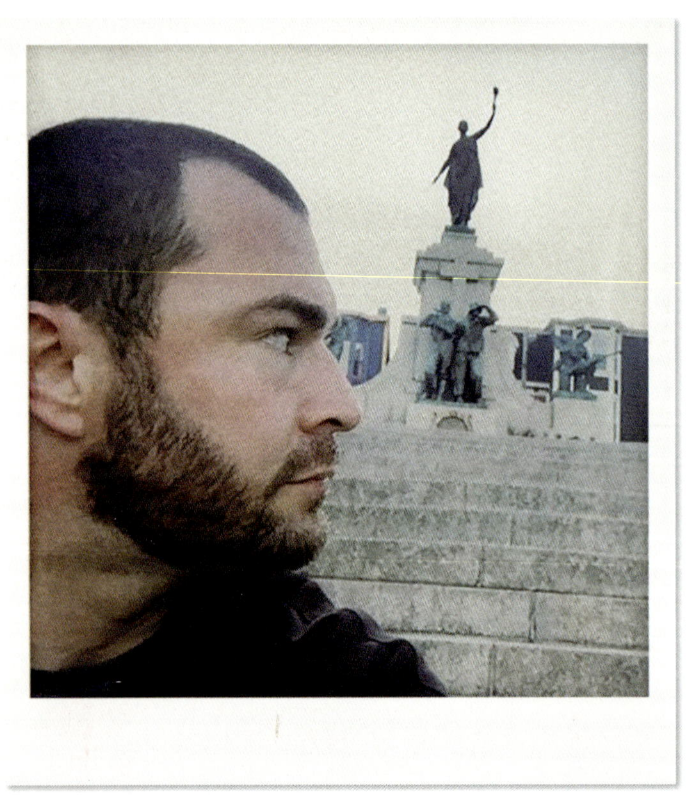

"Being Canadian is about serving my country and being part of something greater than myself. It's like an instinct for me."

JODY MITIC
AUTHOR · POLITICIAN

"FROM COAST TO COAST, IT'S JUST SUCH AN IMPRESSIVE LANDSCAPE. THE LAKES, MOUNTAINS, FORESTS ARE SO INSPIRING FOR ARTISTS OF ALL AGES. AS AN EIGHT-YEAR-OLD, I REMEMBER PAINTING THE ROCKIES ON THE WALL OF OUR BASEMENT AS A BACKDROP TO MY TRAIN SET."

MÉLANIE WATT
CHILDREN'S AUTHOR

What does it mean to be Canadian?

"I have lived in Alberta all my life. When I look out my front door — through the trees and the long grass towards the enormous Rocky Mountains, I am in complete awe of the vast amount of space that I have — that and the electric blue sky that spreads itself over everything, has shaped my life and my writing for the past 40 years. When you feel like you belong somewhere, it gives you courage to let yourself go out into the world fearlessly. **To me, that's what makes me acutely aware that I am Canadian.**"

JANN ARDEN
MUSICIAN · SONGWRITER

d in alberta all my life. when I
my front door - through the free
long glass towards the enormous
mtains, I am in complete awe
vast amount of space that I
hat and the electric blue sky
ads itself over everything, has
y life and my writing for the pa
ars. When you feel like you
mewhere, it gives you the
to let yourself go out into
that

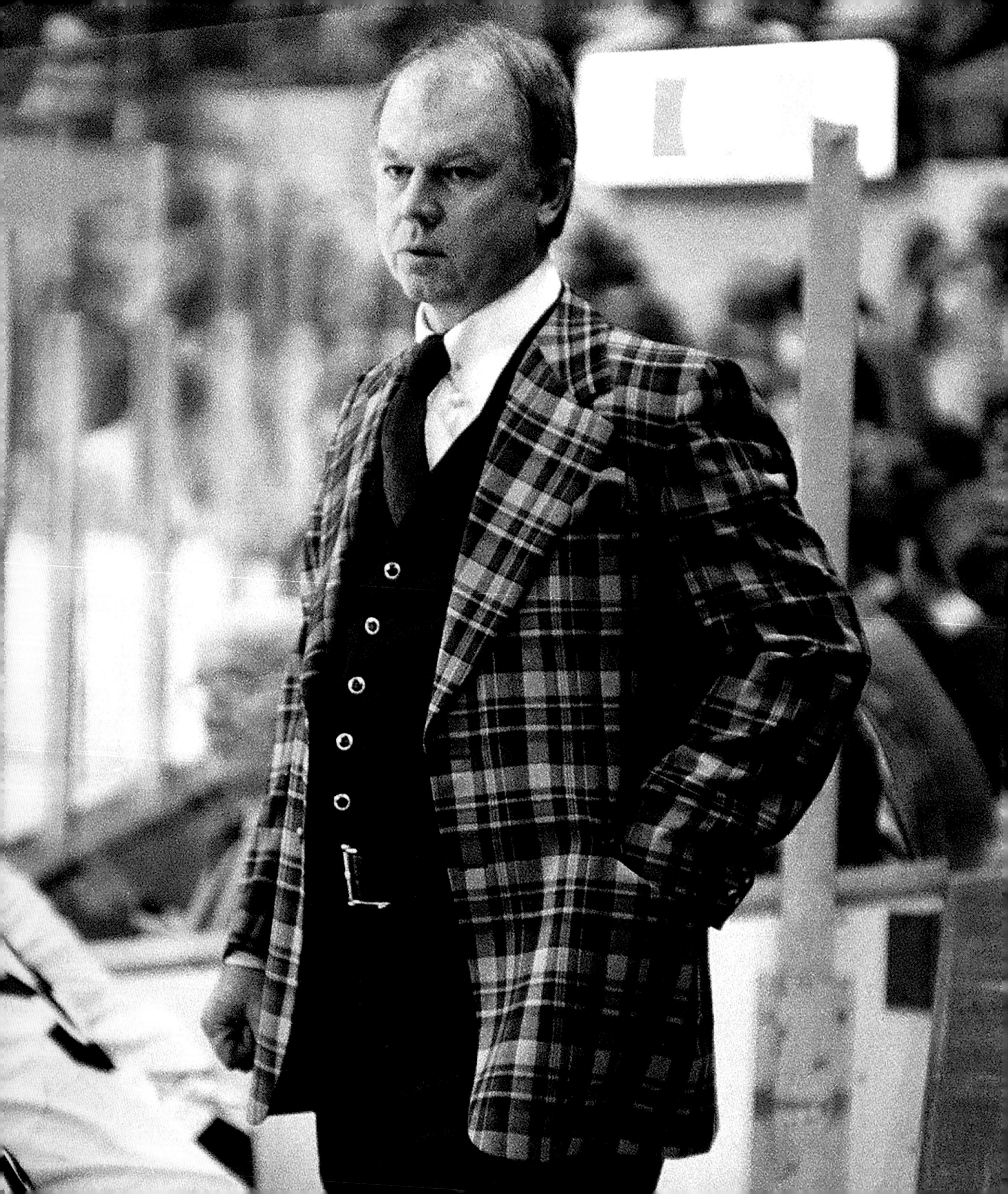

"LOVE, HONOUR, AND RESPECT. THAT'S WHAT IT MEANS TO BE A CANADIAN."

DON CHERRY
SPORTS COMMENTATOR

ter·rasse
/te'räs/

L'expression canadienne-française qui fait référence à une surface plane et pavée à l'extérieur d'un café. L'endroit parfait pour prendre un verre avec des amis les belles soirées d'été.

sour·dough

/'sou( )r,d /

The nickname given to a person residing in the Yukon for more than a year.

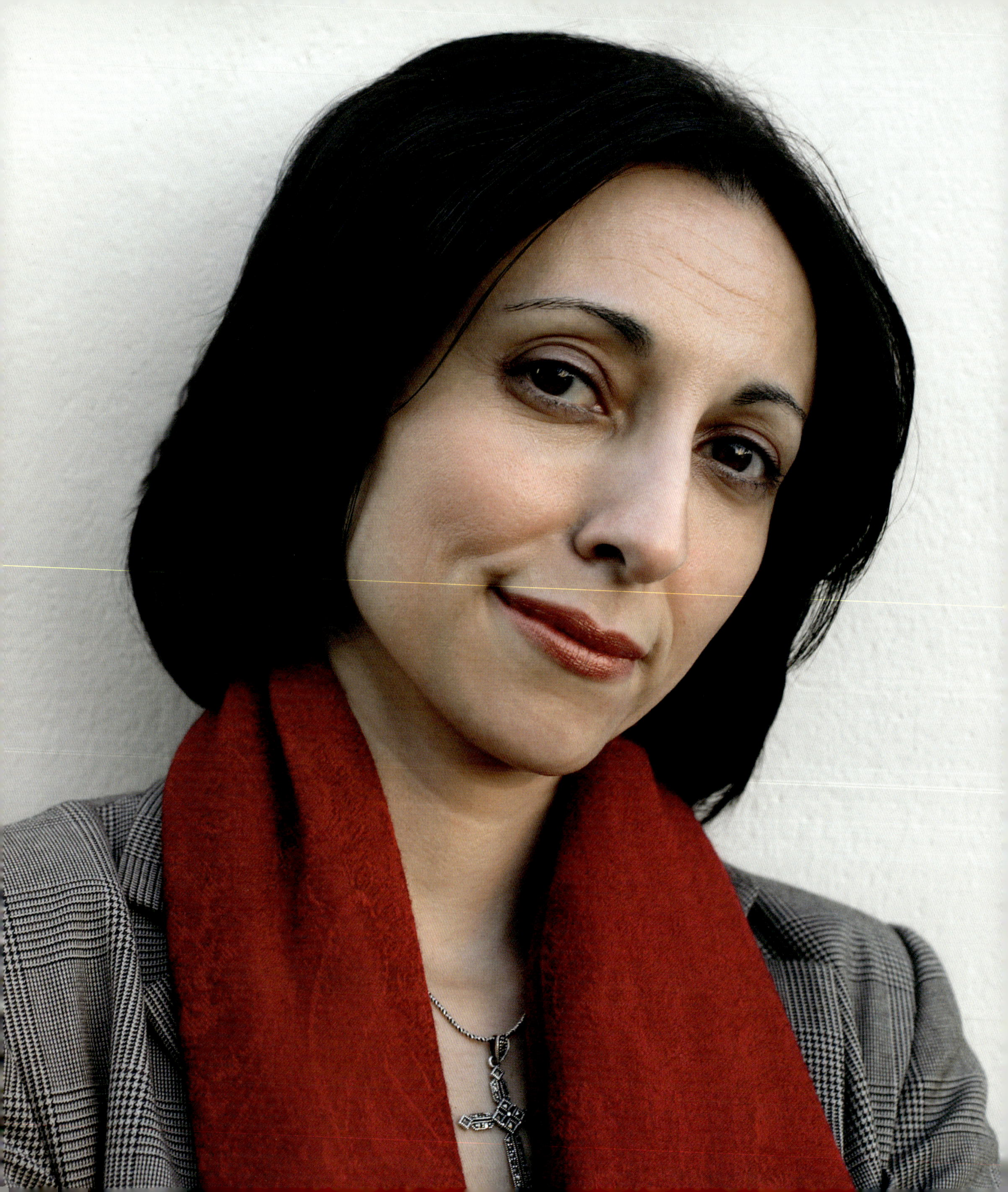

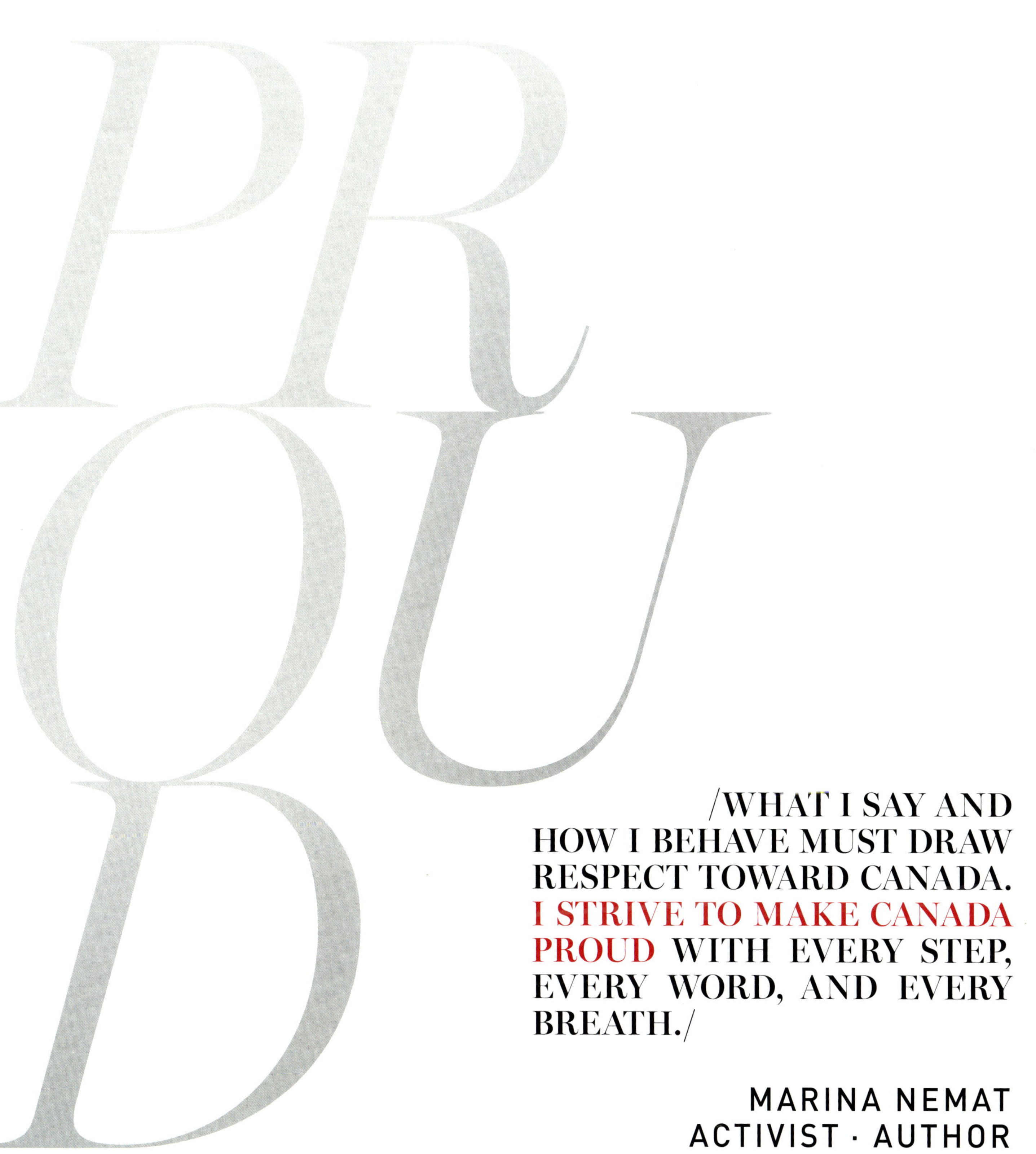

/WHAT I SAY AND HOW I BEHAVE MUST DRAW RESPECT TOWARD CANADA. I STRIVE TO MAKE CANADA PROUD WITH EVERY STEP, EVERY WORD, AND EVERY BREATH./

MARINA NEMAT
ACTIVIST · AUTHOR

ERIC PETERSON · ACTOR

"Years ago, I spent some time on St. Barts, an island in the French West Indies, helping refit a sailboat. I noticed that people often received my greeting of 'Beautiful day!' or 'Can you believe this sunshine?' with puzzlement and a kind of mild astonishment, a reaction that seemed out of kilter with my simple acknowledgment of the lovely day. Eventually it dawned on me that this normal Canadian greeting was a non sequitur here, since every day was beautiful, most of them anyway, and when they weren't, it was probably blowing a hurricane. So I found different things to say when greeting people, but I have to admit I missed, and would sometimes feel homesick for, a good old 'Jeez it's hot.'

Canadians' chronic 'weather commenting' is often presented as a defining Canadian cliché and pejoratively judged as a trivial and banal pastime. But I want to push back a little on this notion of banality.

There is a deceptive utility in the weather comment, and the 'banality' is actually an asset in its efficacy as a societal facilitator, presenting as it does a risk-free topic when initiating a conversation with a fellow citizen. When this banality is coupled with humour, which it often is, such a remark, and the subsequent chuckling agreement, goes a long way in easing those initial tensions of social intercourse.

Greeting with 'a weather comment' could also be seen as an attempt at articulating a shared existential reality. As already noted, the subject of weather provides a benign topic along which you can align points of view or provide a quick consensus — and consensus is one of the chief pleasures of community, not to mention its necessary glue.

Trivializing the sharing of opinions on the 'topic of the weather' might also be to miss its value as a 'gateway' topic, a lure to take on 'stronger,' more contentious subjects. We agreed on the weather. Could we agree on the global economy? And in the rare case where agreement about the weather is not forthcoming — such as on a bright winter day with the temperature the same as that on Mars, with one person wryly observing 'So this is global warming?' to be responded to with 'Climate change is bullshit!' — this might indicate a 'gate' not to proceed through. In this case, in the interests of harmony, a simple 'Yea, f(ing) cold' with a quick exit would be the right choice.

People might be a little surprised to realize that they have engaged in metaphysics when they declare: 'Man, that was a big wind last night! I lost branches.'

When we comment on the weather, we see ourselves in relationship to it, with the tacit acceptance that in this relationship, we are puny but the weather is not. No matter how much we joke or complain about it, no matter how much we claim the topic is trivial and banal, we live by its mandate. Weather is our capricious ruler, bestowing prosperity and pleasure as easily as suffering and ruin; giving us good crops or a great weekend at the beach with the same indifference as it bestows a tornado in which there is loss of life. Minus 40 degrees Celsius, with a wind chill of minus 70 degrees, has a disregard for human welfare that we must hide from, or run from, or die from.

When I was in the south, I missed the north. I got bored with the island paradise and its predictable unceasingly heavenly weather. Not right away, of course, but eventually I hankered for the weather of this cold country and our 'weather comment' with all its banal complexity. I missed 'Fucking cold, eh?'"

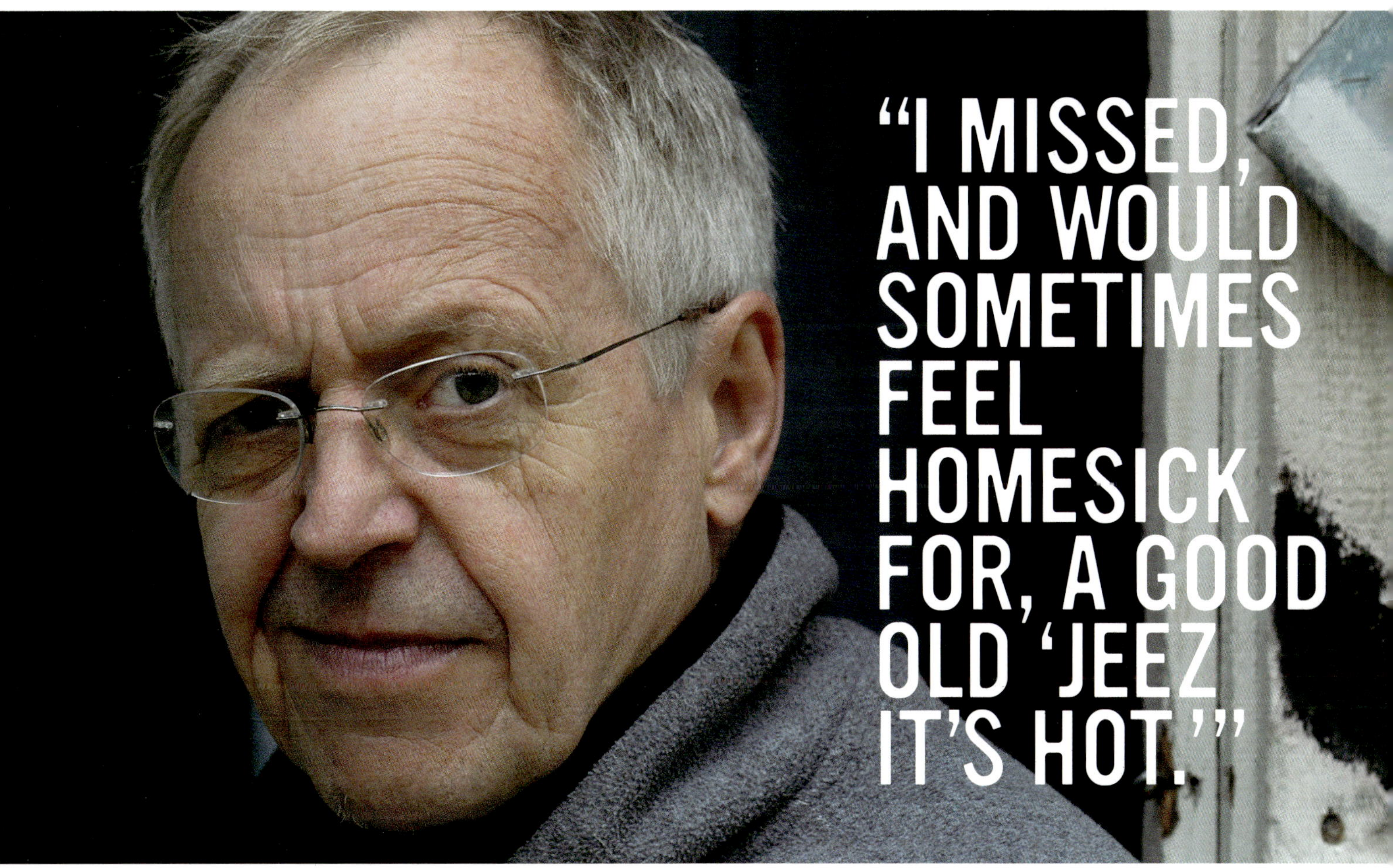
"I MISSED, AND WOULD SOMETIMES FEEL HOMESICK FOR, A GOOD OLD 'JEEZ IT'S HOT.'"

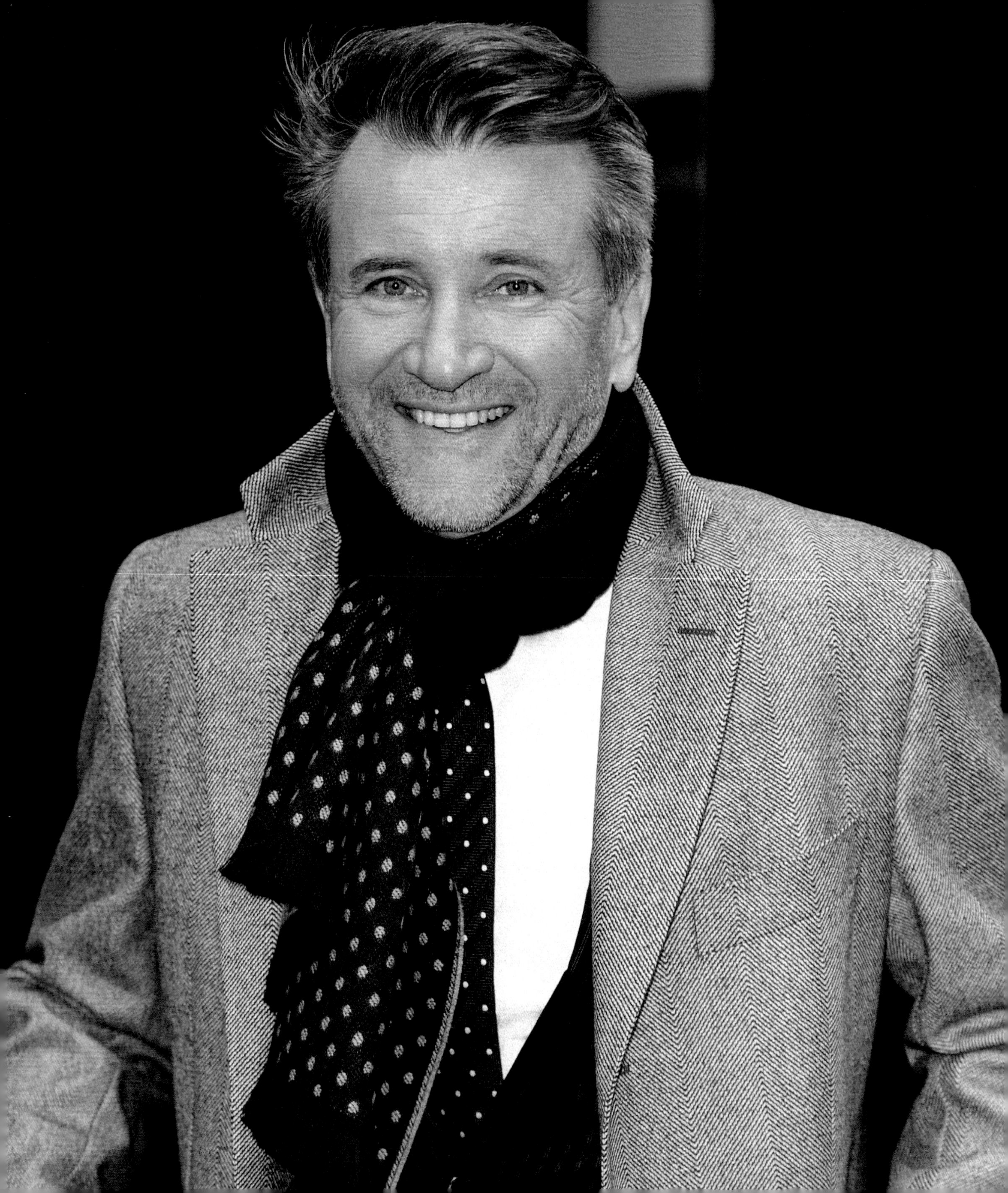

ROBERT HERJAVEC · ENTREPRENEUR

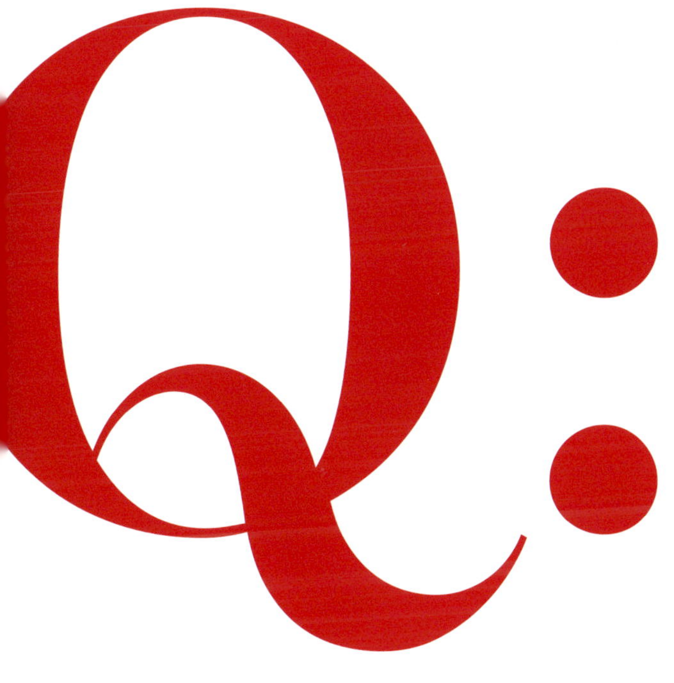

WHAT DOES IT MEAN TO BE CANADIAN?

"Being Canadian means opportunity to me — this country that took me and my parents in when no one else would. It has always meant opportunity to me. It's a land where you can build what you want for your family, for yourself, and for those you love. It is a big country, geographically and metaphorically."

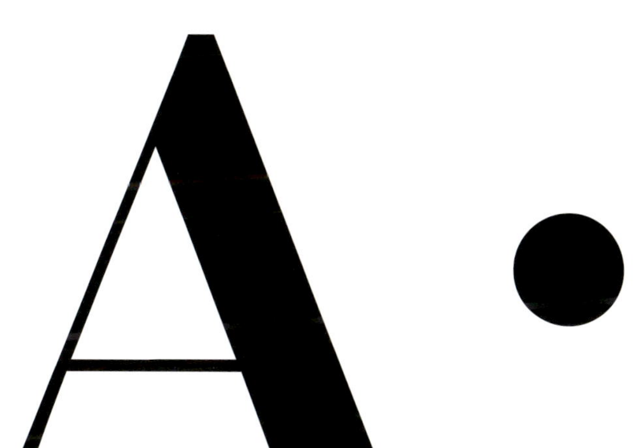

WHAT IS YOUR MOST "CANADIAN" MEMORY?

"Camping with my Mom and Dad — somehow the great outdoors has always signified Canada to me — when I think of Canada, I think of vast open spaces."

THE TRUTH ABOUT CANADA IS...

"The truth about Canada is we can take on the world. We are nice, but as I always say, don't mistake our kindness for weakness."

THE BAY OF FUNDY BOASTS

THE WORLD'S HIGHEST

WHEN THE TIDE RETREATS, ON THE OCEAN FLOOR.

TIDES.

VISITORS CAN WALK

“When I travel, I'm surprised if I meet people who don't appreciate Canada's consummate excellence. I half expect people from other countries to cheer when they learn I'm Canadian, partly because I feel like cheering every time I remember that I am lucky enough to have been born here and live here. The country isn't perfect and there is problematic history to contend with, but it's still a place that fills me with gratitude and amazement.

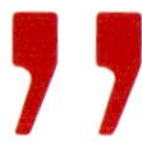

SUSAN JUBY
AUTHOR

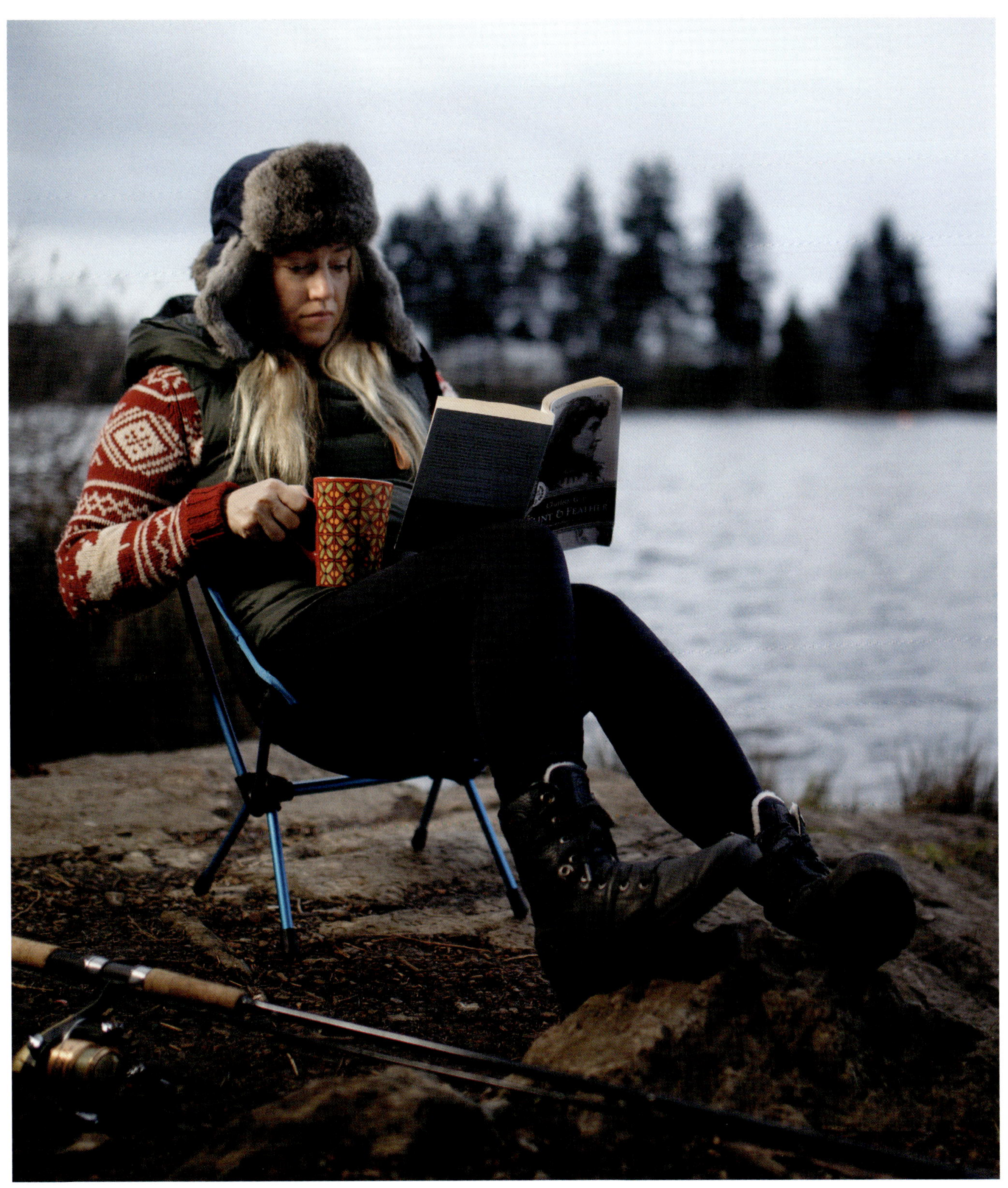

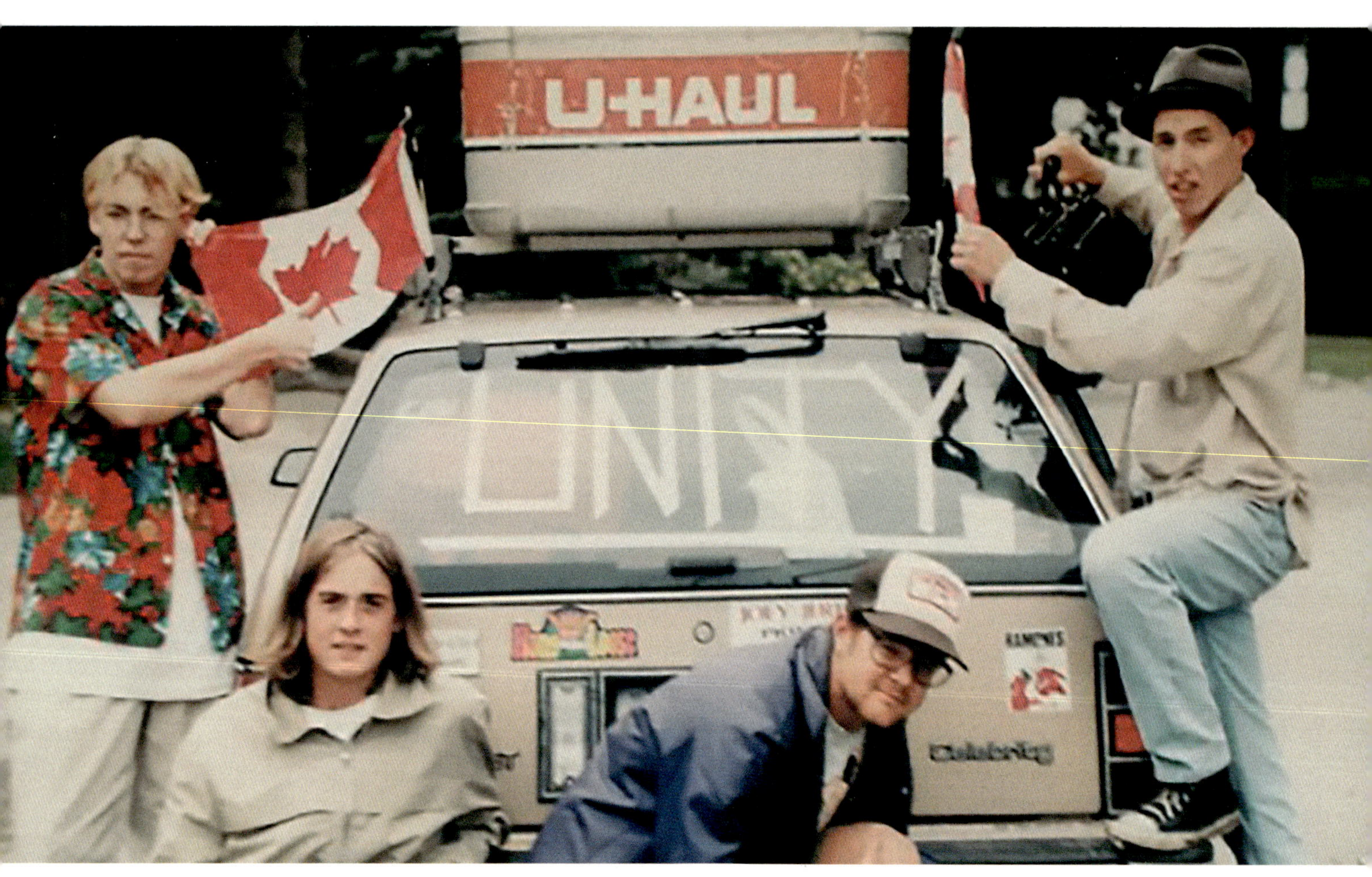
U-HAUL
UNITY

PAUL SPENCE · FILMMAKER

Quelle est la chose la plus canadienne que vous ayez faite?

«C'était en 1995. Je déménageais à Montréal pour poursuivre mes études dans une Chevrolet Celebrity 1987. Quand elle m'a vendu son chevalier vaillant pour $800 sans taxes, j'ai enfin su que ma mère m'aimait. Faque, avec mes trois copains les moins attachés a leur job, on a planifié notre départ de Calgary pour Québec. Une semaine avant notre départ, a travers une table pleine de cannes vides, on a décidé de faire notre part pour sauver le Canada en adoptant un slogan — «We say Oui to Unity», c'était l'année du Référendum après tout. Le 14 Août, le Unity Tour se pointait vers l'est, vers le Québec, vers un destin incertain. Avec un sac de 1000 épingles du drapeau canadien (merci Chrétien), on a traversé notre cher pays. On les offrait dans les truck stop, bars, places publiques, et même à une station service dans la région de la capitale nationale du Québec (Québec), à un certain Guy Lafleur.

Est-ce qu'on a sauvé notre pays? Ché pas, mais quand notre wagon a explosé dans le nord de l'Ontario, un vieux vendeur de chars, apres avoir entendu notre histoire, nous a donné un Ford Thunderbird 1979 pour qu'on puisse poursuivre notre chemin. Petit train va loin.»

Complétez cette phrase : « La vérité à propos du Canada, c'est que... »

«Si tu veux arrêter une bagarre au Canada, offre une bière à chacun des combattants. Les deux, en respectant la 3ième Loi de la Bière Canadienne (En recevant l'offre d'une bière gratis, on n'a pas le choix de la boire), vont tout de suite arrêter de s'engueuler, pour boire la bière. Directement après la première gorgée, ils vont donner leur opinion sur la qualité de la bière, la température, et la différence entre la boire en canne versus en bouteille. Avant même d'avoir calé la dernière goutte, ils vont être entrain d'échanger des top cinq, tout en discutant les difficultés d'être goaler dans une ligue de garage.»

«We say Oui to Unity»

Qu'est-ce que ça veut dire d'être Canadien?

«Tu sais quoi? D'être canadien, c'est comme porter une paire de culottes propres. Personne ne le sait, que tu te promènes en culottes propres, mais crime tu te promènes avec une certaine confiance. Bien sûr qu'on affiche aucune attente d'enclencher une soirée de plaisir jamais vue depuis la scène de sexe de Mon Fantôme d'Amour (Ghost), mais tout se peut. On est prêt. Et c'est ça qui compte. Comme canadien, les situations incroyables, les succès internationaux, ils ne nous arrivent pas a tous les jours- mais quand ils se produisent, on est là avec notre dignité, notre respect pour les concurrents, et surtout, nos culottes propres.»

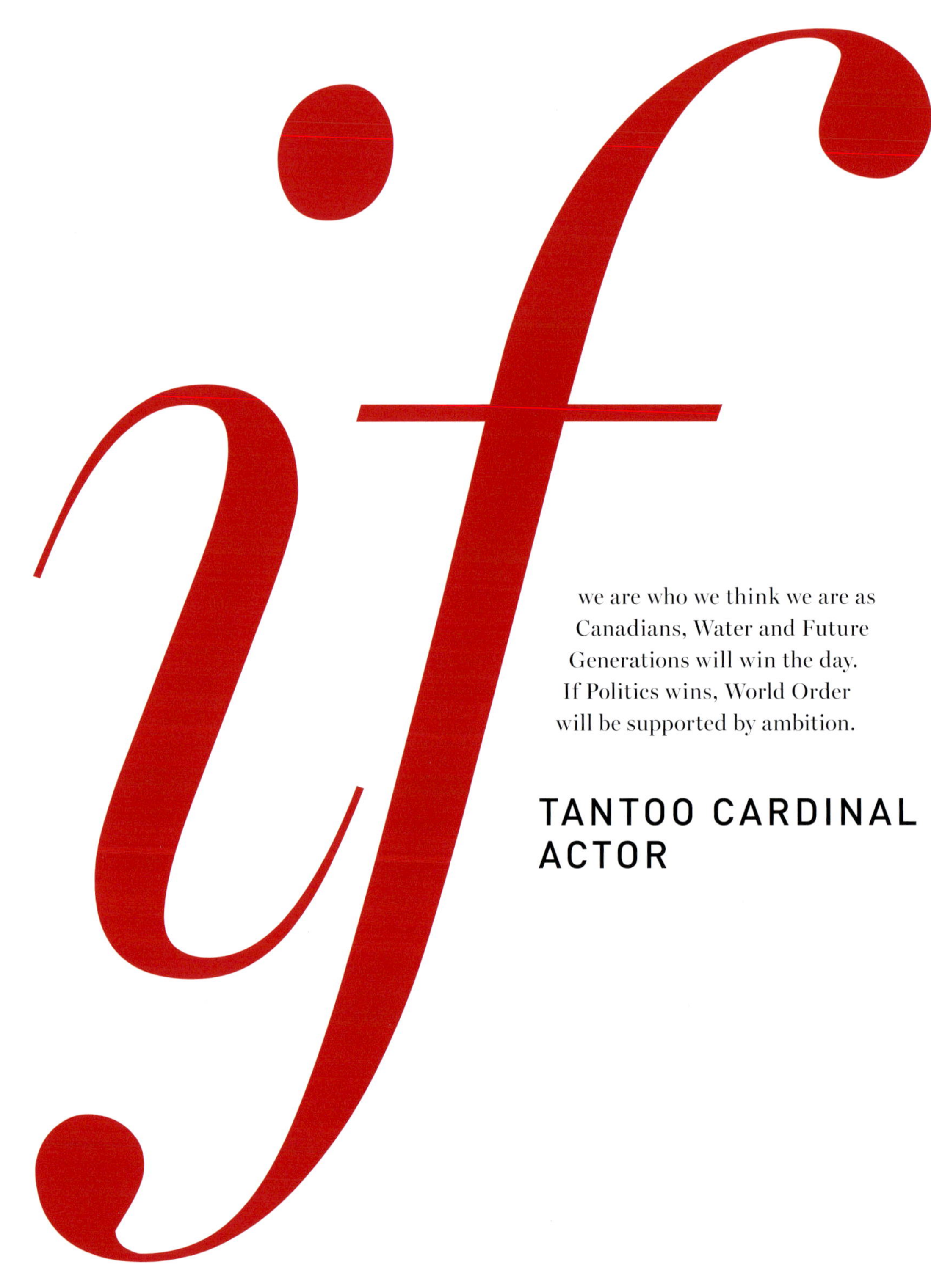

we are who we think we are as Canadians, Water and Future Generations will win the day. If Politics wins, World Order will be supported by ambition.

TANTOO CARDINAL
ACTOR

"My most 'Canadian' memory happened in the summer of 1973. I had a sustained sequence of such moments while backpacking through Europe as a teen for several months. It was just about obligatory for all of us to have a Canadian flag stitched to our backpacks; some added pins to their shirts or hats. The war in Vietnam was ongoing. Protests against it were worldwide, and it was remarkable how differently we were treated as Canadians and how much those recurring moments consolidated for the young version of myself an awareness of identity, pride in being a Canadian and awareness of a distinctive, respected place in the world. **That pride has never gone away, nor has a sense that we need to conduct ourselves so as to be deserving of that respect."**

GUY GAVRIEL KAY
AUTHOR

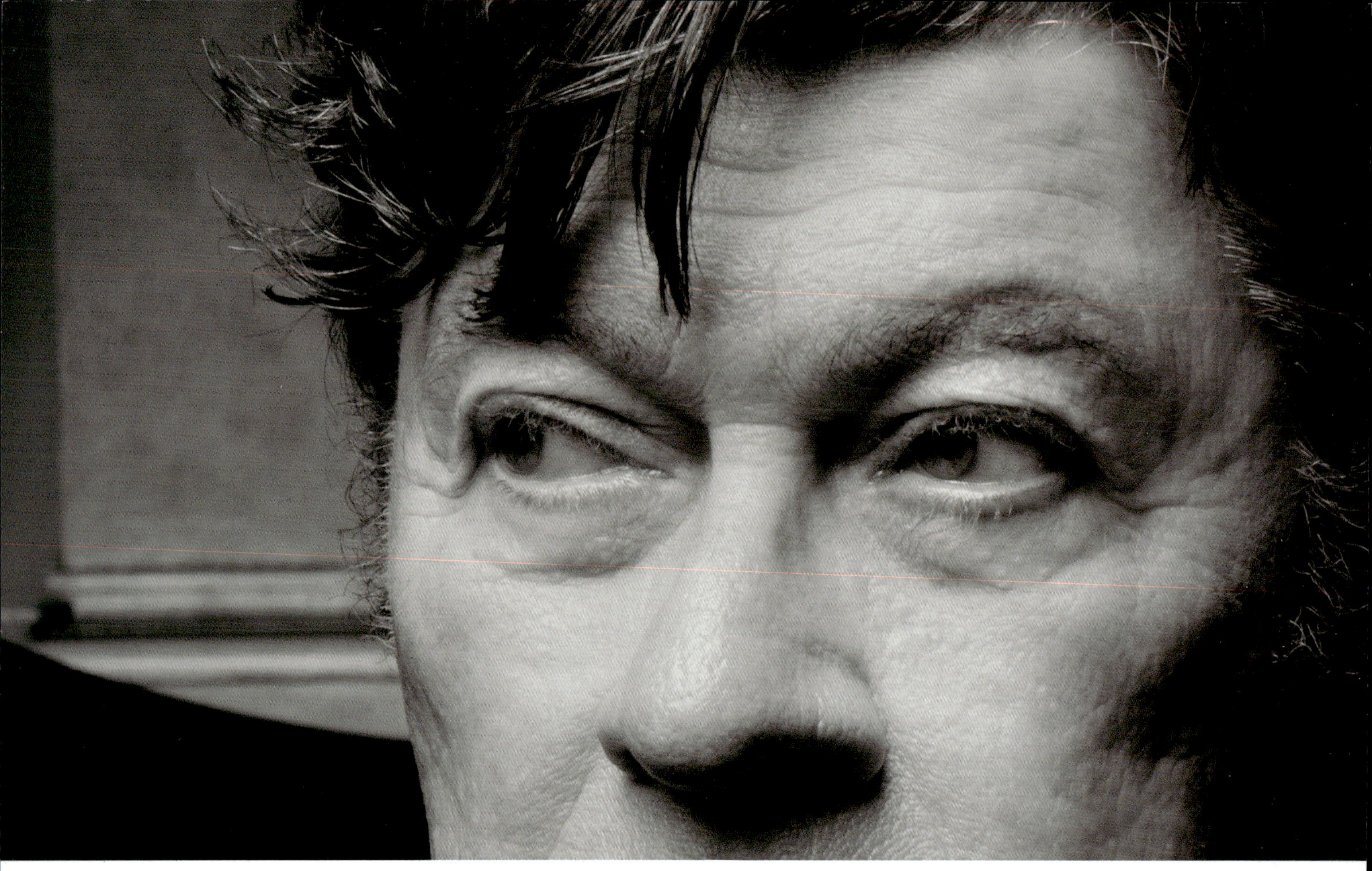

"THESE DAYS, I'M FEELING **MORE PROUD THAN EVER** OF MY CANADIAN ROOTS."

"O Canada. These days, I'm feeling more proud than ever of my Canadian roots. Day after day we witness the madness and sadness around the world, and know deep in the soul of our north country, there is kindness and caring at its core.

Recently, I saw a photo of Prime Minister Justin Trudeau and President Donald Trump sitting together. Something's very wrong with this picture, I thought. Something looks false. Then, the problem became clear. It certainly wasn't Pierre Elliott Trudeau's son; it was this huckster in a big red tie.

A few months back I did a tour of some Canadian cities for my autobiography, *Testimony*. Everywhere I went, you could feel a warmth among the people, and a beauty and serenity in the air.

Yes, I am a proud Canadian, and I want to wish my country a great big Happy 150th Birthday."

ROBBIE ROBERTSON
MUSICIAN · SONGWRITER · AUTHOR

"CLUSTERING AROUND THE DOCK IN NORTHERN ONTARIO."

"My most 'Canadian' memory is the same one every year: clustering around the dock in northern Ontario, unable to feel our toes in the frigid water, swatting away the blackflies, and smiling through the bone-chilling drizzle of the May 24th long weekend, pretending that summer has finally arrived."

DR. SAMANTHA NUTT
FOUNDER OF WAR CHILD · AUTHOR

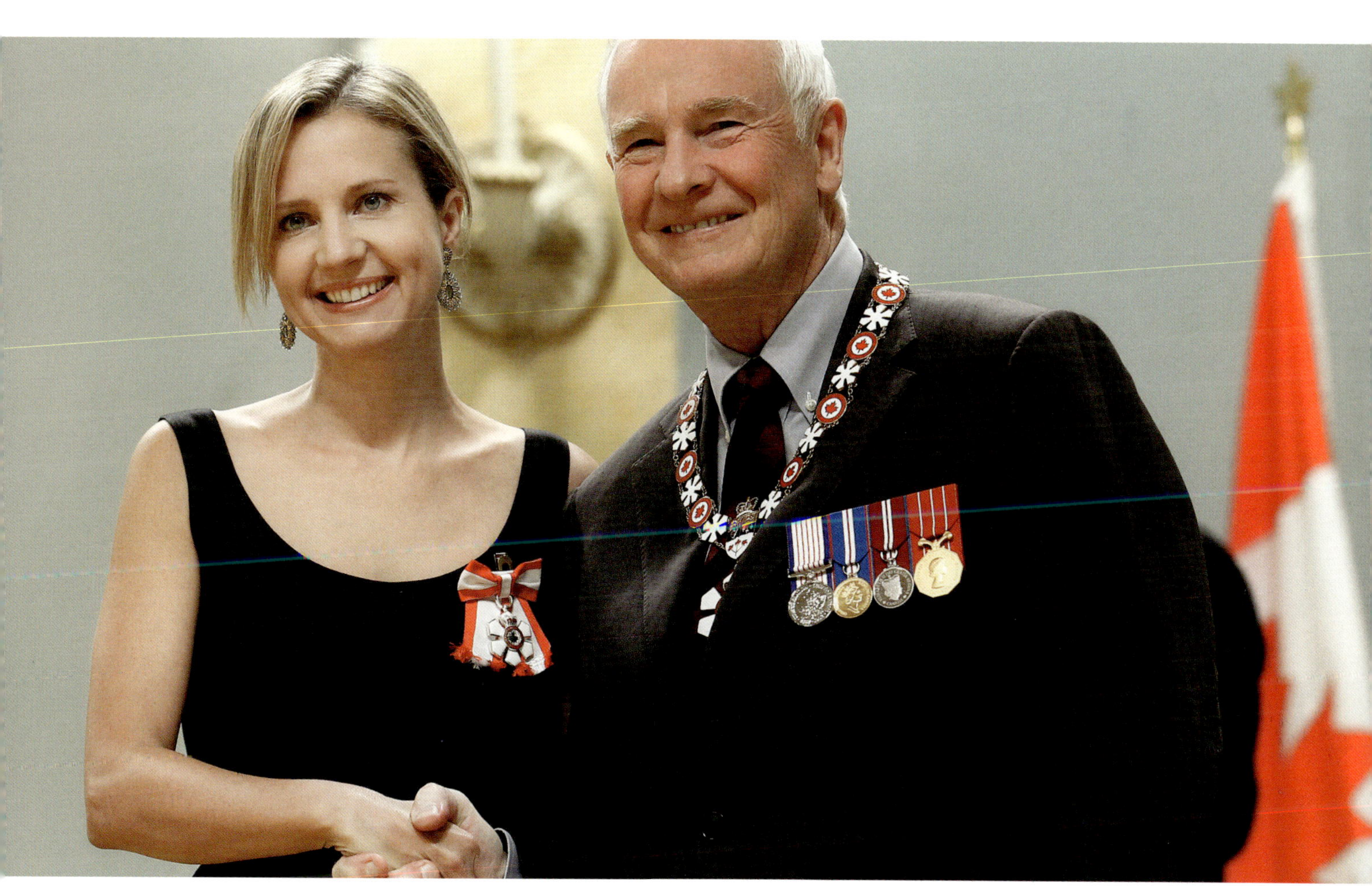

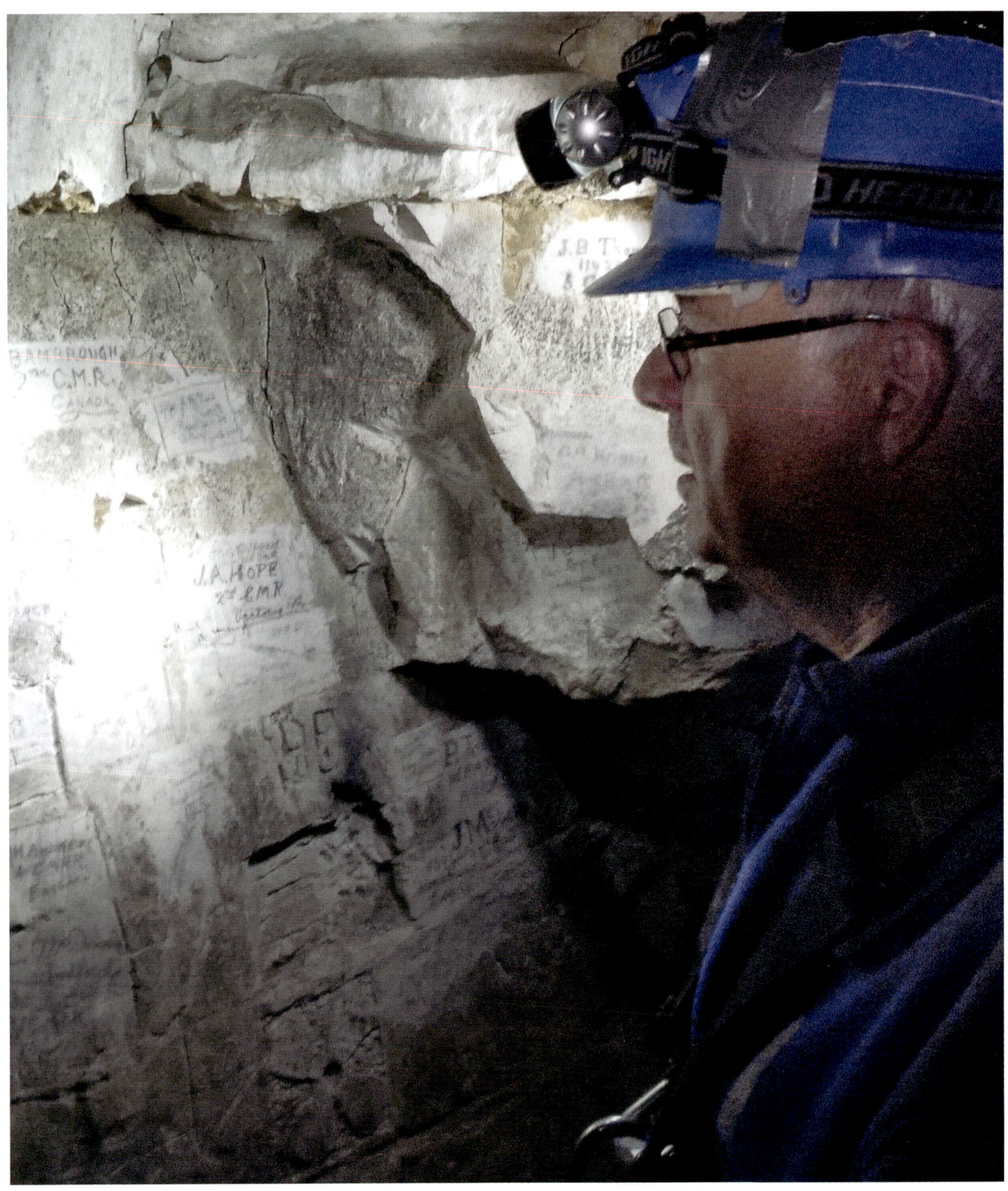
BAMBROUGH
C.M.R.
CANADA
J.A.HOPE
C.M.R

/HUNDREDS OF CANADIAN SOLDIERS STOOD IN THIS SAME SPOT, WAITING FOR THE SIGNAL TO GO UP AND OVER THE TOP./

"I was crawling through the ruins of a tunnel in France, 10 metres below Vimy Ridge, where many feel Canada became a nation during the bloody battles of the First World War. In April of 1917, hundreds of Canadian soldiers stood in this same spot, waiting for the signal to go up and over the top to fight the German enemy. As they waited, many carved their names into the tunnel walls. For some, it may have been the last thing they ever wrote—thousands would die in the ensuing battle. Some etched more than their names: they drew pictures below them. A soldier from Nova Scotia drew a fish, a maple leaf for the chap from Quebec, a canoe for the fellow from Ontario, and a wheatfield for the man from Manitoba. It was deeply emotional to see it, and when I finally got out of the tunnel about two hours later, even though I was on the other side of the world, I have never felt more Canadian than in that moment."

PETER MANSBRIDGE
JOURNALIST

"MY MOST 'CANADIAN' MEMORY IS BEING ABROAD AND REALIZING THERE'S REALLY NO CITY ON EARTH WITH BETTER FOOD THAN TORONTO. THAT, AND EVERY TIME I'VE EVER GONE CAMPING AND HAD A SWIM IN A COOL LAKE."

HANNAH SUNG
JOURNALIST

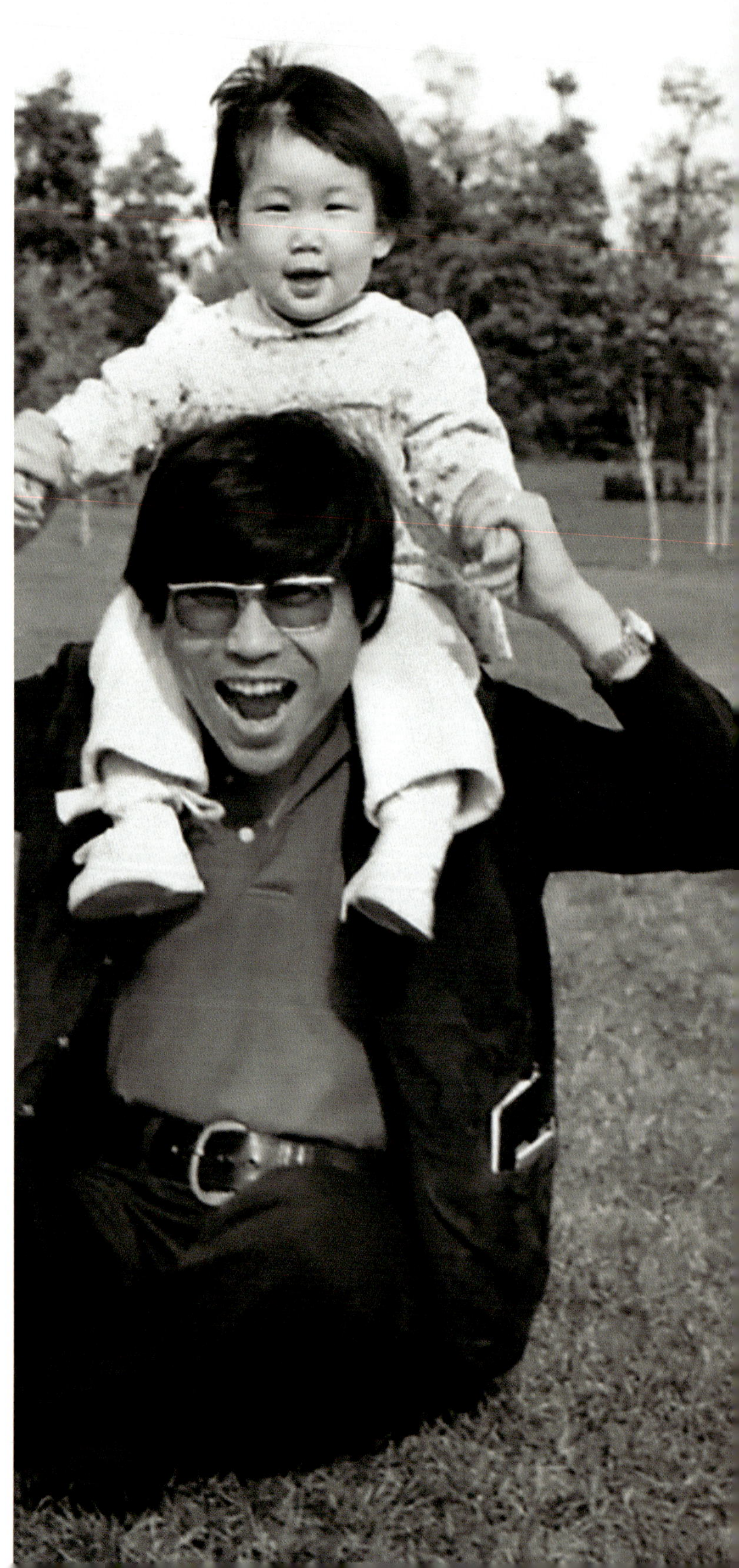

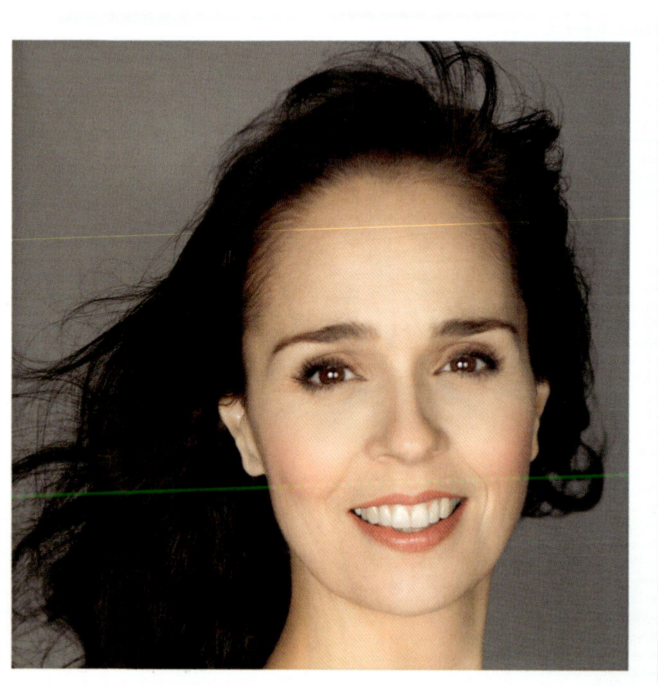

"I remember feeling the sound in an Inuit drum circle somewhere deep inside my body. I was in the Arctic with a group of people that Peter Gzowski had asked to come with him and speak about literacy. We were in a school gymnasium where the Inuit had welcomed us by playing their powerful instruments. Like a train whistle, a loon call, or a whale song, the sacred drumbeat rattled inside of me and I felt connected to this country in a way I had never experienced before."

CYNTHIA DALE · ACTOR

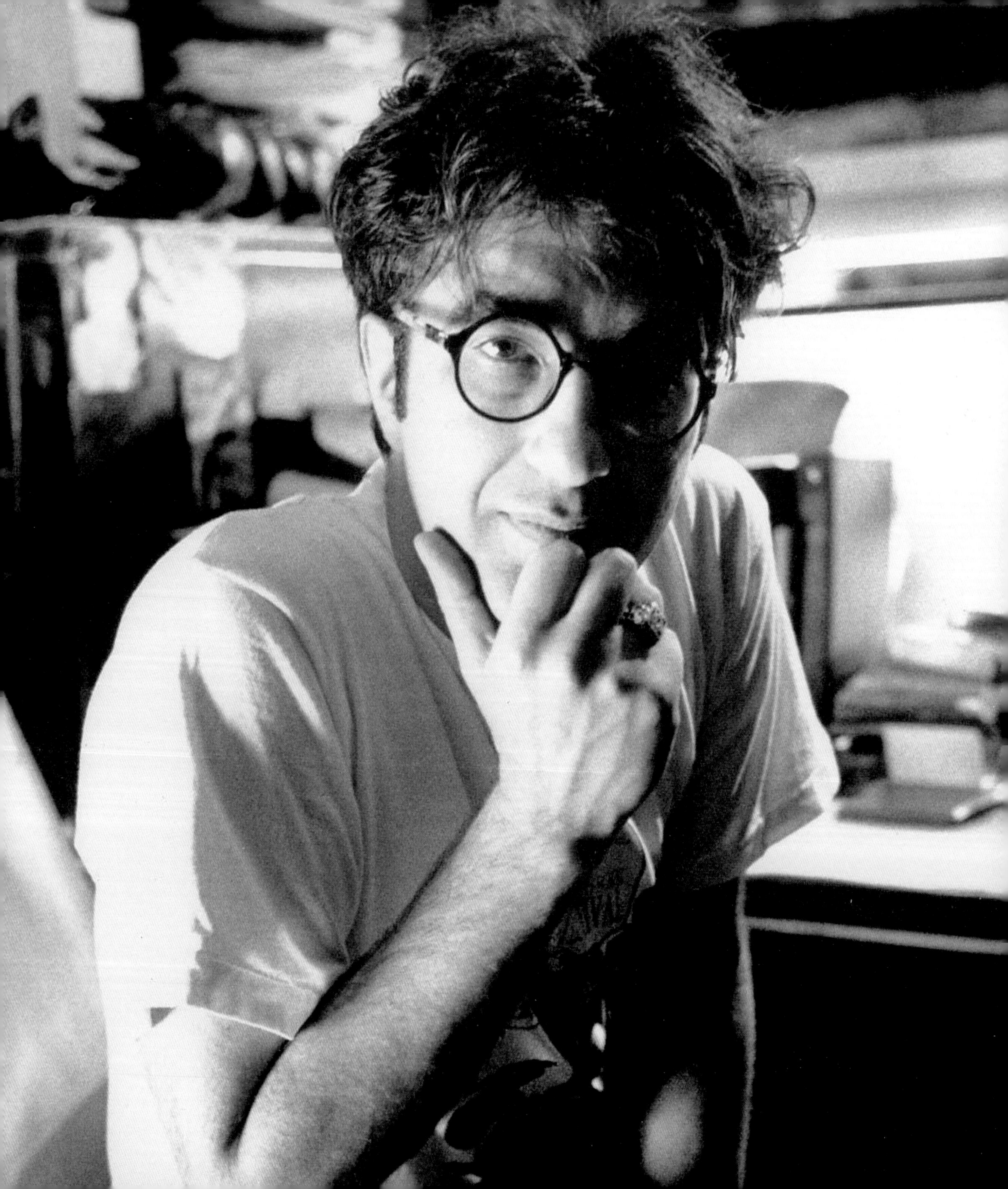

ATOM EGOYAN · DIRECTOR

"What makes me proud to call myself Canadian is to be part of an ongoing experiment that is unlike anything else going on in the world. No where else can one find so many people from so many parts of this planet making such an earnest and hard-fought attempt to get along with each other. It's not always easy, and there are certainly hard questions ahead, but we are having those conversations in an open and honest way."

THE BEST WAY TO ENDEAR YOURSELF TO A CANADIAN IS...

"TO HAVE A SENSE OF HUMOUR AND BE KIND."

COCO ROCHA, MODEL

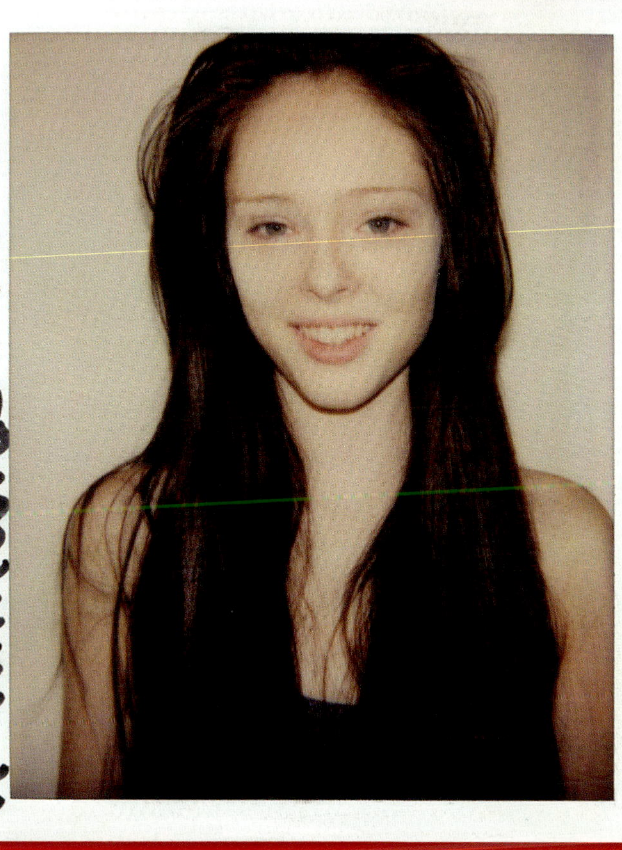
COCO ROCHA
17 VANCOUVER
9.6.06

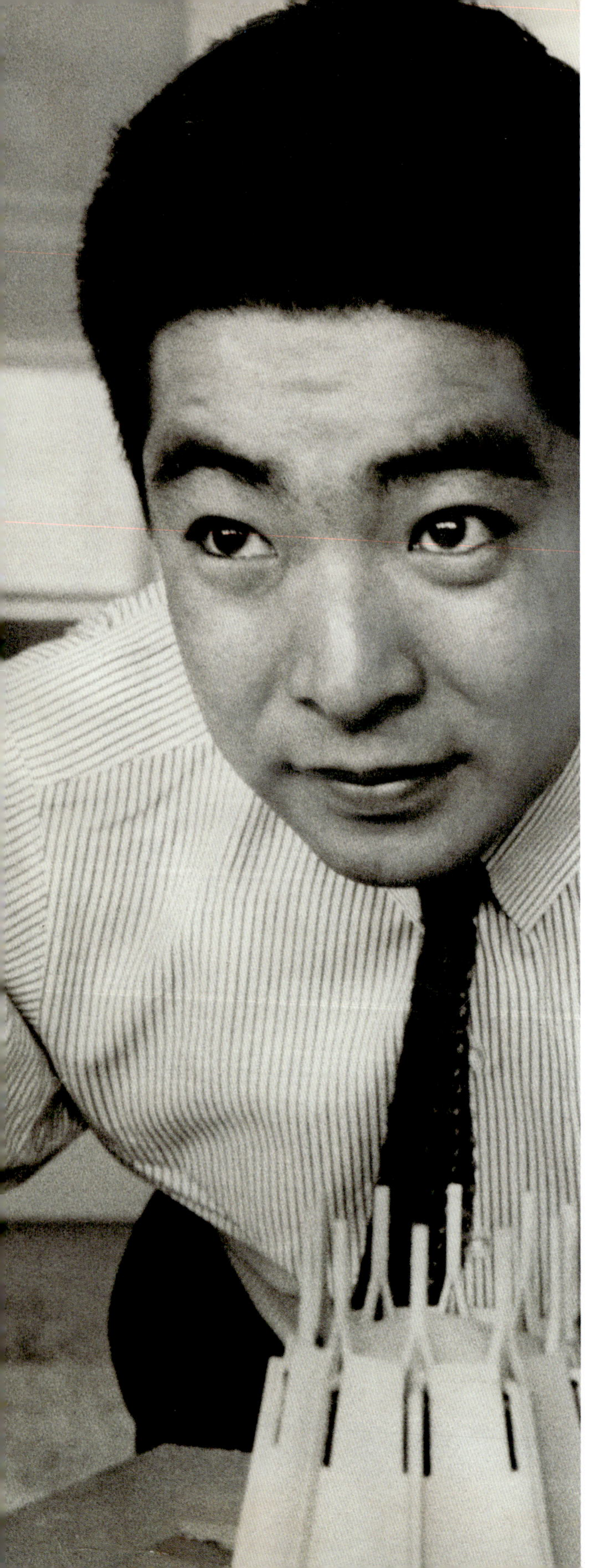

"I EXPERIENCED THE MAGNIFICENCE, THE POWER, AND THE BEAUTY OF NATURE."

"At age 12, I was in despair.

Not only did my country, Canada, label me an 'enemy alien,' Canada arrested and made my father a prisoner of war for peacefully fighting the contradiction of Canada going to war overseas to defend democracy and individual rights, while back home making shambles of 22,000 lives. Canada, with its insensitively conceived actions of separate and conquer, caused my mother to suffer physically and lose the only baby brother I could have had. And Canada incarcerated her and my two younger sisters in an internment camp in the Rockies, where I was taunted 'disease, disease' for my childhood scars by my fellow Japanese Canadian inmates.

In desperation, I built a secret lookout and bathed in the icy Slocan River. The lookout, outside the usual confines of the camp, on the other side of Little Mountain, offered a challenge — my first foray into architecture — a tree house. Not to be caught by the RCMP, I built it by myself. Camouflaged with natural materials, it was nearly invisible, and beautiful (I was never caught). When finished, it was a place of peace and solitude, a place to think and contemplate, a place to open my eyes and heart. It was my university.

From this higher perch, I experienced the magnificence, the power, and the beauty of nature in Canada. Moreover, directly below on the ground, I was exposed to, for the first time, and overwhelmed by the intricacies and the minute details of nature, each square foot of ground different from the next and the next. Is the whole world like this? This discovery gave me a thought that I, 'little ol' me,' could have a place in this vast world, in Canada, and perhaps allow me to do something great like the magnificent Rockies.I was given hope, a dream for my future, and an initial understanding about optimism, ideas, and balance needed for creativity and contribution.

The tree house saved me during my youthful duress and nurtured my positive rethink of Canada and my community. Thus in 1958 I started another challenge — an architectural/planning practice — with [my wife] Sachi, who was to be a single unpaid partner. With two babies and total savings of $392, we were determined to make a difference.

'Centennial' was in the air. Ontario needed an 'Institution of International Significance' (former premier John Robarts). Mr. Ray Connell, former minister of Public Works, offered me the commission. I first refused. He finally told me to listen: 'We are looking for a young architect with imagination, talent, and a lot of guts. That's you. We asked many established architects whom they would recommend if they were not doing the project. The name most often recommended was yours.'

What a wonderful, convincing minister. What honour coming from older, established architects. What an opportunity in 1964 to create a transformative museum. (In 2013 I was informed that with its hands-on learning, the Ontario Science Centre had spawned over 335 new museums worldwide based on its philosophy and spirit.)

Other Canadian challenges followed: the Canadian Embassy in Japan, the Canadian War Museum in Ottawa, the Meewasin Valley 100-year plan in Saskatchewan. They led our office to other transformative projects worldwide: the 124-kilometre-long Wadi Hanifa Restoration Project (by largely bioremediation), and the 83-acre Centennial Historical Centre and the National Museum in Riyadh, Saudi Arabia, among other international projects. We worked hard, but we owed so much to our Canadian experience and to Canada for letting us try new visions, concepts, and ideas.

In Canada 150, I continue to believe in the potential of Canada becoming a great world leader in true, healthy democracy — total equality, inclusion, and service to the community — with compassion, civility, and balance of economy, nature, and development.

Sachi and I will continue our best to reach for this golden Canada.

Happy Canada 150! Go Canada go!"

RAYMOND MORIYAMA
ARCHITECT

"THOUGHT I WAS IN CANADA FOR A SECOND."

"My most 'Canadian' memory has to be when I was taking photos in New York for the Love Trumps Hate protest. A man in front of me dropped his cellphone. I picked it up and gave it to him. He turned to me smiling and said in a joking manner, 'Thanks, brother! Thought I was in Canada for a second. Sometimes I forget how nice New Yorkers can be, too.' I laughed and said, 'I'm actually Canadian. I'm just here taking photos of the protest.' He was shocked. He then stopped me and said, 'I love you, man,' and gave me a hug."

YASIN OSMAN
PHOTOGRAPHER

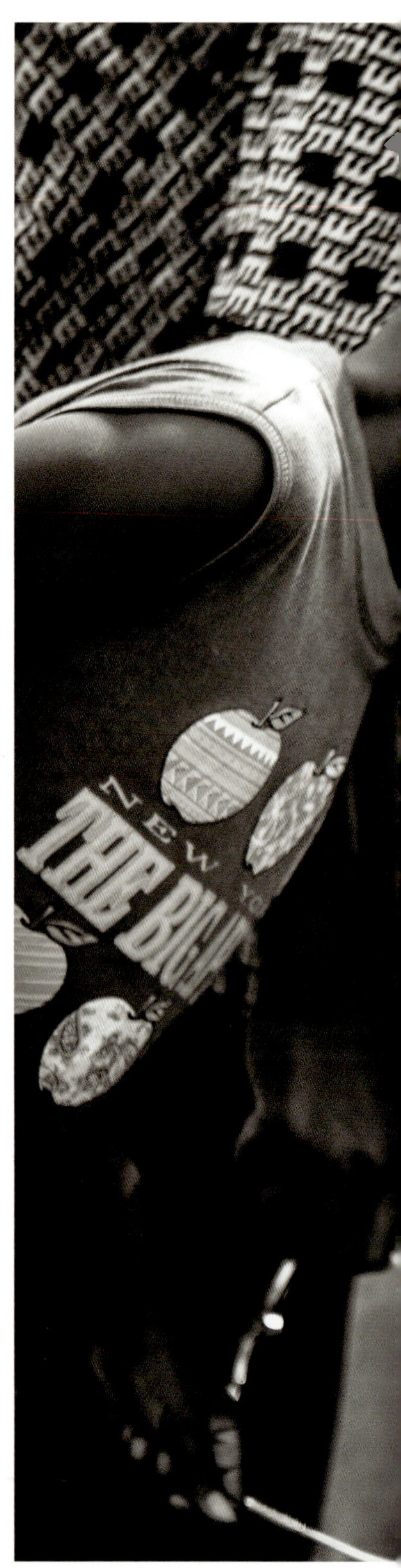

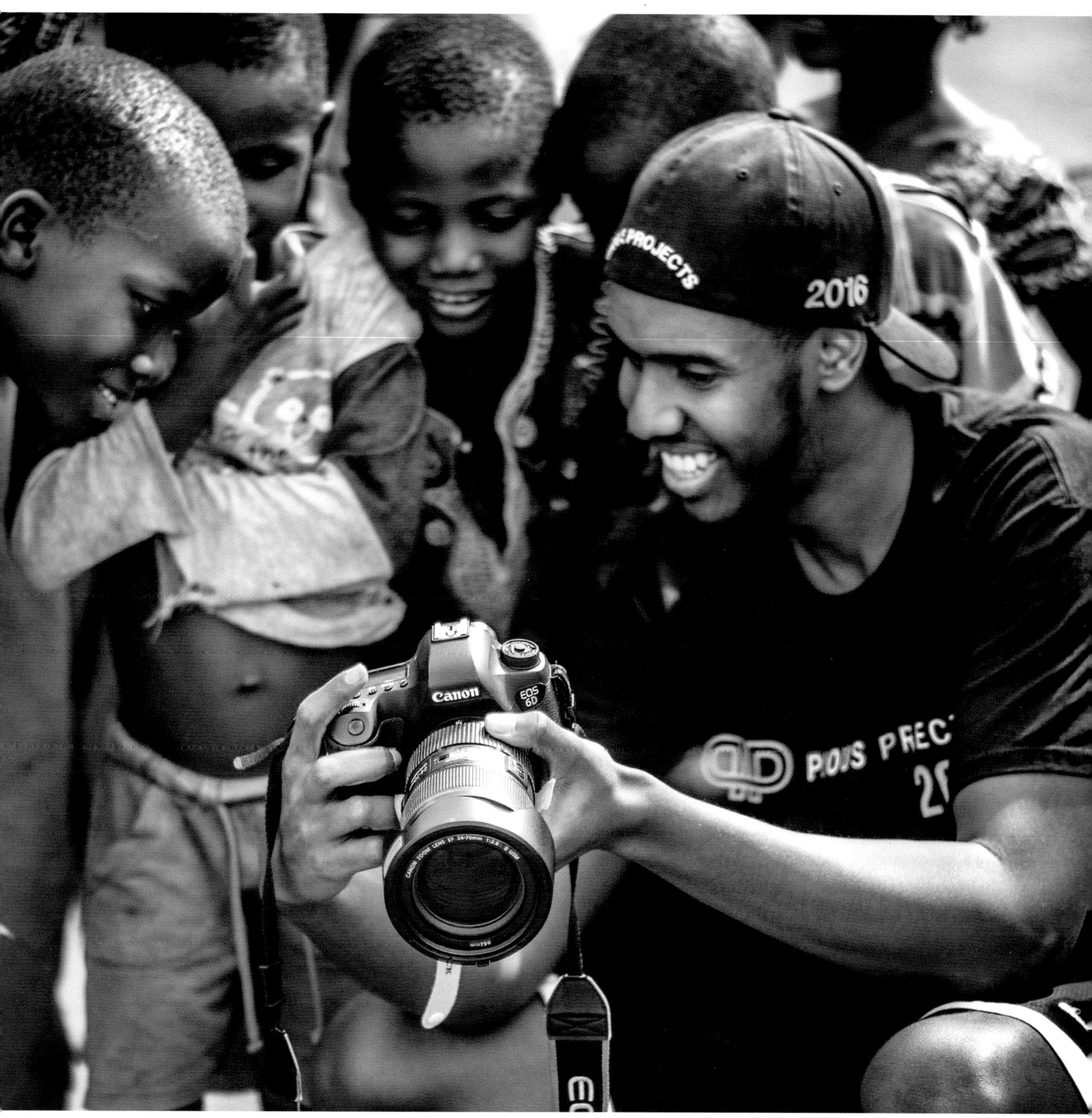
PROJECTS
2016
Canon
EOS 6D

NEWFOUNDLAND HELD DOMINION STATUS AS

ITS OWN

UNTIL 1949 WHEN IT

CONFEDERATION.

COUNTRY

JOINED THE CANADIAN

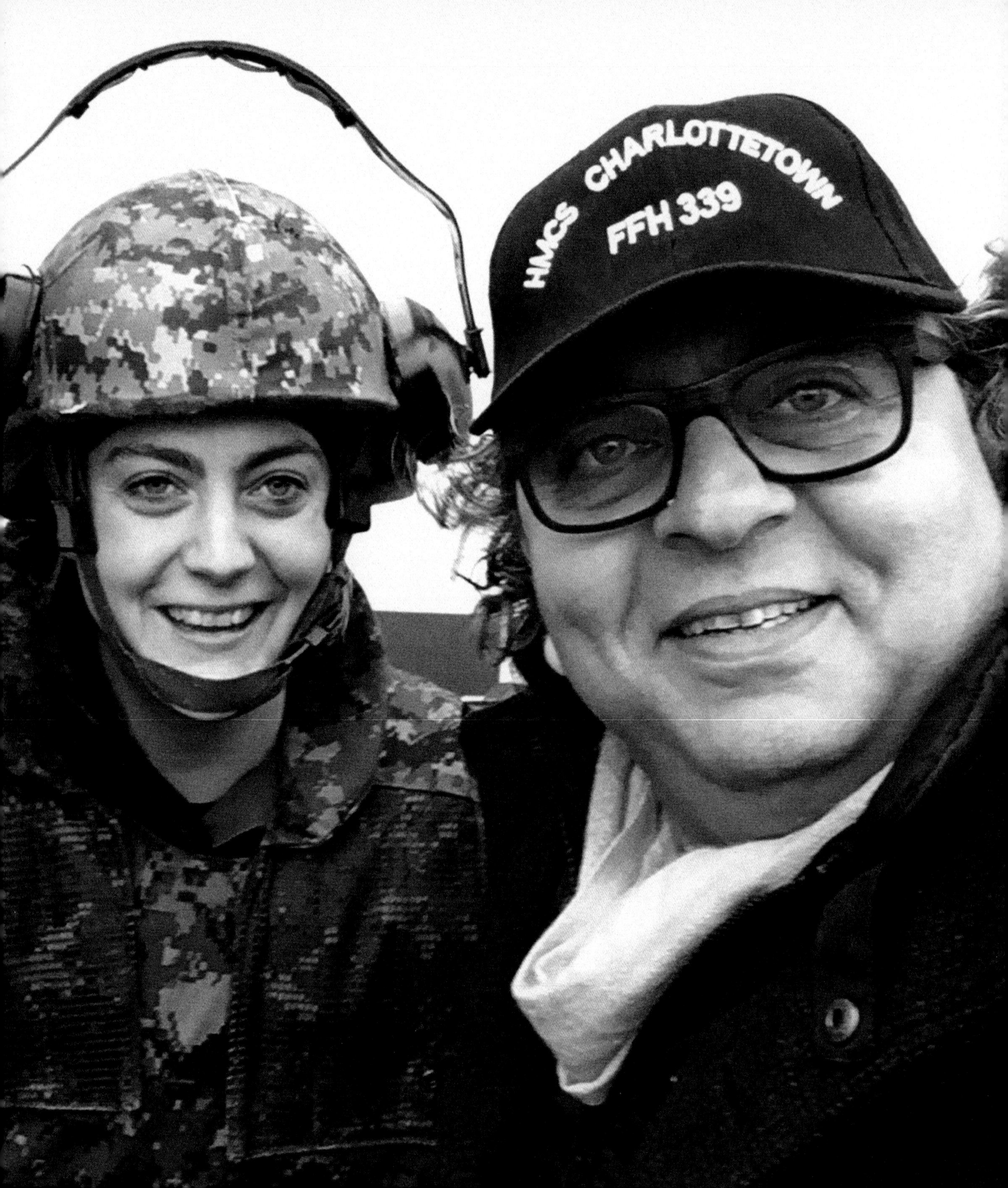
HMCS CHARLOTTETOWN
FFH 339

VIKRAM VIJ · CHEF · AUTHOR

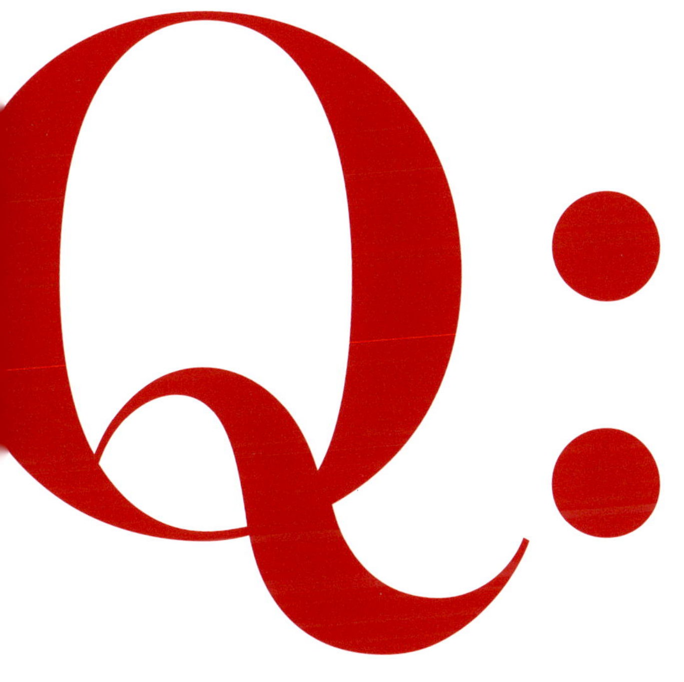

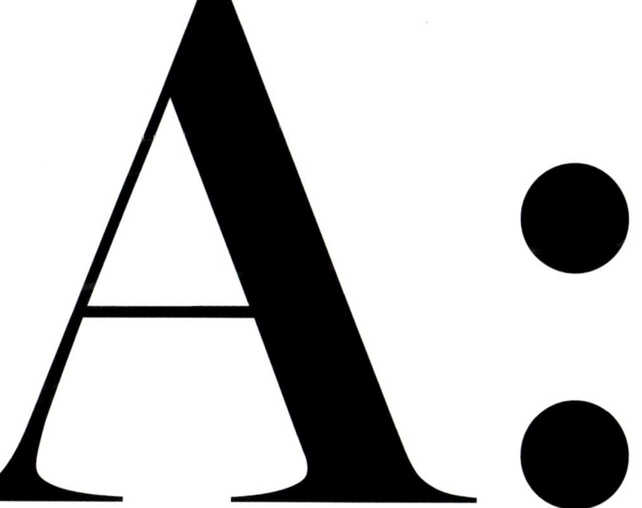

OK, THIS IS A PRETTY CANADIAN MOMENT...

"Walking up Parliament Hill in Ottawa and then being asked by PM Justin to come and have a brief chat in the PM's office."

WHAT IS YOUR MOST "CANADIAN" MEMORY?

"Being on the ship HMCS Charlottetown and cooking for the troops in Kuwait. It showed me that democracy should not be taken for granted, that it needs to be protected, and that our men and women (in uniform) do that for us every day."

WHAT MAKES YOU PROUD TO CALL YOURSELF CANADIAN?

"That I can be who I am; whatever I wear, whatever my religious background is... I am a Canadian first."

WHAT IS YOUR
BIRTHDAY WISH FOR CANADA?

"TO REMAIN AS WONDERFULLY ECCENTRIC, ECLECTIC, AND CHEERFULLY CONTRADICTORY AS EVER."

WILL FERGUSON · AUTHOR

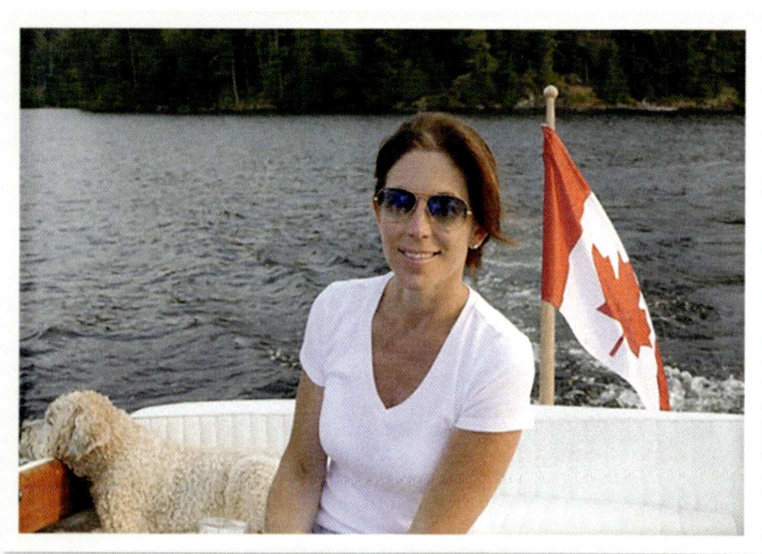

"Dear Canada, I hope you always remember who you are, where you came from, and what makes you wonderful. You are unique and exquisite and I hope you always cherish your natural beauty, as it's what makes you so breathtakingly captivating."

SARAH RICHARDSON · DESIGNER

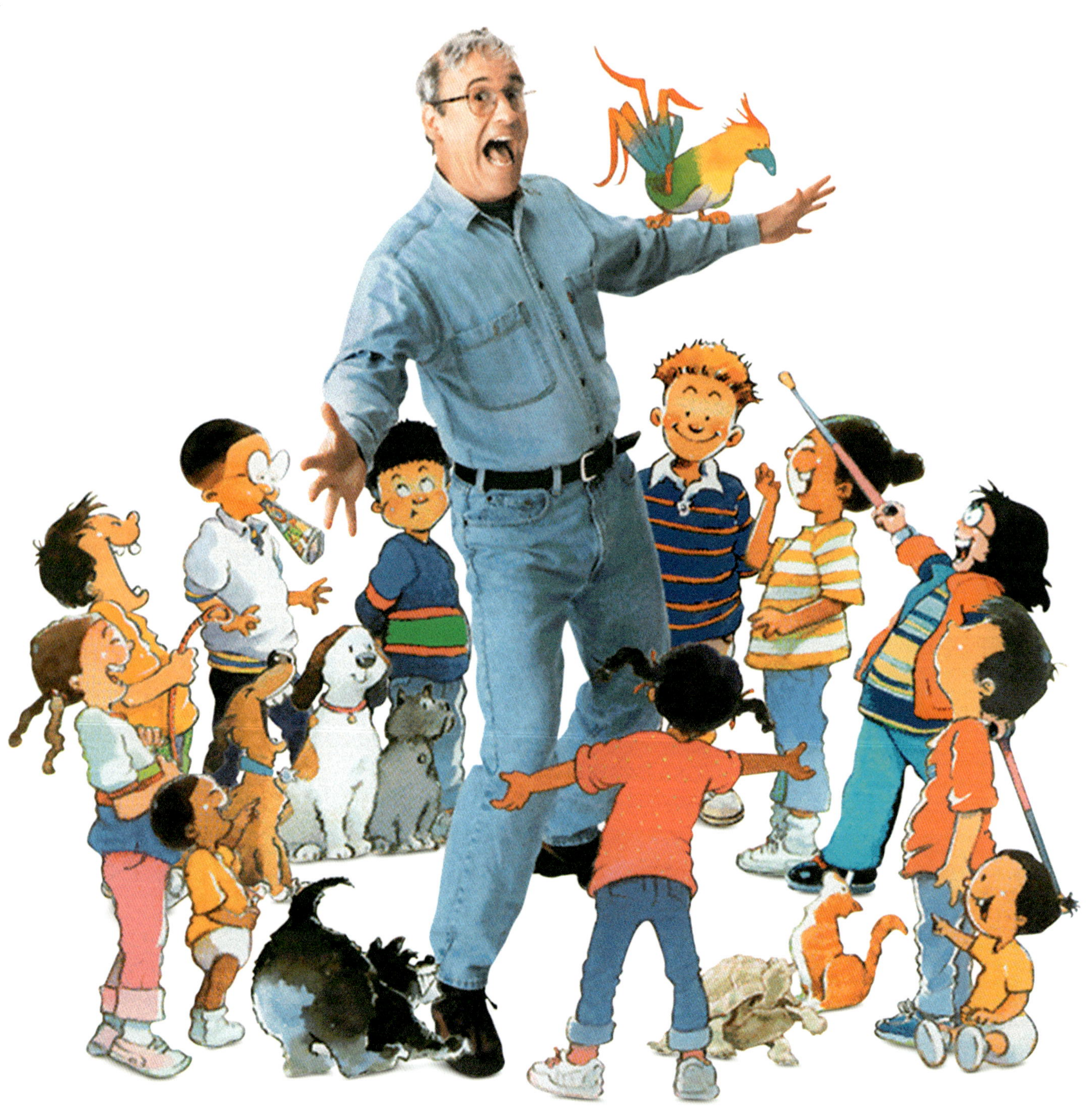

THE TRUTH ABOUT CANADA IS...

"IT IS A GREAT COUNTRY TO LIVE IN."

ROBERT MUNSCH
CHILDREN'S AUTHOR

"I was travelling with two friends in Normandy, France, and one day we were having coffee in a café in Courseulles-sur-Mer, which had been liberated by the Canadians on June 6, 1944. When I asked for our bill, the café owner pointed to a young man leaving the café and said, 'No need, he paid for it.' Puzzled, I asked why. He replied, 'He saw your Canadian lapel pins.' I was never more proud to be a Canadian."

MICHAEL MARTCHENKO
ILLUSTRATOR

sor·ry
/'särē,'sôrē/

What Canadians say when someone else bumps into us on the sidewalk.

cae·sar
/'sēzər/

A spicy mix of vodka, hot sauce, Worcestershire sauce, and clam and tomato juice perfected by Calgary bartender Walter Chell in 1969.

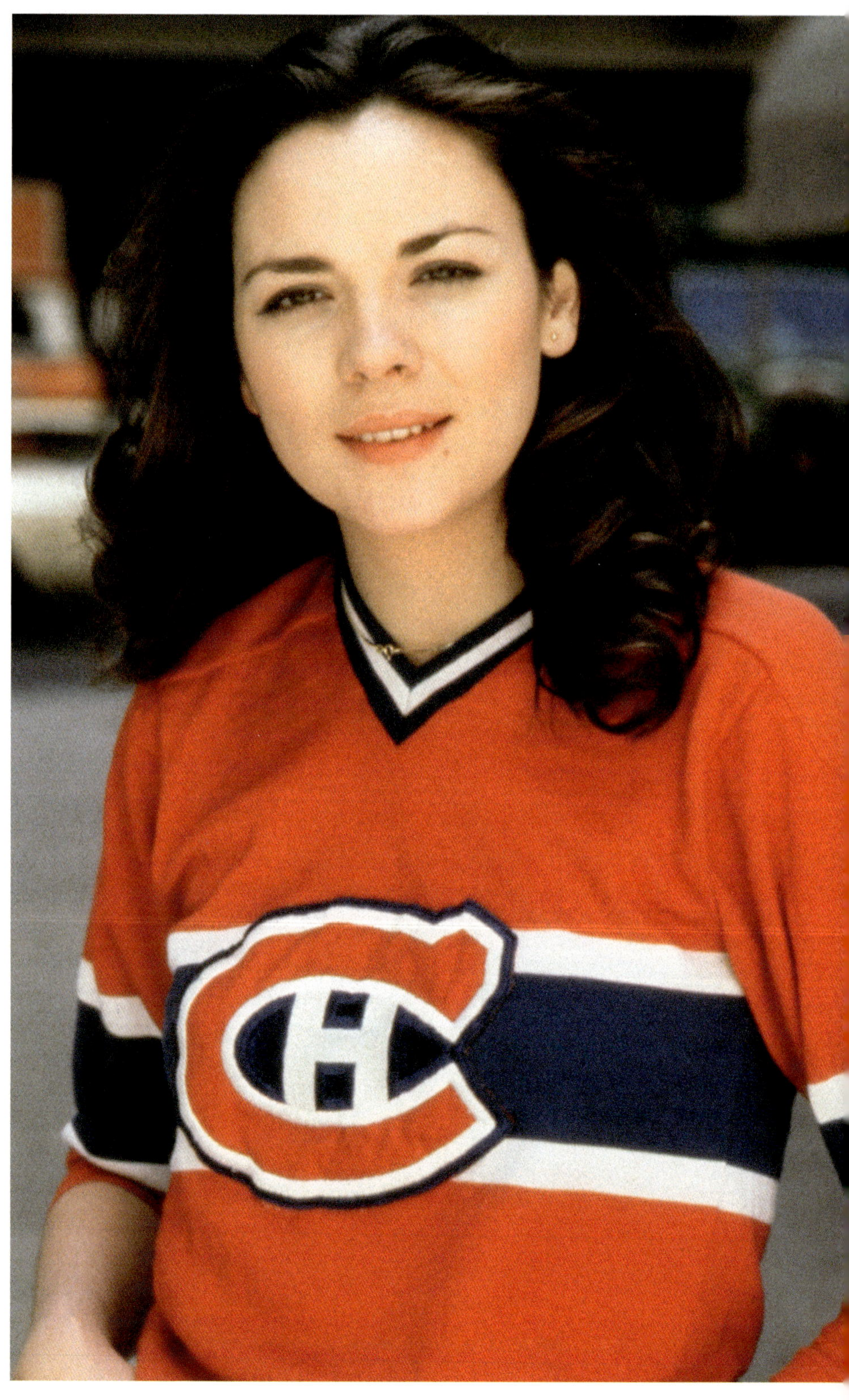

“I FEEL NATIONALISTIC WITHOUT FLYING A FLAG AND I’M LIKELY TO TEAR UP WATCHING TELEVISED ICE SKATING COMPETITIONS.”

KIM CATTRALL · ACTOR · PRODUCER

"MY BIRTHDAY WISH FOR CANADA IS THAT CANADIANS

BECOME MORE ENGAGED WITH HERITAGE

—BOTH NATURAL HERITAGE AND HUMAN HERITAGE."

ROBERT BATEMAN · ARTIST

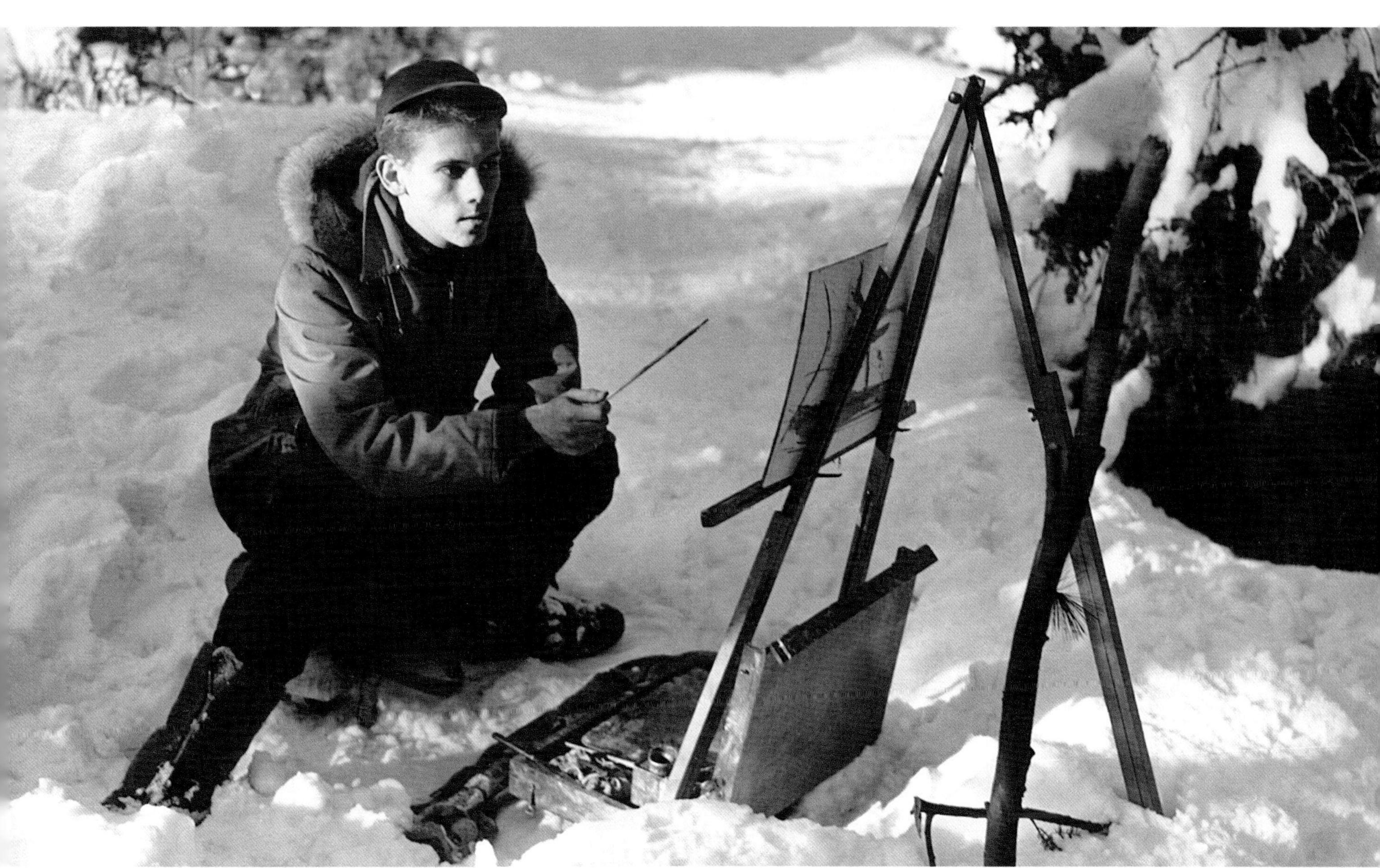

ONTARIO'S WASAGA BEACH

IS THE **LONGEST**

BEACH IN THE

FRESHWATER WORLD.

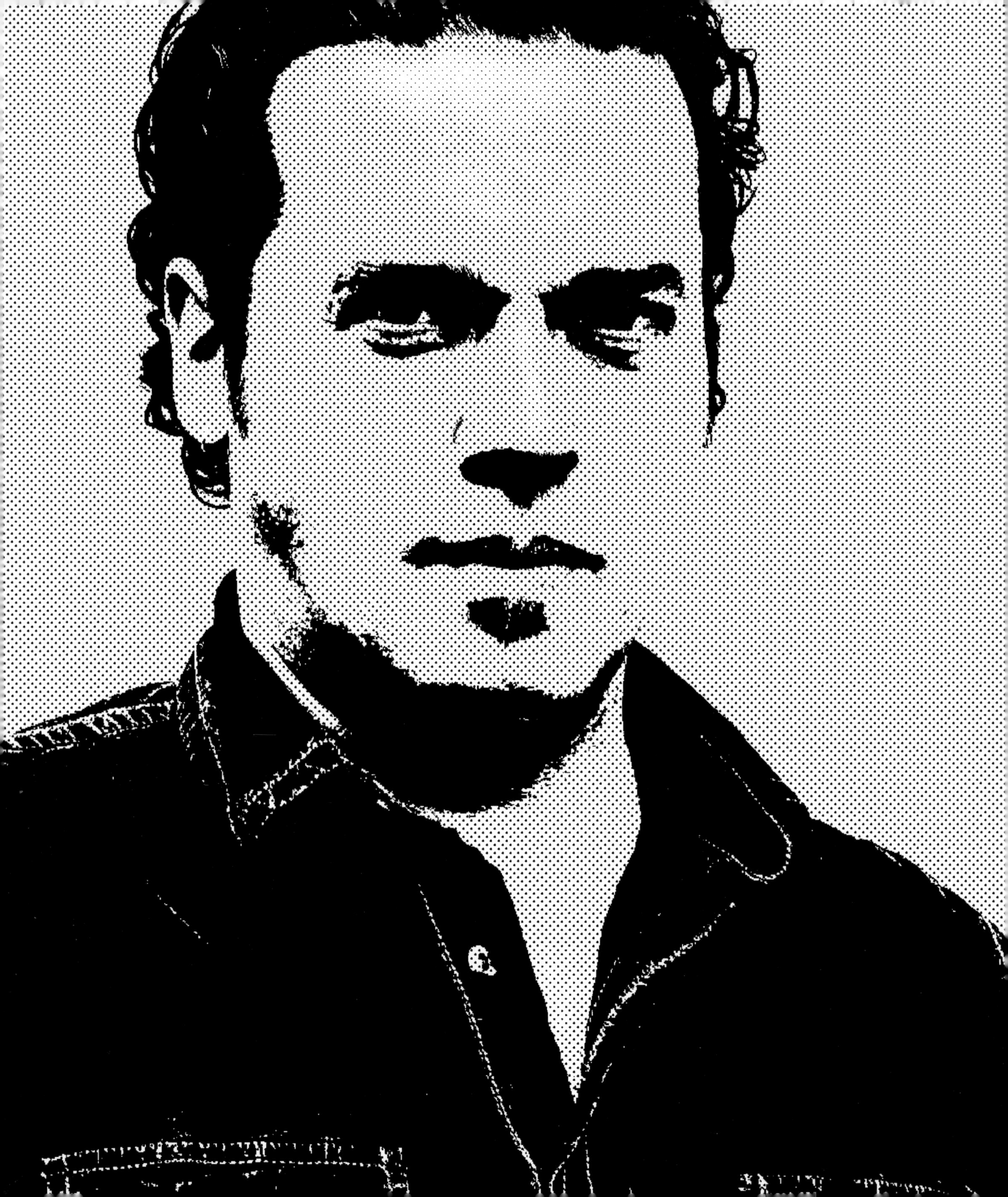

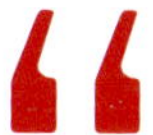

My most 'Canadian' memory happened a number of years ago. I invited a first-generation Basque-American from California, a six-foot-seven surfer from Virginia, and an Asian/Native American inner-city tough guy from New Orleans to come moose hunting with me in the Arctic lowlands of James Bay. Suffice to say that they were city people. We did everything we could to try and scare away any potential game. We sang old rock classics at the top of our lungs. **We created loud games with rocks on the riverbank at dusk instead of practising our cow-moose-in-estrus calls, we stayed up all night by the fire talking and laughing and then rose at noon.** My Cree brother, guide, and legend, William, later told me he never had a hunting party like that one before. The two moose we harvested fed a lot of good families in the winter that followed.

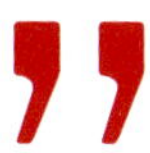

JOSEPH BOYDEN · AUTHOR

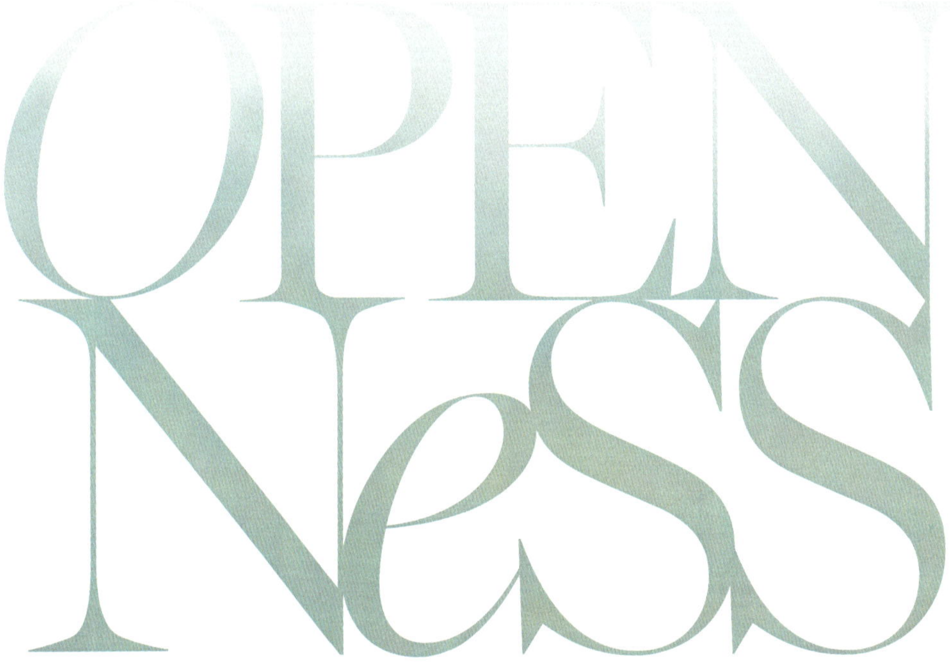

"My birthday wish for Canada is that we continue to be an example and leader of progressive change in the world. To me, being Canadian means embracing diversity, inclusivity, equality, and openness. The most powerful moment of being Canadian that I have experienced was when I arrived home from captivity in Somalia and I realized just how many Canadians had been part of making that possible for me through incredible generosity, prayer, and support."

AMANDA LINDHOUT
HUMANITARIAN · AUTHOR

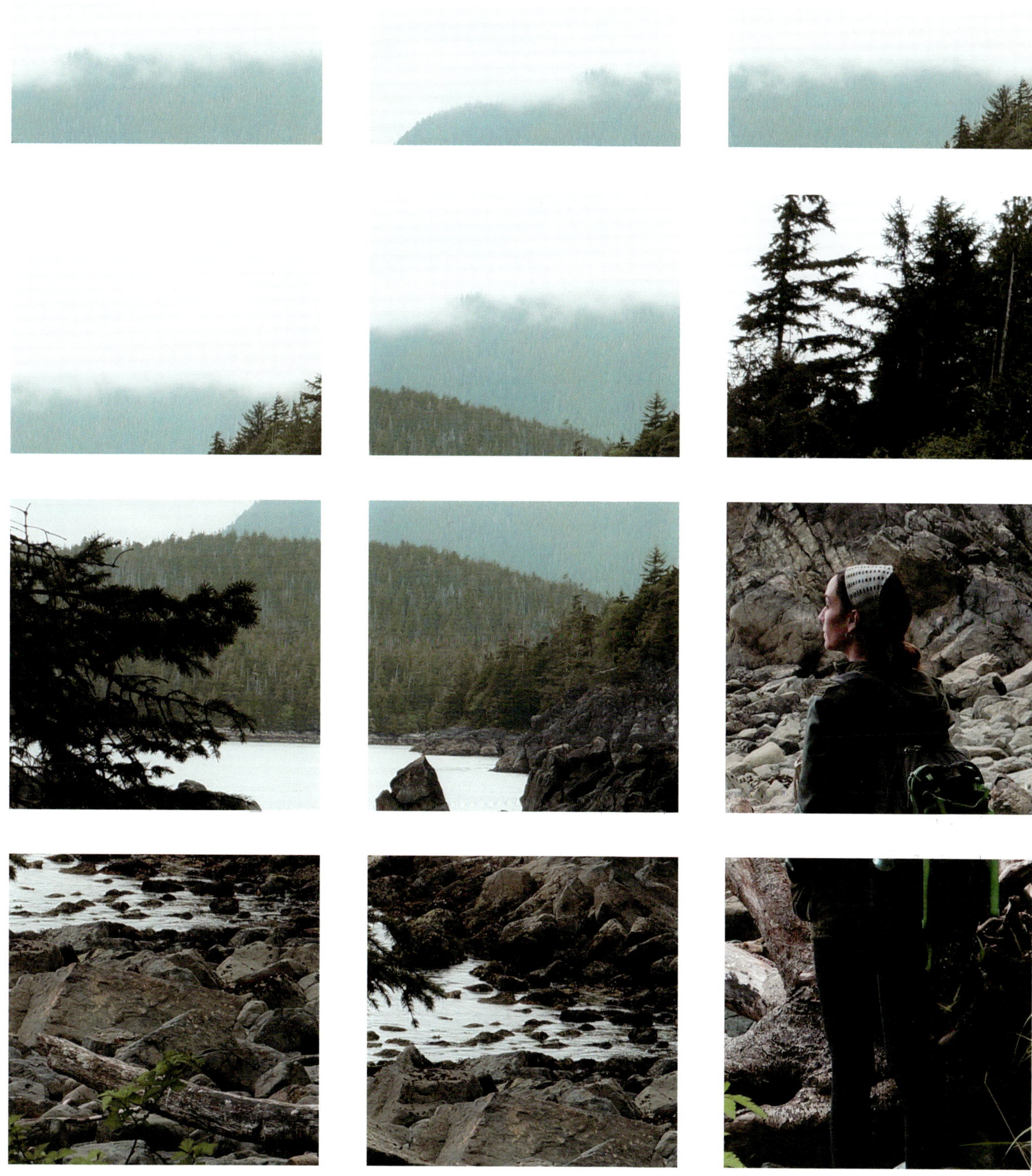

do·nair
/'donər/

A late-night snack of shaved beef covered in a tangy sweet sauce wrapped in a pita; invented by Peter Gamoulakos in Halifax.

cinq·à·sept /'sengk-a-SET/

L'expression québécoise qui fait référence aux heures entre la fin de la journée de travail et le souper, où l'on se réunit pour passer de bons moments ensemble.

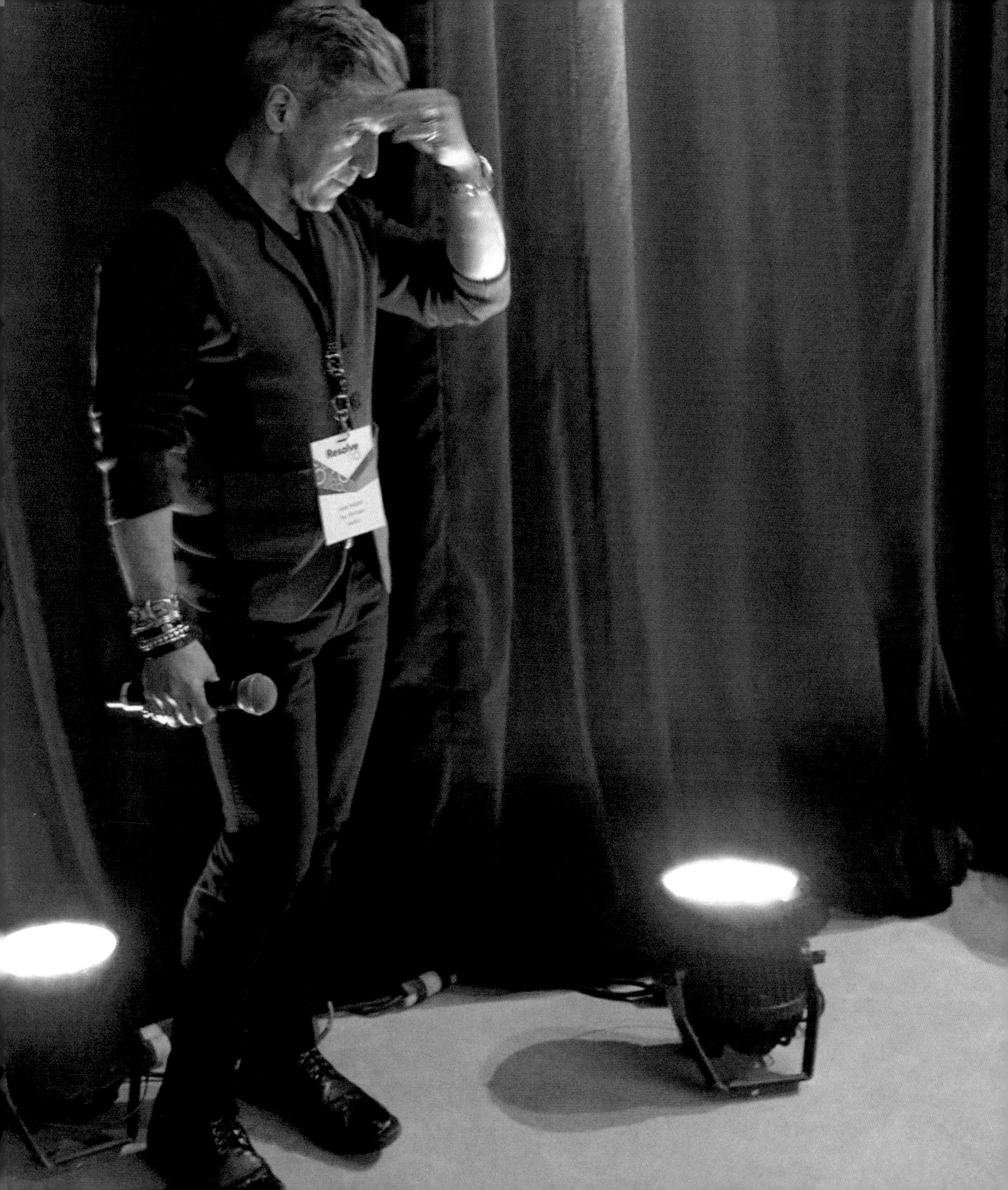

WHAT DOES IT MEAN TO BE CANADIAN?

"WHEN YOU GET AN EMAIL INVITING YOU TO BE PART OF A PRESTIGIOUS LITERARY PROJECT LIKE THIS, AND YOUR FIRST THOUGHT IS 'THIS MUST'VE BEEN MEANT FOR SOMEONE ELSE.'"

ANDY NULMAN
CO-FOUNDER OF JUST FOR LAUGHS

“IN A FEW HUNDRED YEARS, SOME ARCHAEOLOGIST WILL BE DIGGING AT EXACTLY THAT SPOT IN AFRICA AND THINK THERE WAS AN ODD CANADIAN COMMUNITY IN THE MIDDLE OF THE BUSH!”

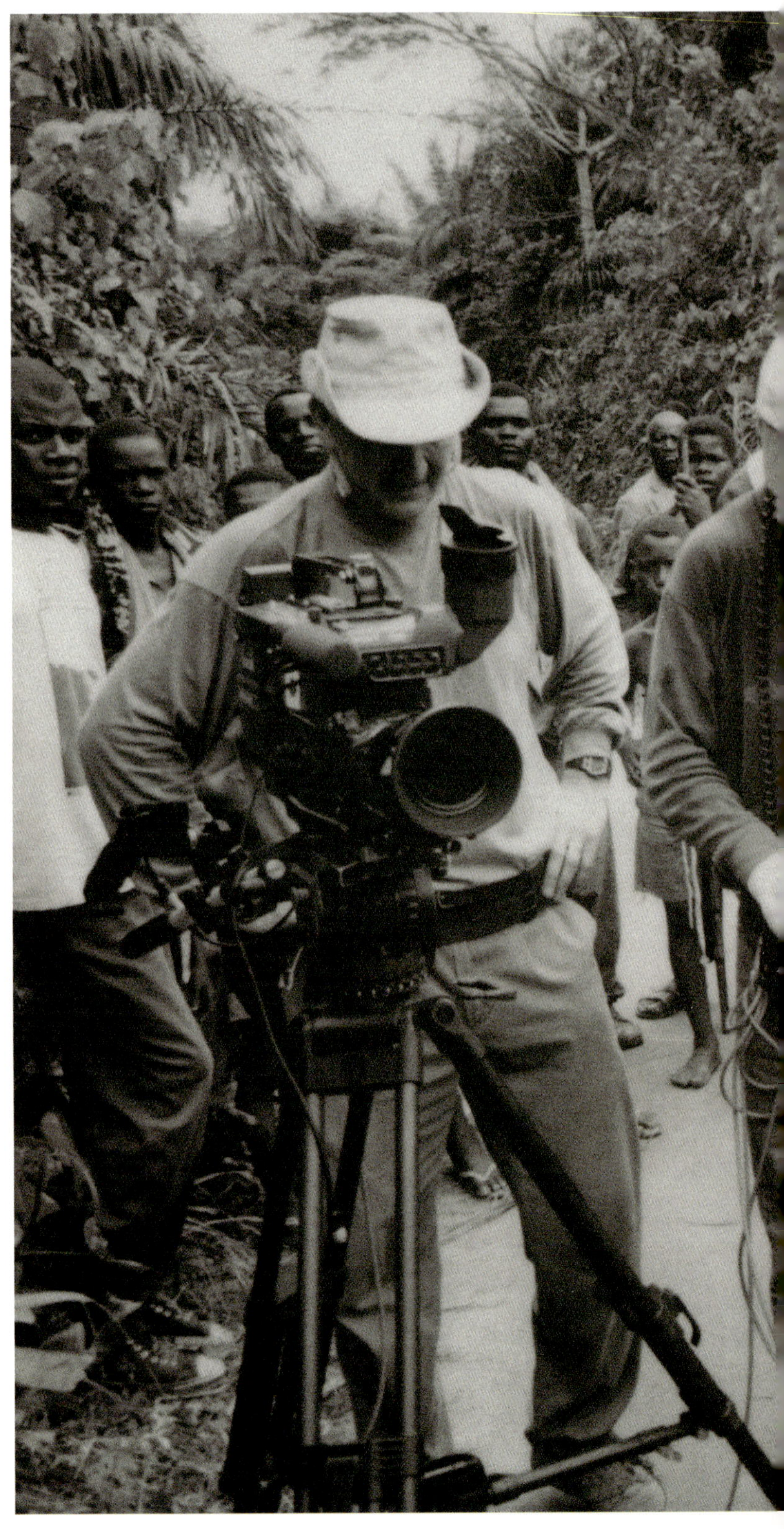

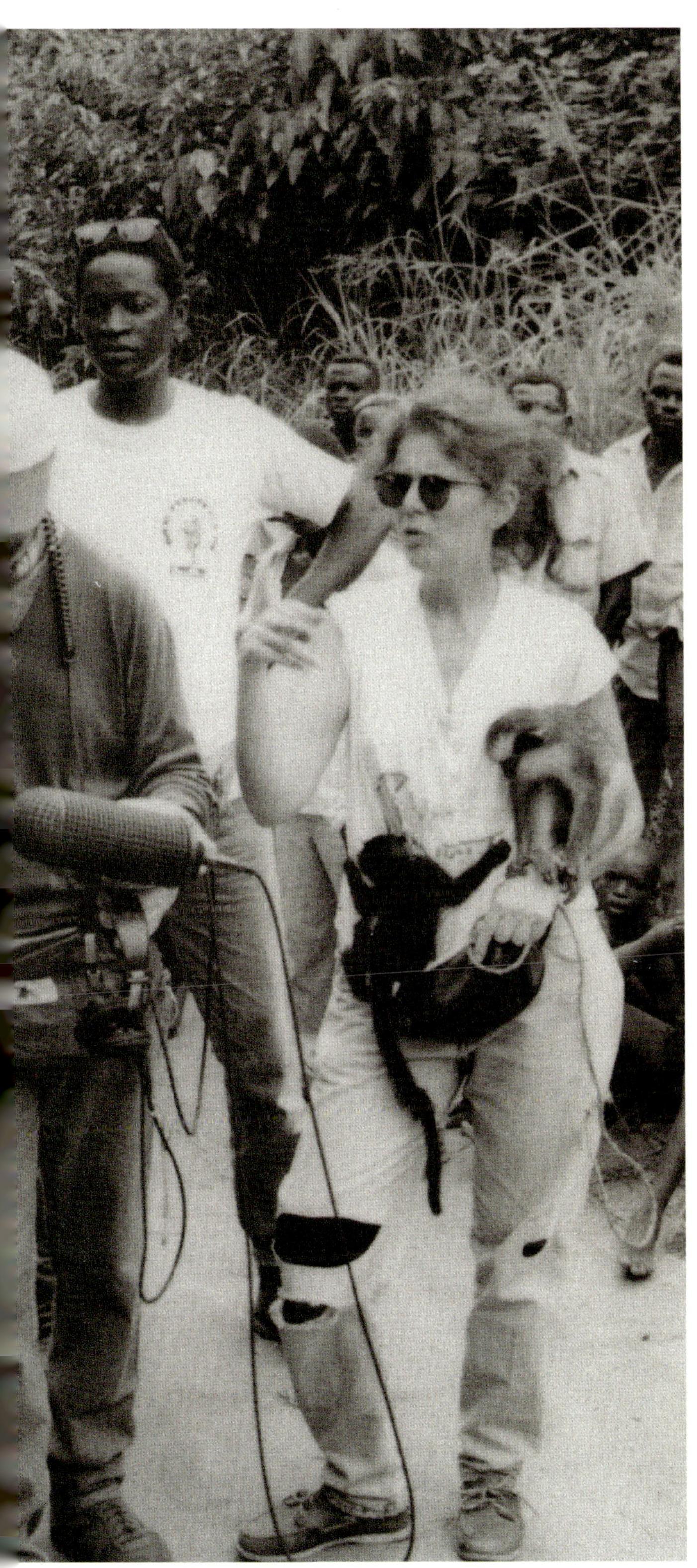

What is your most "Canadian" memory?

"I always bring little trinkets and gifts to hand out to kids when I'm shooting overseas. Years ago, I was filming an Ebola outbreak in Zaire and I brought a huge bag of Canadian flag pins and T-shirts so that I'd always have a little something when I was inevitably surrounded by kids when shooting a scene. Well, I might have overdone it. I returned to a village after a couple of weeks to film some additional shots of the villagers. But when I panned across the kids' faces, half of them were wearing these lapel pins as earrings and I couldn't get a clean shot without having a Canadian flag somewhere in it. Not quite the Zaire shot I needed. In a few hundred years, some archaeologist will be digging at exactly that spot in Africa and think there was an odd Canadian community in the middle of the bush!"

RIC ESTHER BIENSTOCK
DOCUMENTARY FILMMAKER

THE BEST WAY TO ENDEAR YOURSELF TO A CANADIAN IS...

"NOT TO PANIC WHEN YOU COME FACE-TO-FACE WITH A BEAR."

JOHN FIRTH · AUTHOR

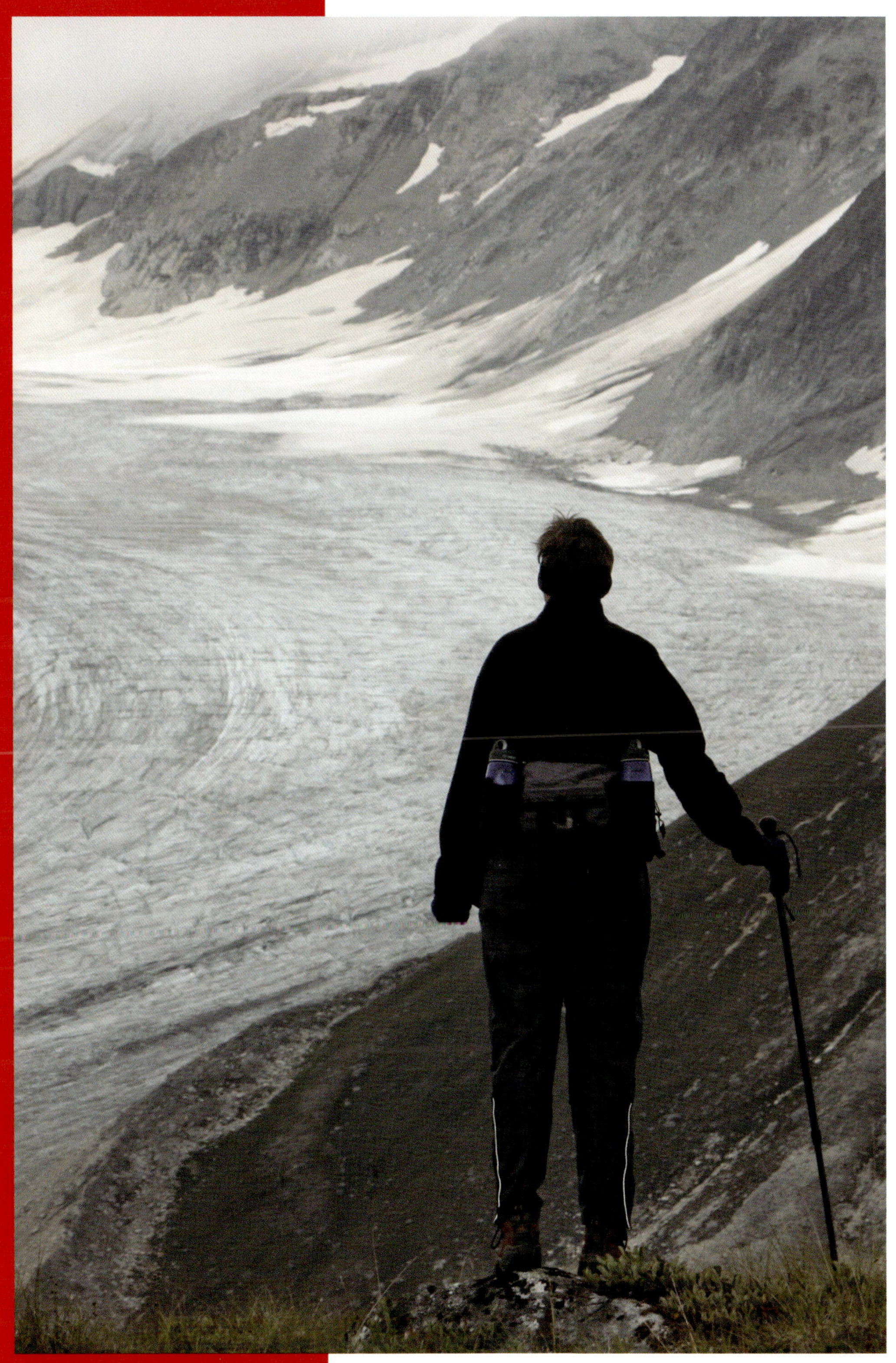

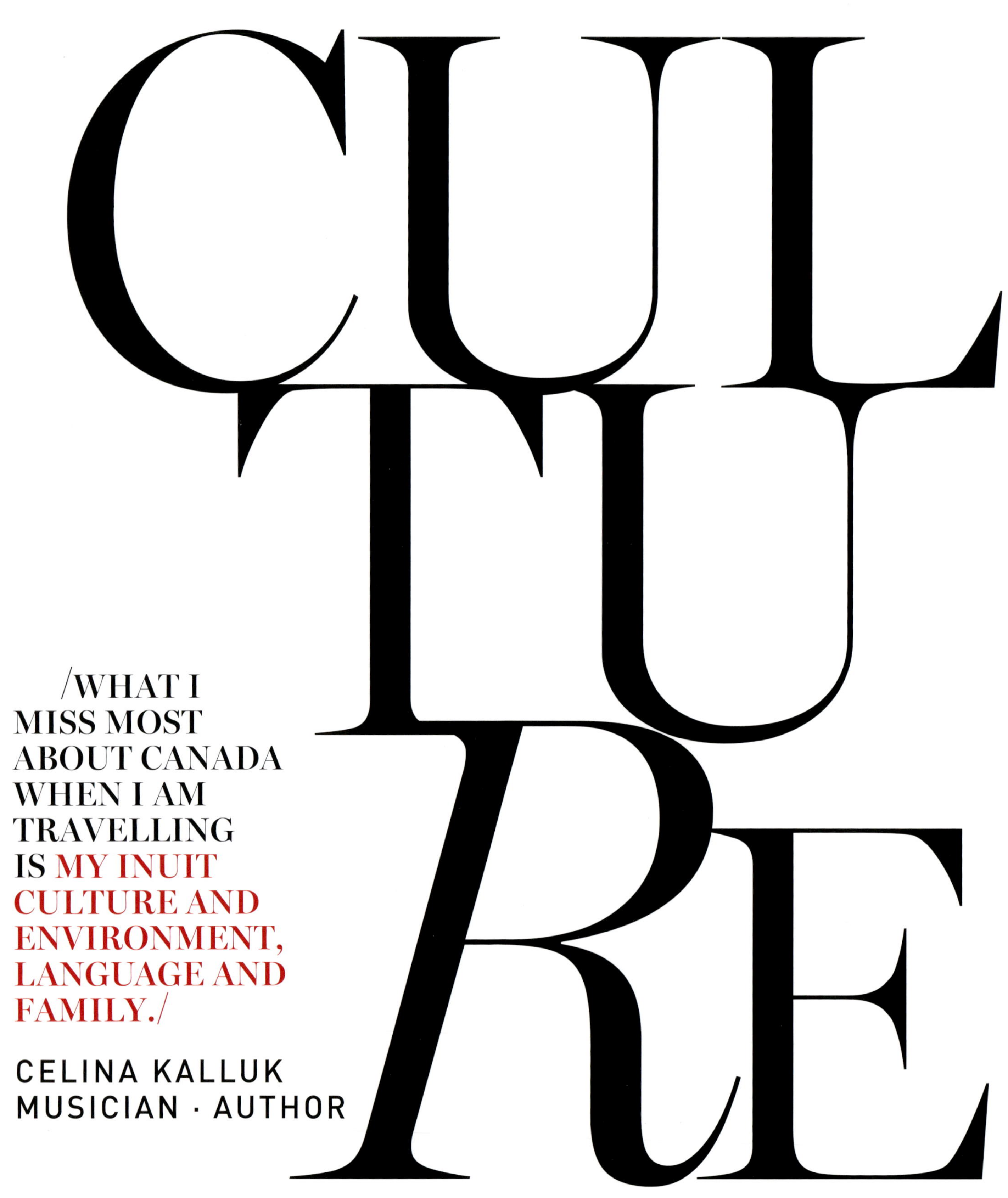

/WHAT I MISS MOST ABOUT CANADA WHEN I AM TRAVELLING IS MY INUIT CULTURE AND ENVIRONMENT, LANGUAGE AND FAMILY./

CELINA KALLUK
MUSICIAN · AUTHOR

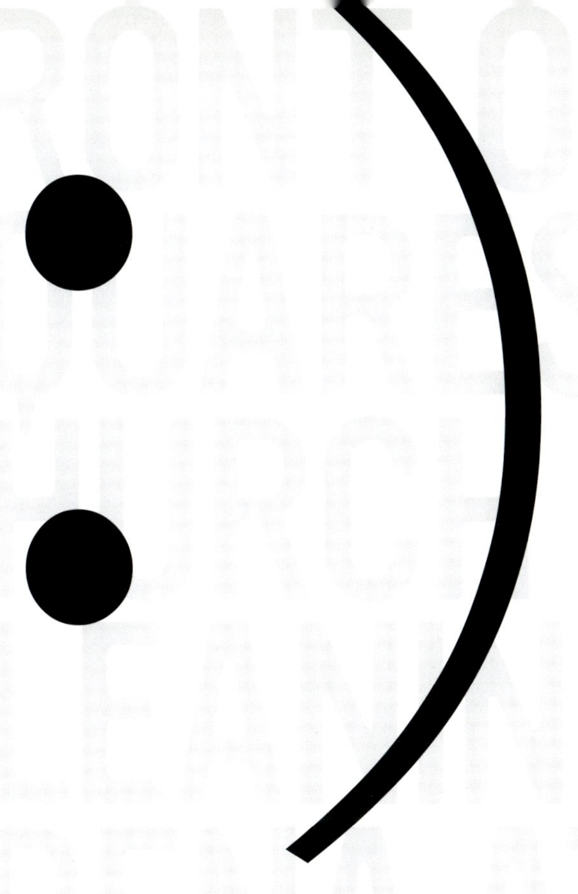

"Canada is wobbly picnic tables in front of mirrory lakes, crumbly date squares and Nanaimo bars in mouldy church basements, that cold, refreshing cleaning-type smell at the front of the arena at six in the morning, wet open umbrellas standing on the floor beside the boot tray inside the dentist's office, gooey cheese curds and steaming gravy dripping off plastic forks at two in the morning, that day the entire maple tree explodes into a uniform bright yellow, samosas and shawarma and ceviche on the same corner, a pile of splintery old hockey sticks in the garage, misty rainbows glittering over Niagara Falls, listening to afternoon storytelling on public radio, debating what flavours are actually in All Dressed chips, confidently knowing how to say 'cottage cheese' and 'orange juice' and 'mustard' in French, seeing someone from TV in the grocery store and deciding it's probably best not to bother them, owning way too many ice scrapers but somehow none of them are in your car on the first snowstorm, both people saying sorry after you bump someone with the mall entrance door, supporting a very specific NFL team for no reason whatsoever, walking by a group of kids playing cricket in the park after school, sitting in Muskoka chairs under blankets complimenting the person who built this campfire, not even thinking if you can drink the water out of this tap, **and bright red suns slowly setting over golden hay bales beside the highway...**"

NEIL PASRICHA
AUTHOR

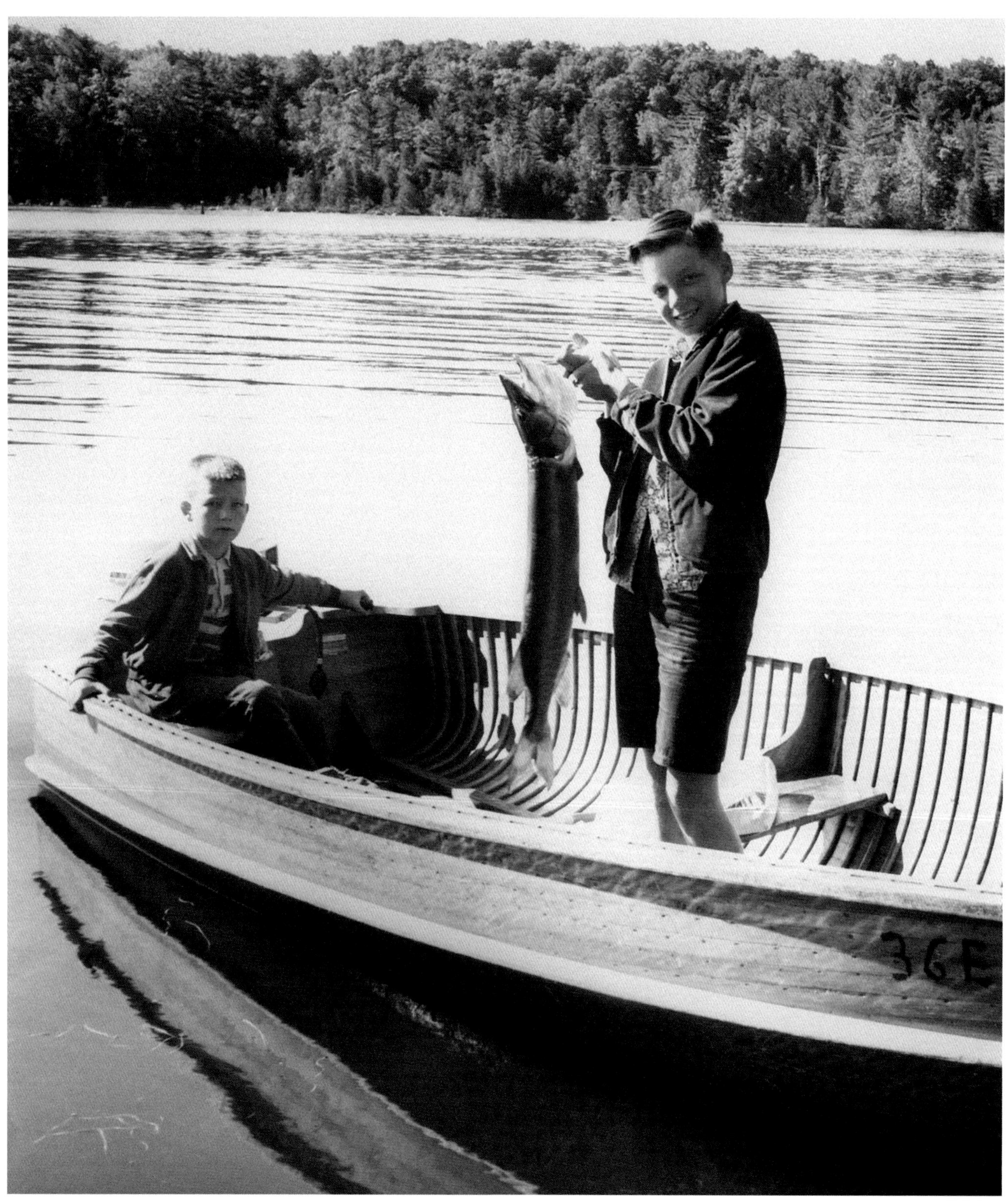
36E

EDWARD BURTYNSKY · PHOTOGRAPHER · ARTIST

What is your most "Canadian" memory?

"I was 13, camping and fishing with my father and brother on Lovesick Lake, north of Peterborough, Ontario, in Burleigh Falls. The camping was great, but the fishing was a little lacklustre; fishing from the shore, we just weren't having any luck. Our small group was approached by a rugged First Nations man — Dallas, as he introduced himself — his wooden leg thudding against the earthen floor. We later discovered the leg was a result of his service in the Second World War. Dallas immediately recognized the flaw in our fishing strategy and offered to take us out on his boat — an unexpected generosity from this complete stranger. Though my father was hesitant, nervous perhaps, to accept the offer, I'm sure it was near-impossible for him to refuse the enthusiasm of his two bright-eyed, excited children who'd come along on this trip hoping to catch some fish. Very early the next morning Dallas returned, 'Are you ready to go?'

The lake was every bit as beautiful and eerie as you'd expect that early in the morning—quiet, still, and blanketed in a thick, deep mist waiting to rise toward the sun. I could barely see the granite shoreline and fast-moving current beyond the imperfect wood of Dallas' boat. Eventually, we were anchored somewhere near the centre of Lovesick and, handing me a rod with a massive lure ready to go, Dallas encouraged me to keep letting out the line. I can still feel my nerves bristling beneath the arms of my jacket.

After letting out the line and waiting patiently, I felt some resistance in the rod. It was unlike anything I'd ever felt fishing before, and I was convinced I'd actually caught the bottom of the lake. Dallas disagreed and told me to begin reeling in. I did, and much to my thrill and surprise, it was a very large muskie fighting against the current and my 13-year-old grip.

It took us three intense hauls and attempts with the net to get this muskie out of the water, but finally it was ours. That wild fish got a bit of me too, between its razored teeth — I don't advise anyone to get their fingers near an angry muskie's mouth! A hard-won prize, nearly as long as I was tall back then, and that night, Dallas' granny served a muskie feast.

It was an opportunity and experience afforded me as a young man, a young Canadian — one of the many I had growing up here — one that instilled in me a deep love for and long-lasting connection to these landscapes. A loving appreciation for nature, for what is all around us. What has been given to us. It's a memory from a time when I could still view and experience nature as only a child can — a world that as adults we lament and feel a deep sense of lovesickness for, as that time and those places begin to fade away. As that young Canadian boy, I was able to see and experience the landscapes around me the way the planet had intended, and not how we as humans have repurposed the intention of that land. It's a trip I'll never forget."

THE TRUTH ABOUT CANADA IS...

"THAT THERE IS NO SINGLE TRUTH. WE ARE A
OUR FIRST NATIONS AND FROM EVERYWHERE

OUR TRUTH IS IN
WHICH BELONG TO

NATION BORN FROM
ELSE ON EARTH,

OUR STORIES,

THE WORLD."

KIM ECHLIN · AUTHOR

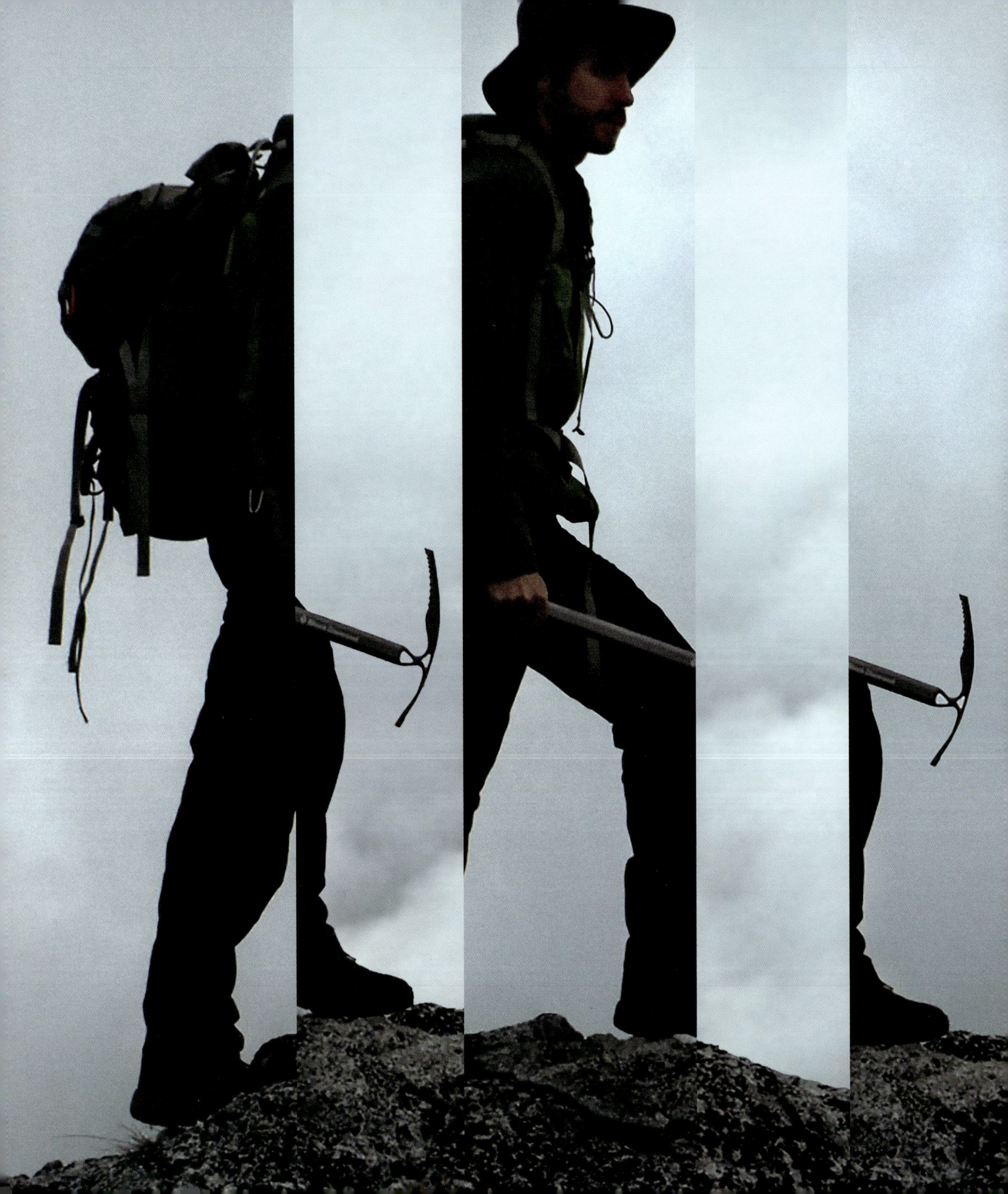

"My most 'Canadian' memories are of growing up in the countryside around Fenwick, Ontario. My brother and I had chores like cutting firewood and keeping the fire going in the furnace. In March, we'd collect sap from the sugar maple trees to make our own syrup. Our pastimes were pond hockey, fishing, and wandering the woods. Every spring, a big snapping turtle would come to the woods near our house from a pond down the road to lay her eggs. Snapping turtles can live for a very long time (over 100 years), so this went on all through my childhood. The same turtle would come each year, choose a spot she liked, dig a big hole, and then lay her eggs in it. It was exciting to witness — especially since the turtle came from over half a kilometre away and would return to her home pond each time. Two to three months later, the eggs would hatch and we would have baby snapping turtles in the ponds and swamps. I always thought they looked like little dinosaurs. We'd sometimes keep one or two as pets and then release them when they got bigger.

It was especially sad then, to see a turtle killed on roads by vehicles that drove over them. One of our neighbours even had a 'turtle crossing' road sign to try to get traffic to drive slower. My father, when he'd be driving my brother and me to hockey practice or wherever and we'd see a turtle on the road, would pull the truck over, get out, pick the turtle up, and carry it across the road to save it. He had trapped muskrats and occasionally hunted, but it just seemed senseless to him to let turtles be needlessly killed on roads by oncoming traffic.

To this day, my brother and I, whenever we see a turtle crossing a road, still pull over and help it across."

ADAM SHOALTS
AUTHOR · EXPLORER

ROBERT LANTOS · PRODUCER

"I just recently came upon this picture. It was taken on June 23, 1963, by my uncle Pali at what was then called Aéroport Dorval (more about this in a minute). It was shot just a couple of minutes after my parents and I landed from Montevideo, via Santiago and New York, on the very first flight of our lives. Leading the way is my mother, Agnes, followed by me and my father, Laszlo. These were our first steps into our new country. It was the final chapter of an odyssey that began years earlier and had led our little family from Hungary through a detour to Uruguay, where we waited for five years for the visa that would allow us to immigrate to our chosen land — Canada.

We did not know much about our new country. We knew that Lester B. Pearson, reputedly a fair-minded man, was prime minister. We knew that unlike Communist Hungary and a Uruguay then ruled by the military, it was a stable democracy. We knew that admission to university was based on merit, not political affiliation. We knew that there was freedom of speech. We knew that Jews were not persecuted. And that was more than enough.

We also knew that it would be considerably colder than in Uruguay, so we came well prepared. Which explains my mother's fur coat — in June.

But 'Aéroport' and all these French signs? No one had mentioned anything about French. My mother, who had an extraordinary talent with languages, was fluent in English. My father and I had been hard at work taking English lessons in Montevideo, without much progress. But French? What was that all about?

What began as a surprise turned out to be one of the many bounties of this great nation of ours. In order to navigate through my teenage years in Quebec, I learned English and French more or less in tandem. Bilingual Montreal became my teacher and my playground. I quickly fell in love with the city and with its people. (Though not its winters.) After years of growing up in Latin America, the rhythm and cadence of French temperament and music suited me fine.

In time my parents opened a Hungarian pastry shop, and I, after a stint at Northmount High, spent six glorious years at McGill University, dividing my time between four noble pursuits: academics, new-left radical politics, waterpolo — and girls. (Not always in that order.)

Both official languages came in handy. English, with my university courses; French, with my girlfriends. Both have been integral to my life since. My very first girlfriend, Marthe, was Québécoise, as was my first love, Renée. Robert Charlebois and Gilles Vigneault were my favourite crooners, outranked only by Leonard Cohen. I began my filmmaking career in French, with *L'Ange et la Femme.*

My new country's first of many gifts to me was the rich and vibrant bilingual culture that I had stumbled into so unexpectedly **— and which has stayed with me and enriched my life."**

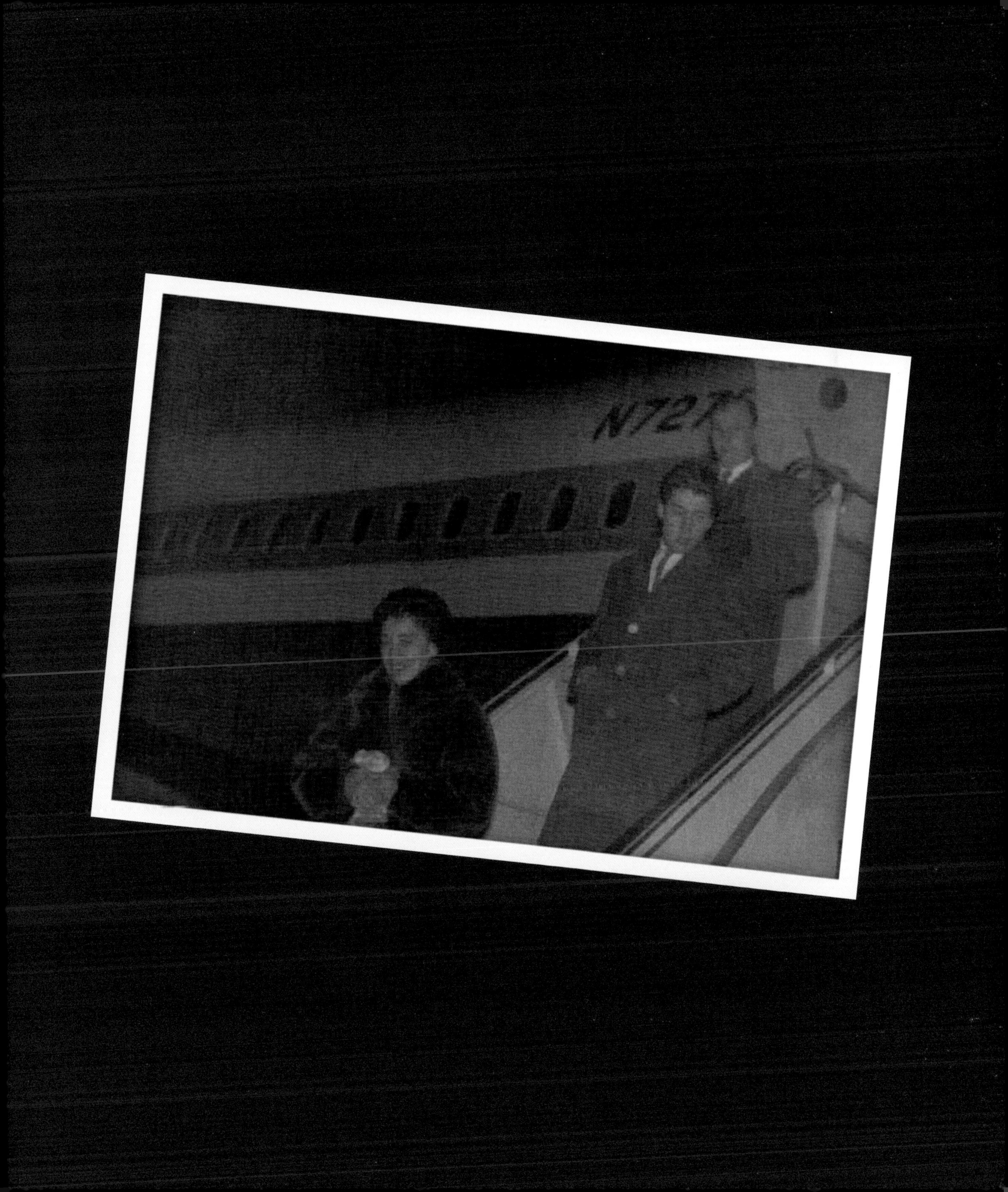

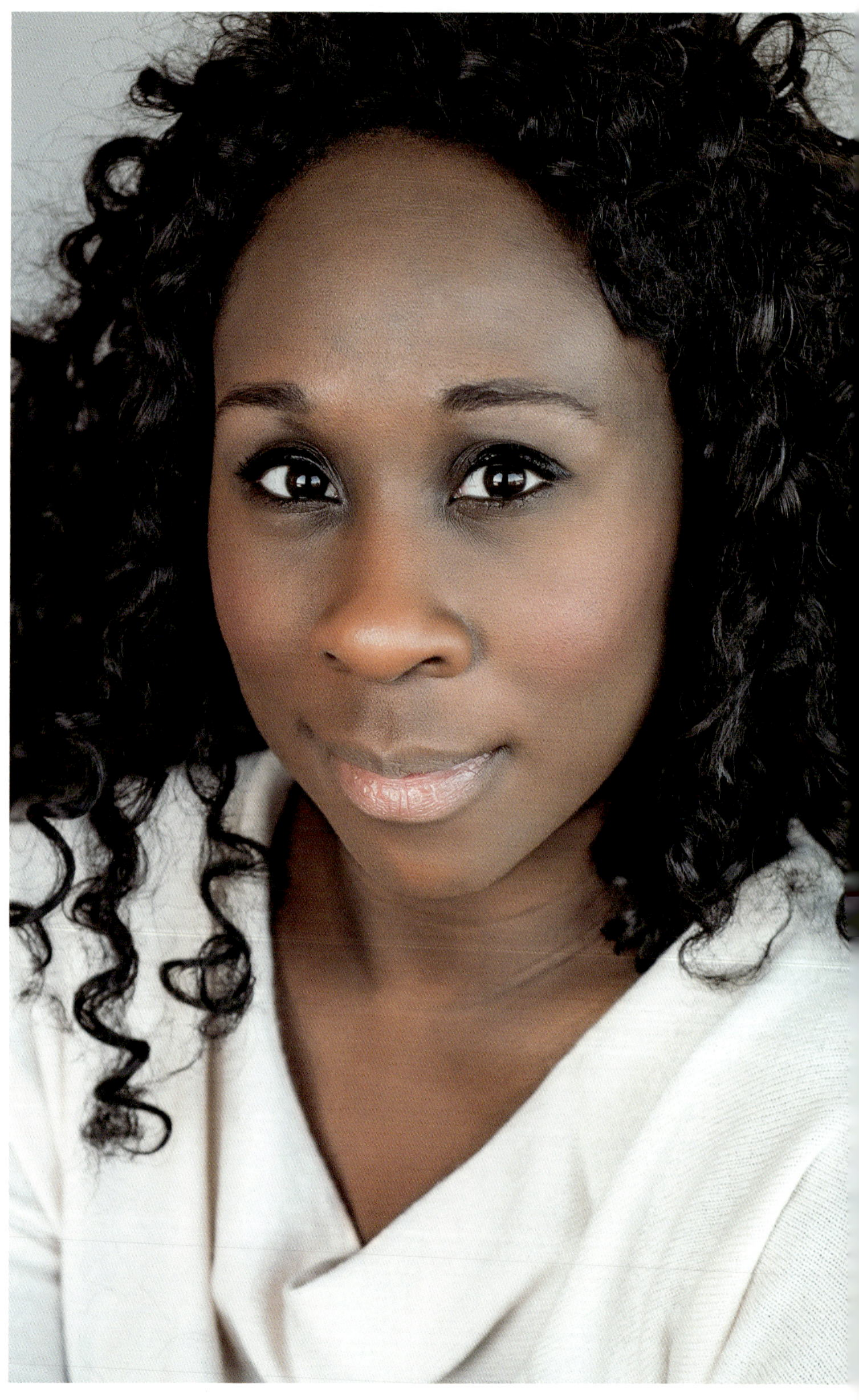

My most 'Canadian' memory: it was a typical Calgary winter, astonishingly cold, the snow piled in high banks. Our elementary school cleared its back field to make a rink, and there, upon its glistening surface, my class was sent to skate, most of us for the first time, pushing chairs before us for balance. **Afterwards we gathered inside, where we were treated to hot chocolate laced with maple syrup and an afternoon of French songs.** It felt like such an occasion then, before it became commonplace. An afternoon among the ice, and the comforts of a hot, sweet drink.

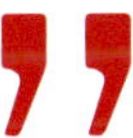

ESI EDUGYAN
AUTHOR

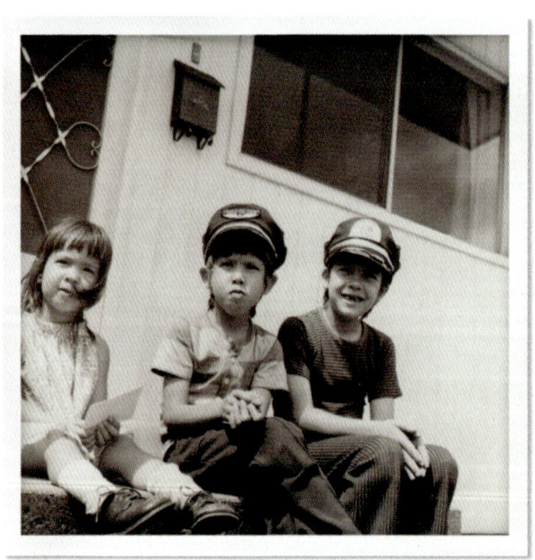

/CANADA IS THE COUNTRY
I CHOOSE TO LIVE IN./

TERRY FAN
AUTHOR·ILLUSTRATOR

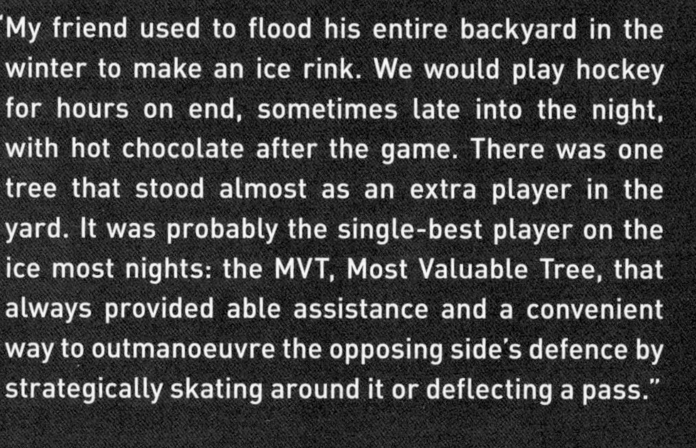

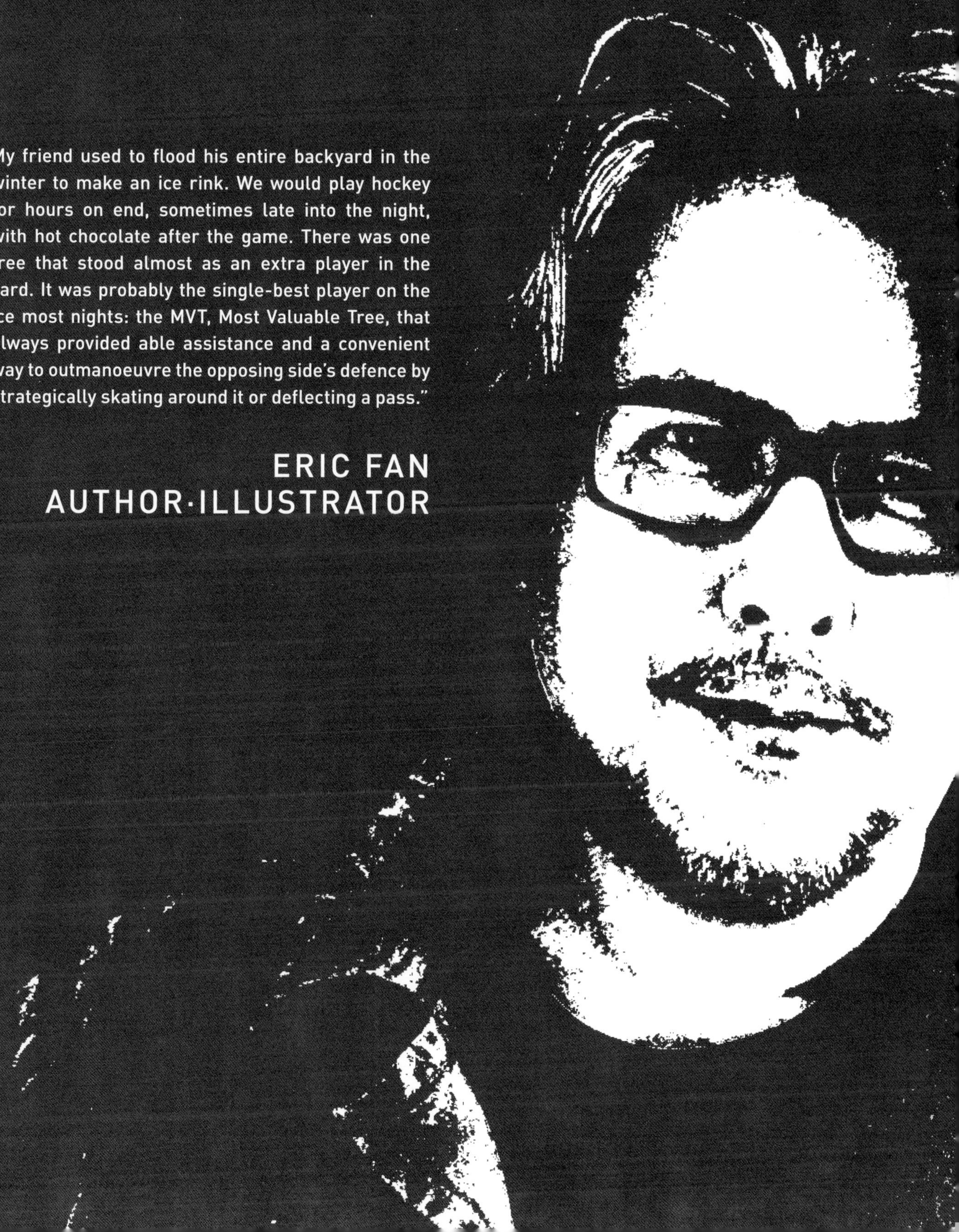

"My friend used to flood his entire backyard in the winter to make an ice rink. We would play hockey for hours on end, sometimes late into the night, with hot chocolate after the game. There was one tree that stood almost as an extra player in the yard. It was probably the single-best player on the ice most nights: the MVT, Most Valuable Tree, that always provided able assistance and a convenient way to outmanoeuvre the opposing side's defence by strategically skating around it or deflecting a pass."

ERIC FAN
AUTHOR·ILLUSTRATOR

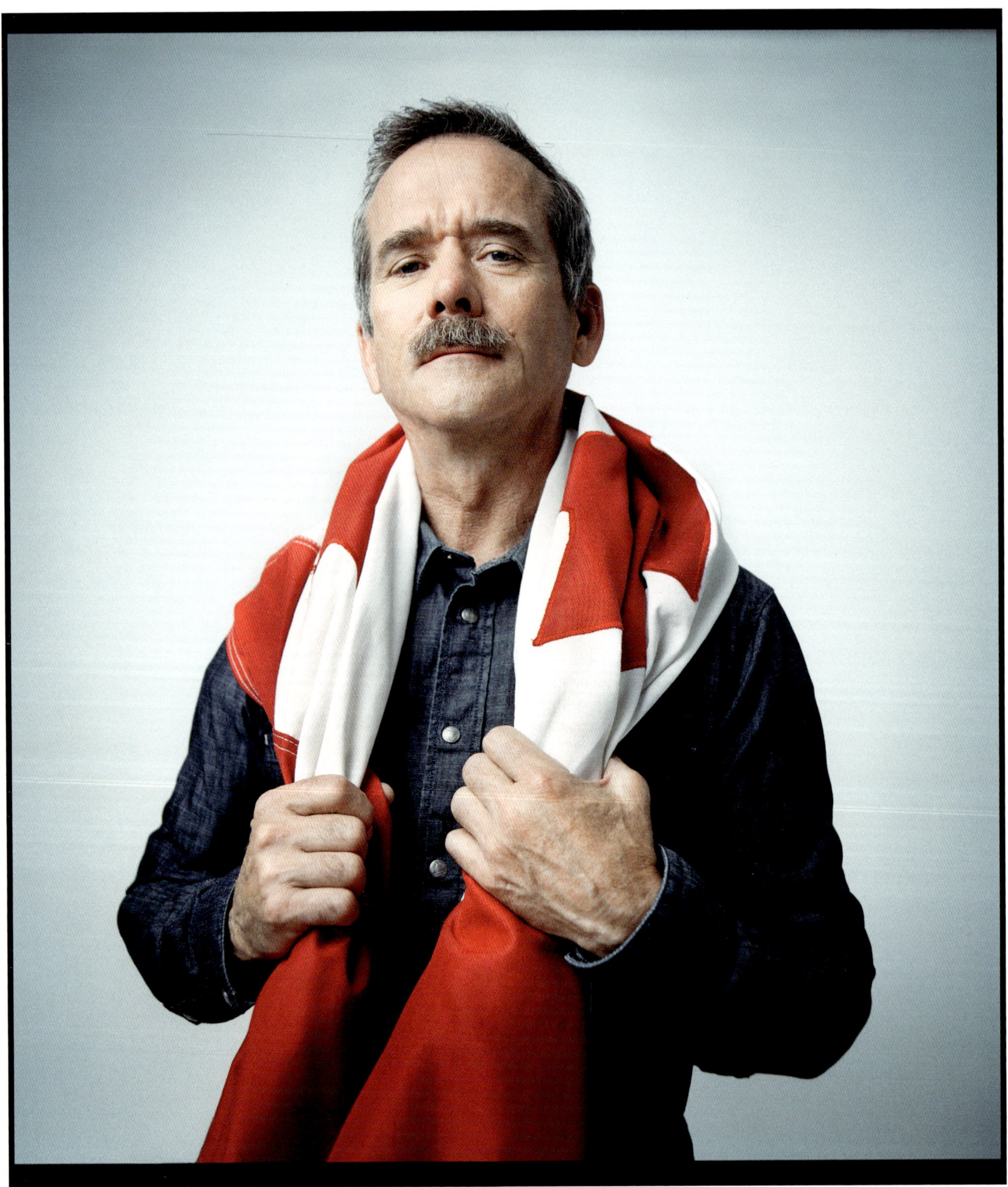

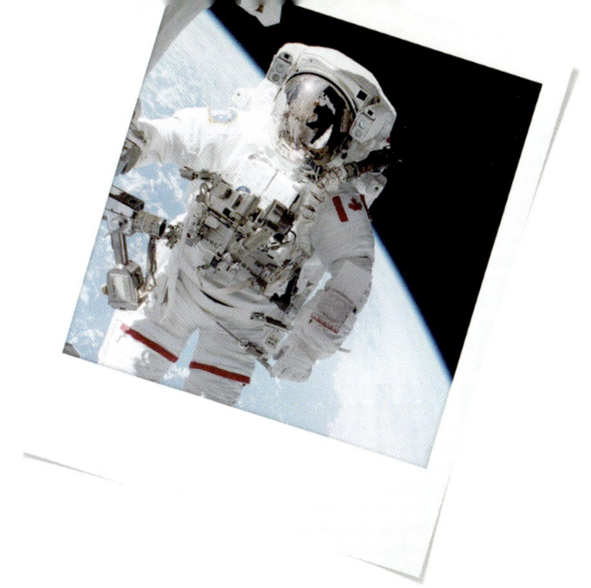

"My most 'Canadian' memory is soaring high above the Earth, floating weightlessly, our spaceship approaching Canada. I'd just finished our country's first spacewalk, building Canadarm2 onto the International Space Station, and Houston said it was time to climb back into the airlock. But Canada was starting to roll beneath my feet, and I lingered for a last look.

Off to my left I could see all the way across the Great Lakes, out to the Prairies. Hudson Bay loomed far on the horizon, and the Atlantic twinkled blue to my distant right. Below me the Maritimes and the St. Lawrence flowed past, a living map of our history, cities and farms, our giant land, my home. I did my best to look everywhere at once, to try and cement this rare perspective and moment into my memory forever.

Just as I was about to reluctantly call Houston and tell them I was coming in, I heard the crackling sound of music beginning. To my astonishment it was *O Canada*, loud and clear in my headset. And not just any version, but the strong, familiar voice of Roger Doucet, singing it before an NHL hockey game. Fellow Canadian Steve MacLean had organized the recording to be played down in Mission Control, and it brought tears to my eyes. I felt my body stiffen to attention as I held onto the spaceship with one hand, the words and music pouring into my spacesuit, our whole East Coast below.

As the anthem ended, I thanked Houston for the honour; thanked my parents, wife, and everyone who had helped me get to this rare place; and silently thanked my lucky stars. Even though I was off the planet, as far from home as anyone of us has ever been, I have never felt more completely, proudly Canadian."

CHRIS HADFIELD · ASTRONAUT · AUTHOR
INTERGALACTIC ROCK STAR

Nous tenons à remercier toutes les personnes qui ont contribué à ce livre de leur générosité, tant avec leur temps qu'avec leurs souvenirs, et chaque créateur de culture canadien qui s'efforce d'améliorer nos vies.

Un merci tout spécial à Louise Dennys, qui est toujours là, tant pour les écrivains que pour les détaillants de livres. Vos efforts réfléchis sont évidents partout dans le livre.

Thank you to each of you who contributed to this book for being so very generous with your time and your memories, and to every Canadian culture maker who helps make our lives better.

A special thank you to Louise Dennys, who is always there — for writers and for booksellers. Your thoughtful efforts are evident throughout the book.

INDEX

PHOTO CREDITS

THE PAINTED FLAG. Acrylic on canvas. Charles Pachter, 1981, 4
Source: 123RF Limited. Photo by Songquan Deng, 7
Source: The Canadian Press. Photo by Peter Bregg, 8
Source: Getty Images. Photo by Pal Hansen. Getty Images Contour Collection, 11
DRESSED TO KILL. Acrylic on canvas.Charles Pachter, 2012, 12
Courtesy of Barbara Reid, 15
(Left) Source: The Canadian Press. (Right) Courtesy of Wayne Gretzky, 16
Source: Getty Images. Photo by Ken Faught. Toronto Star Collection, 18–19
Courtesy of Geddy Lee, 21
Source: Alamy Stock Photo, 23
Source: Alamy Stock Photo, 26
Courtesy of Frank Viva, 29
Courtesy of Emily Haines, 30
Source: Alamy Stock Photo, 33
Source: Trunk Archive. Photo by Peter Hapak, 34
Courtesy of Kirstine Stewart, 37
Courtesy of Wayne Bourque, 38
Courtesy of Charlotte Gray, 41
Source: Getty Images. Photo by Mathis Weinand. Getty Images Entertainment Collection, 42
Courtesy of Lawrence Hill, 45
Courtesy of Yann Martel, 48
Source: Alamy Stock Photo, 51
Courtesy of Douglas Cardinal, 52
Source: Getty Images. Photo by Ullstein Bild. Ullstein Bild Collection, 55
Source: Stocksy United. Image by Christian McLeod, 56–57
Courtesy of Oliver & Bonacini Events and Catering. Photo by CTV, 59
Courtesy of Judith Thompson, 60
Courtesy of Daniel MacIvor, 63
Courtesy of Ami McKay, 64
Source: Getty Images. Photo by Dimitrios Kambouris. WireImage Collection, 67
Source: The Canadian Press. Photo by Michael Bell, 68
Courtesy of Susin Nielsen, 71
Courtesy of Ann-Marie MacDonald, 73
Source: Getty Images. Photo by Smallz & Raskind. Getty Images Contour Collection, 74
Courtesy of Susur Lee, 76
Source: Getty Images. Photo by Keith Beaty. Toronto Star Collection, 79
Source: Getty Images. Photo by Dan Burn-Forti. Getty Images Contour Collection, 83
Courtesy of Arkells. Photo by Brandon Newfield, 84
Courtesy of Jeanne Beker, 86–87
Courtesy of Eric McCormack, 88
Courtesy of Farzana Doctor. Photo by Mark Raynes Roberts, 91
Courtesy of Ricardo Larrivée, 92
Courtesy of Jully Black, 95
Source: Getty Images. Photo by Charley Gallay. Getty Images Entertainment Collection, 96
Source: Getty Images. Photo by Boris Spremo. Toronto Star Collection, 99
Source: Getty Images. Photo by Reg Innell. Toronto Star Collection, 100
Courtesy of Karen Kain, 101
Courtesy of Chantal Kreviazuk. Source: Warner Music Canada, 103
Source: Alamy Stock Photo, 104
Courtesy of Oliver & Bonacini Events and Catering, 107
Courtesy of Piers Handling, 113
Source: Getty Images. Photo by Emma MacIntyre. Getty Images Entertainment Collection, 114
Courtesy of Sugar Sammy, 117
Courtesy of Nadia Litz, 118-119
Courtesy of Penguin Random House. Photo by Stephen Lowe, 121
Courtesy of Michael Smith. Photo by Heckbert Studio, 122
Source: Getty Images. Photo by Ethan Miller. WireImage Collection, 125
Courtesy of Carrie-Anne Moss, 126
Courtesy of Jody Mitic, 128
Courtesy of Jann Arden, 130-131
Source: Getty Images. Photo by Steve Babineau. National Hockey League Collection, 132
Source: Alamy Stock Photo, 136
Source: Getty Images. Photo by Rene Johnston. Toronto Star Collection, 139
Source: Getty Images. Photo by Ray Tamarra. GC Images Collection, 140
Courtesy of Susan Juby, 145
Courtesy of Paul Spence, 146
Courtesy of Robbie Robertson. Photo by David Jordan Williams, 150–151
Source: Alamy Stock Photo, 153
Courtesy of Peter Mansbridge, 154
Courtesy of Hannah Sung, 156
Courtesy of Cynthia Dale, 157
Source: Alamy Stock Photo, 158
Courtesy of Coco Rocha, 161
Source: Getty Images. Photo by Harold Whyte. Toronto Star Collection, 162
Courtesy of Yasin Osman, 164–165
Courtesy of Vikram Vij, 168
Courtesy of Sarah Richardson, 171
Illustrations copyright © Michael Martchenko, 172
Source: Alamy Stock Photo, 176
Courtesy of Robert Bateman, 179
Source: Alamy Stock Photo, 182
Courtesy of Amanda Lindhout. Photo by Florian Guerithault, 185
Courtesy of Andy Nulman, 188
Courtesy of Ric Esther Bienstock, 190–191
Courtesy of John Firth, 193
Courtesy of Edward Burtynsky, 196
Courtesy of Adam Shoalts, 200
Courtesy of Robert Lantos, 203
Courtesy of Esi Edugyan, 204
Courtesy of Terry Fan, 206
Courtesy of Eric Fan, 207
Source: Getty Images. Photo by Christopher Wahl. Getty Images Contour Collection, 208
Courtesy of Chris Hadfield, 209

ris Hadfield Margaret Laurence Bryan Webb Chantal Kreviazuk Peter Oliver Nellie Cournoyea
ordon Pinsent Carrie-Anne Moss Douglas Cardinal The Rankin Family Wade Dav
hn Firth Pierre Bourgault Norval Morrisseau Deborah C
Michael Crummey La Bolduc Joseph Boyden
eg Joy Oscar Peterson Stephen Leacock Ric Esther Bienstock Don Cherry
Alan Thicke Peggy Baker
von Deschamps Bachman-Turner Overdrive The Kids in the Hall Zoe Whittall Monty Ha
si Edugyan Richard Wagamese Cynthia Dale Ricardo Larrivée Jeff Lemire Hubert Aqui
ohn Candy Roy Dupuis Michael Bonacini Gabriel Dumont Jane Urquhart Lorne Michaels Drake
illes Vigneault Edward Burtynsky Heather O'Neill The Tragically Hip Clara Hug
teve Nash Mavis Gallant Hubert Reeves Jully Black Norman Jewison Jean-Mar
Terry Fan Simonie Michael A.M. Klein Al Purdy Barbara Rei
ené Richard Cyr
Loreena McKennitt Raymond Massey Frank Gehry
amuel Bronfman Martin Picard Lynn Coady Stompin' Tom Connors The Weeknd William McDouga
ufus Wainwright Will Ferguson Robert Thomas Allen Jean Drapeau Lise Payet
arian Engel Michael Ondaatje Yousuf Karsh Olivier Guimond Robert Batema
vril Lavigne Vincent Lam Lucy Maud Montgomery Judith Thompson Sir Frederick Carte
ise Arbour Maynard Ferguson Stan Rogers Margaret Atwood Shar
avid Suzuki Prime Minister Justin Trudeau Leon Edel Susan Musgrave Christoph
aomi Klein Ron Sexsmith Lisa Moore Viola Desmond Maurice Richard Corey Hart
dy Mitic Feist Louis de Buade de Frontenac Guy Gavriel Kay Atom Egoyan Gregory Charle
arzana Doctor Rick Mercer André Alexis William Giauque The Band Yasin Osman Dennis L
irstine Stewart Timothy Findley Leonard Cohen Ronnie Hawkins Jacque
Mike Myers Ethel Blondin-Andrew Frédéric Back Barenaked Ladies Eden Robinso
enys Arcand Paul Spence Ralph M. Steinman Eric Peterson Wayne and Shuster Louise Penn
aul Okalik Charlotte Gray Mitsou Antonine Maillet Deepa Mehta Jack
Jacques Ferron Piers Handling Ivan Reitman David Adams Richard
arles Pachter Mélanie Watt Sharon, Lois & Bram Susanna Moodie Jean-Paul Riopelle Malin Åkerma
arah Richardson Rohinton Mistry Chief Dan George Dan Aykroyd Sylvia Fraser Jessie Oonark
usan Juby Sheila Watt-Cloutier Cirque du Soleil Michael Smith
rederick G. Banting Ami McKay Stéphane Dompierre Sean Michaels John Kim Bell
om Longboat
dney Altman David Foster Donald Sutherland Kim Cattrall Jeanne Beker